CONNECT with WORDS

GRADE 3

School Specialty Publishing

Send all inquiries to:
School Specialty Publishing
8720 Orion Place
Columbus, OH 43240-2111

ISBN 0-7696-7433-X

1 2 3 4 5 6 7 8 9 10 POH 12 11 10 09 08 07

AMERICAN
EDUCATION
PUBLISHING™

Columbus, Ohio

Table of Contents

About The Book

Connect With Words is designed to help students increase their vocabulary skills with cross-curricular, grade-appropriate words and activities.

Activity Pages

Connect With Words is divided into 36 weeks, which is the average length of the school year. Each book is broken down into three-week units with a review lesson at the conclusion of each unit. The activity pages in the book focus on important words from different subject areas.

Keywords

A keyword is listed at the bottom of each activity page. This keyword is the link that connects students to the online activities via the CD, providing extra practice.

How to Use the CD

After inserting the CD into your computer, first follow the directions to register for the online activities database. Your registration is free and good for one year. After you have registered, click on the unit that your student is currently working on. Then, click on the appropriate keyword. This will take you to an online database of activities related to that keyword. You may choose to download up to 200 activities, which you may then print. Also included on the CD is a printable progress chart so your student can keep track of his or her progress through the workbook.

For further explanation of the online database, CD, or for technical help, refer to the help me file located on the CD.

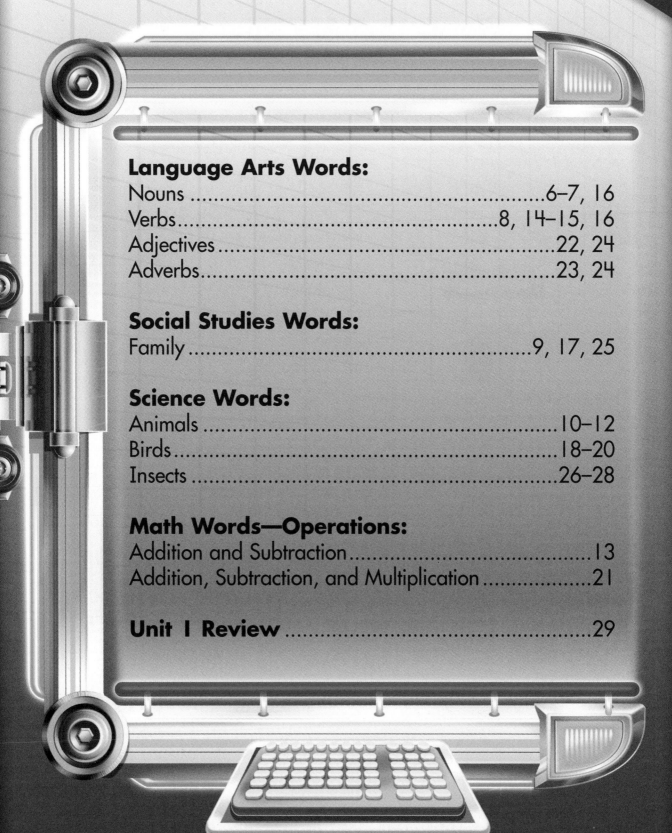

UNIT 1

Name:_____

Words That Are Nouns

A **noun** names a person, place, or thing.

person		• chef • postman • florist
place		• meadow • beach • island
thing		• bowl • doorknob • jacket

Directions: Read the story. Then, circle all the nouns.

There is a magical chef who lives on a small, windy island off the coast of Ireland. His name is Happy O'Reilly, and people travel from all over the world to see Happy. He has jolly red cheeks, twinkling blue eyes, and a smile for everybody. He lives by himself in a small, stone cottage that has a giant stone fireplace right in the middle. In that magical fireplace, he makes his potato bread and vegetable beef stew that will cure any sickness. In the summertime, he makes his apple cobbler dessert, which will keep a smile on your face for an entire year! Go visit Happy O'Reilly—if you can find him!

Nouns

6

Name:_____

Words That Are Nouns

Nouns can also name **ideas**. Ideas are things we cannot see or touch, such as **bravery**, **beauty**, and **honesty**.

Directions: Read the sentences. Then, underline each idea noun. Some sentences may contain more than one.

1. Respect is something that you must earn.

2. We value highly truth and justice.

3. The beauty of the flower garden was breathtaking.

4. You must learn new skills in order to master new things.

5. His courage impressed everyone.

6. She finds peace out in the woods.

7. Their friendship was amazing.

8. The man's honesty in the face of such hardship was refreshing.

9. The dog showed its loyalty toward its owner.

10. Trouble is brewing.

11. The policeman's kindness calmed the scared child.

12. The boy had a fear of the dark.

Nouns

7

Name:_____

Words That Are Verbs

The word that tells what is happening in a sentence is called a **verb**. Verbs are action words.

Directions: Write a verb from the Word Bank on each line to complete the sentences.

Word Bank				
discovers	dances	eats	drives	shoots

1. Duffy _____ his new, red car.

2. The lady _____ on the stage.

3. Coby _____ the arrow at the target.

4. Judy _____ pumpkin pie.

5. The archaeologist _____ the hidden doorway.

Directions: Write two sentences using verbs from the Word Bank.

Word Bank				
creates	hammers	builds	mows	scrubs

1. _____

_____

2. _____

_____

Verbs

8

WEEK 01
social studies

Name: _____

Words About Family

Directions: The puzzle below has two of the words from the Word Bank in it. Find and circle the words. Look across and down.

Word Bank					
brother	cousin	aunt	mom	sister	dad

l	m	e	r	x	f	y	h
c	o	u	s	i	n	s	t
y	m	a	a	r	n	m	z
g	w	i	t	b	i	v	s

Now, make your own puzzle. Write the words from the Word Bank in the blank puzzle below. Write some words across and others from top to bottom. Make some words cross each other. Fill the extra squares with other letters. See if someone else can find the words in your puzzle!

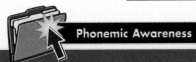

Phonemic Awareness

9

UNIT 1

Name:_____

Words About Animals

Directions: Read about animals that hibernate. Answer the questions. Then, color the animals that hibernate.

Have you ever wondered why some animals hibernate? Some animals sleep all winter. This sleep is called **hibernation**.

Animals get their warmth and energy from food. Some animals cannot find enough food in the winter. They must eat large amounts of food in the autumn. Their bodies store this food as fat. Then, in winter, they hibernate. Their bodies live on the stored fat. Since their bodies need much less food during hibernation, they can stay alive without eating anymore food during the winter.

Some animals that hibernate are **bats**, **chipmunks**, **bears**, **snakes** and **turtles**.

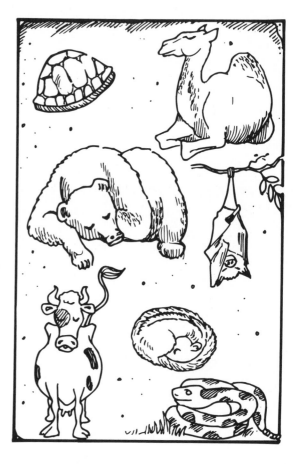

1. What is hibernation? _____

2. When do animals hibernate? _____

3. Where do animals get their warmth and energy? _____

4. Do animals need more or less food when they are hibernating? _____

5. What are two animals that hibernate? _____

Name:_____

Words About Animals

A **food chain** is a series of living things in which each living thing serves as food for the next. For example, bats eat insects and are therefore above them in the food chain.

Directions:

1. Color the pictures.
2. Cut out the pictures and glue them on cardboard.
3. Create a mobile with string and a hanger. Arrange the animals in the order of the food chain from last to first.

Page left blank for cutting activity.

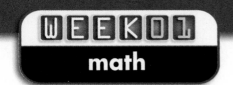
Name:_____

Words About Addition and Subtraction

Directions: Write **add** or **subtract** on the line to tell how to solve each problem. **In all** is a clue to add. **Left** is a clue to subtract. The first one is done for you.

1. There are 6 red birds and 7 blue birds. How many birds in all? _____add_____

2. The pet store had 25 goldfish, but 10 were sold. How many goldfish are left? _____

3. There are 8 black cats and 3 brown cats. How many cats in all? _____

4. The store had 18 puppies this morning. It sold 7 puppies today. How many puppies are left? _____

5. There were 11 cats this morning. Someone bought 2 black cats. How many cats are left? _____

UNIT 1

Name:_____

Words That Are Verbs

Sometimes an action verb needs help from another verb called a **helping verb**.

Common Helping Verbs					
am	can	does	is	shall	will
are	could	had	may	should	would
be	did	has	might	was	
been	do	have	must	were	

Directions: Underline the action verb in each sentence. Then, choose the best helping verb to complete each sentence. Write it on the line.

1. Jasmine's family _____ planning a recycling project.
(is   had   are)

2. They _____ talking to their neighbors.
(is   may   are)

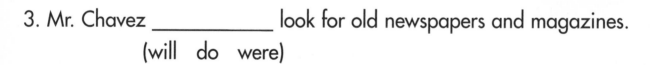

3. Mr. Chavez _____ look for old newspapers and magazines.
(will   do   were)

4. The Ong children _____ gathering bags to collect plastic bottles.
(should   are   did)

5. Jasmine _____ open a lemonade stand to make some money.
(have   was   might)

6. Mrs. Zanuto said she _____ drive us to the recycling center.
(would   be   are)

Name:_____

Words That Are Verbs

The words **is**, **are**, and **am** are special verbs.

Use **is** with one person, place, or thing.
Example: Mr. Wu **is** my teacher.

Use **are** with more than one person, place, or thing, or with the word you.
Examples: We **are** studying mummies.
                You **are** happy.

Use **am** with the word **I**.
Example: I **am** happy today.

Directions: Write **is**, **are**, or **am** to complete each sentence correctly.

1. My house _____ brown.

2. My favorite color _____ blue.

3. We _____ baking cookies today.

4. I _____ going to the movies on Saturday.

5. My friends _____ going with me.

6. What _____ your phone number?

7. You _____ standing on my foot.

8. I _____ four feet tall.

9. Charles and I _____ playing football.

10. Denver _____ east of Los Angeles.

Verbs

15

Name:_____

Words That Are Nouns and Verbs

A **noun** names a person, place, or thing. A **verb** tells what something does or what something is. Some words can be used as both nouns and verbs.

Directions: Write a word from the Word Bank to complete each pair of sentences.

Word Bank			
mix	kiss	brush	crash

1. Did your dog ever give you a _____?

(noun)

   I have a cold, so I can't _____ you today.

(verb)

2. I brought my comb and my _____.

(noun)

   I will _____ the leaves off your coat.

(verb)

3. Was anyone hurt in the _____?

(noun)

   If you aren't careful, you will _____ into me.

(verb)

4. We bought a cake _____ at the store.

(noun)

   I will _____ the eggs together.

(verb)

Name:_____

Words About Family

Directions: Use the words in the Word Bank to complete the puzzle about family.

Word Bank
cousin   son   sister   grandma   grandpa   uncle   aunt

Across
1. The child of your aunt and uncle
5. Your mother's mother
7. Your father's father

Down
2. Your mother's child, a boy
3. Your girl sibling
4. Your father's brother
6. Your mother's sister

Name:_____

Words About Birds

Directions: Looking at a bird's feet can tell you a lot about how they are used. Look at the pictures. Unscramble each bird's name. Then, draw a line to match the bird's name to the sentence that best describes it.

kawh
_____

"My webbed feet are great for swimming."

ckud
_____

"My feet are great for walking up trees."

noreh
_____

"I use my feet with long toes to wade in the water and mud."

reckwoodep
_____

"I use my strong, powerful feet to catch small animals."

Name:_____

Words About Birds

Directions: The shape of a bird's bill can tell you about what it eats. Look at the pictures. Unscramble each bird's name. Then, draw a line to match the bird's name to the sentence that best describes it.

noreh

_____

"I pound holes in wood to find insects."

bumminghird

_____

"I use my long bill to get nectar from flowers."

panicel

_____

"I use my strong bill to crack open seeds."

reckwoodep

_____

"I use my sharp bill to tear the flesh of animals."

kawh

_____

"I stab at small fish with my sharp bill."

dinalcar

_____

"I scoop up large mouthfuls of water and fish."

Birds

19

UNIT 1

Name: _____

Words About Birds

Directions: Use the Word Bank to write the word that best describes each kind of bird's bill.

Word Bank		
preying	straining	seed-eating
probing	fish-eating	insect-eating

1. _____:
short, thick bill for crunching seeds – grosbeak, finch

2. _____:
strong, sharp hooked bill for tearing flesh of prey – owl, hawk

3. _____:
slender, pointed bill for picking up insects – warbler, swallow

4. _____:
broad, flat bill for straining food from mud – duck, goose

5. _____:
long, slender bill for searching for food in mud or flowers – hummingbird, flamingo

6. _____:
long, sharp bill for spearing or with a pouch – heron, pelican

Words About Addition, Subtraction, and Multiplication

Directions: Write **add**, **subtract**, or **multiply** on the line to tell how to solve each problem. Then, solve the problem. The first one is done for you.

1. There were 12 frogs sitting on a log by a pond, but 3 frogs hopped away. How many frogs are left?

   __subtract__   __9__ frogs

2. There are 9 flowers growing by the pond. Each flower has 2 leaves. How many leaves are there?

   _____ _____ leaves

3. A tree had 7 squirrels playing in it. Then 8 more came along. How many squirrels are there in all?

   _____ _____ squirrels

4. There were 27 birds living in the trees around the pond, but 9 flew away. How many birds are left?

   _____ _____ birds

Name:_____

Words That Are Adjectives

Adjectives are describing words that give more information about something. They make writing more interesting.

Examples:			
What Kind:	**white** egg	**small** car	**messy** room
How Many:	**five** flags	**lots** of books	**a half-dozen** donuts
Which One:	**those** ducklings	**that** lamp	**this** bowl

Directions: Look at each picture. Then, write a word that describes it.

1.  _____   4.  _____

2.  _____   5. _____

3.  _____   6.  _____

Name:_____

Words That Are Adverbs

Adverbs are describing words. They describe verbs. Adverbs tell **how**, **when**, or **where** the action takes place.

Examples:

How	When	Where
slowly	yesterday	here
gracefully	today	there
swiftly	tomorrow	everywhere
quickly	soon	

Directions: Underline the adverb in each sentence. Then, write on the line whether the adverb tells **how**, **when**, or **where**. The first one is done for you.

1. The children ran <u>quickly</u> home from school.   how

2. They will have a spelling test tomorrow.   _____

3. Slowly, the children filed to their seats.   _____

4. The teacher sat here at her desk.   _____

5. She will pass the tests back later.   _____

6. The students received their grades happily.   _____

Directions: Write three sentences of your own using any of the adverbs above.

1. _____

2. _____

3. _____

Adverbs   **23**

Name:_____

Words That Are Adjectives and Adverbs

Directions: Write **ADJ** on the line if the bold word is an adjective. Write **ADV** if the bold word is an adverb. The first one is done for you.

1. ____ADV____ That road leads **nowhere**.

2. _____ The squirrel was **nearby**.

3. _____ Her **delicious** cookies were all eaten.

4. _____ Everyone rushed **indoors**.

5. _____ He **quickly** zipped his jacket.

6. _____ She hummed a **popular** tune.

7. _____ Her **sunny** smile warmed my heart.

8. _____ I hung your coat **there**.

9. _____ Bring that **here** this minute!

10. _____ We all walked **back** to school.

11. _____ The **skinniest** boy ate the most food!

12. _____ She acts like a **famous** person.

13. _____ The **silliest** jokes always make me laugh.

14. _____ She must have parked her car **somewhere**!

15. _____ Did you take the test **today**?

Adjectives, Adverbs

24

Name:_____

Words About Family

Directions: Use the words in the Word Bank to write five sentences about the picture. Then, color the picture.

Word Bank				
brother	sister	mom	grandpa	cousin

1. _____

2. _____

3. _____

4. _____

5. _____

UNIT 1

Name:_____

Words About Insects

Directions: Read about insects. Then, color the body parts of the insect. Color the head red, the thorax yellow, and the abdomen blue.

The largest group of animals belongs to the group called invertebrates—or animals without backbones. This large group is the **insect** group. Insects are easy to tell apart from other animals. Adult insects have three body parts and six legs. The first body part is the **head**. On the head are the mouth, eyes and antennae. The second body part is the **thorax**. On it are the legs and wings. The third part is the **abdomen**. On it are small openings for breathing.

Directions: Draw an insect. Be sure it has the correct number of body parts, legs, wings, and antennae. Fill in the information on the lines.

Insect's name _____

Length _____

Where found _____

Food _____

Name:_____

Words About Insects

Directions: Use the hints and the Word Bank to write the correct insect name to answer each riddle.

1. I have stout, spiny forelegs.
   I eat insects, including some of my own kind.
   I camouflage well in my surroundings.
   My forelegs make me appear to be praying.
   What am I? _____

2. I have clear wings.
   My body is quite round.
   The males of my species make long, shrill sounds in summer.
   Some of us take 17 years to develop.
   What am I? _____

3. I have two pairs of long, thin wings.
   I eat mosquitoes and other small insects.
   I live near lakes, ponds, streams and rivers.
   My abdomen is very long . . . as long as a darning needle.
   What am I? _____

4. I am a type of beetle.
   My young are often called glowworms.
   My abdomen produces light.
   What am I? _____

5. I like warm, damp, and dark places and come out at night.
   Humans hate me.
   I am a destructive household pest.
   I am closely related to grasshoppers and crickets.
   What am I? _____

Word Bank		
lightning bug		termite
cicada	dragonfly	praying mantis

© 2007 School Specialty Publishing

Name:_____

Words About Insects

Directions: Read about butterflies and moths. Then, answer the questions.

Butterflies and moths belong to the same group of insects. They both have two pairs of wings. Their wings are covered with tiny  scales. Both butterflies and moths undergo metamorphosis, or a change, in their lives. They begin their lives as caterpillars. Butterflies and moths are different in some ways. Butterflies usually fly during the day, but moths generally fly at night. Most butterflies have slender, hairless bodies; most moths have plump, furry bodies. When butterflies land, they hold their wings together straight over their bodies. When moths land, they spread their wings out flat.

1. What are three ways that butterflies and moths are alike?

   a. _____

   _____

   b. _____

   _____

   c. _____

   _____

2. What are three ways that butterflies and moths are different?

   a. _____

   _____

   b. _____

   _____

   c. _____

   _____

Name:_____

Unit 1 Review

Directions: Use a word from the Word Bank to complete each sentence. Then, on the line beside each sentence, write whether the word you wrote is a noun, verb, adjective, or adverb.

Word Bank			
slowly	strong	bake	plan
toast	beauty	soon	new

1. My dad made _____ for breakfast. _____
2. My brother wants a _____ mountain bike for his birthday. _____
3. My aunt will _____ where to go on her trip. _____
4. The animals will find a place to hibernate _____ . _____
5. The _____ of my mother's garden amazed the neighbors. _____
6. I ride my bike _____ beside the busy street. _____
7. I asked my grandma to _____ some cookies for me. _____
8. A hawk uses its _____ feet to catch small animals. _____

Directions: Write **add**, **subtract**, or **multiply** on the line to tell how to solve each problem. Then, solve the problem. Write the answer on the line.

1. There are 3 bats in a cave. Then, 5 more fly in. How many bats in all?

_____ _____

2. Three children are outside catching lightning bugs. Each child catches 4 bugs and puts them in a jar. How many lightning bugs are there in all?

_____ _____

3. There are 15 fish in the pond. A bear catches 9 of them for its dinner. How many fish are left?

_____ _____

4. Five moths are flying around a lamppost. Five more moths fly over to join them. How many wings do they have in all?

_____ _____

29 © 2007 School Specialty Publishing

Name:_____

Words That Are Pronouns

A **pronoun** is a word that can take the place of a noun. **He**, **she**, **it**, **they**, **him**, **her**, and **them** are all pronouns.

Directions: Read each sentence. Write the pronoun on the line that takes the place of each bold noun.

Example: The **monkey** dropped the banana. ___It___

1. **Dad** washed the car last night. _____

2. **Mary and David** took a walk in the park. _____

3. **Peggy** spent the night at her grandmother's house. _____

4. The baseball **players** lost their game. _____

5. **Mike Van Meter** is a great soccer player. _____

6. The **parrot** can say five different words. _____

7. **Megan** wrote a story in class today. _____

8. They gave a party for **Teresa**. _____

9. Everyone in the class was happy for **Ted**. _____

10. The children petted the **giraffe**. _____

11. Linda put the **kittens** near the warm stove. _____

12. **Gina** made a chocolate cake for my birthday. _____

13. **Pete and Matt** played baseball on the same team. _____

14. Give the books to **Herbie**. _____

Name:_____

Words That Are Pronouns

A **pronoun** is a word that can take the place of a noun.

Directions: Read each underlined noun. Then, in the box above it, write a pronoun from the Word Bank that could replace it. Some pronouns may be used more than once.

Word Bank								
she	it	we	he	his	I	him	they	your

1. Uncle Nick petted the cat as <u>Uncle Nick</u> walked to the kitchen.

2. <u>The children</u> crowded up to the kitchen door.

3. Granny Little said, "<u>Granny Little</u> wouldn't believe it if <u>Granny Little</u> didn't see it with these old eyes."

4. Lucy said, "<u>The cat</u> is very cute."

5. <u>Will and I</u> left to get some leftovers for the cat.

6. <u>Uncle Nick</u> went upstairs to write <u>Uncle Nick's</u> life story.

7. <u>Granny Little</u> whispered, "Don't bother <u>Uncle Nick</u>."

8. I told Uncle Nick, "<u>Lucy and Will</u> want to read <u>Uncle Nick's</u> book."

Pronouns

32

© 2007 School Specialty Publishing

Name:_____

Words That Are Pronouns

Use the pronouns **I** and **we** when you or a group that you are in is doing the action.

Example: I can play ball. **We** can play ball.

Use **me** and **us** when talking about something that is happening to you or a group that you are in.

Example: They gave **me** the ball. They gave **us** the ball.

Directions: Circle the correct pronoun that completes each sentence. Then, write it on the line.

Example: _____We_____ are going to the zoo today.   (We,) Us

1. _____ wish we did not have to go so soon.   I, Me

2. Eric threw the ball to _____ .   me, I

3. They made dinner for _____ last night.   we, us

4. _____ am your new teacher.   I, Me

5. Mom told _____ to go to bed.   me, I

6. _____ got our test scores yesterday.   Us, We

7. They let _____ borrow their car.   us, we

8. That book belongs to _____ .   me, I

9. She is taking _____ with her to the store.   I, me

10. Meredith and _____ play after school.   I, me

Name:_____

UNIT 2

People Words

Directions: Use the words in the Word Bank to write about the people in the picture. Then, color the picture.

Word Bank				
girl	teenagers	mother	man	people

1. _____

2. _____

3. _____

4. _____

5. _____

People Words

34

Name:_____

Words About Dinosaurs

Directions:

Color the dinosaurs.

Cut out the dinosaurs and glue them onto cardboard.

Match the dinosaurs with the descriptions. Write each dinosaur's name on the back of its picture.

Assemble the dinosaurs with string and a hanger to make a mobile.

Triceratops: large dinosaur; three horns, one over each eye and one over its nose; large shield of bone protected its neck

Parasaurolophus: large dinosaur; big crest curved backward from its head to beyond its shoulders

Tyrannosaurus: giant meat-eater; large head; jaws filled with sharp teeth

Brontosaurus: giant dinosaur; weighed almost 40 tons; massive body and tail; front legs shorter than its hind legs

Ankylosaurus: body covered with armored plates; large bony club on the end of its tail

UNIT 2

Page left blank for cutting activity.

Name:_____

Words About Dinosaurs

Directions: Find and circle the hidden words in the puzzle. Look forward, backward, up, down, and diagonally. When you have located the words, write the remaining letters at the bottom of the page to spell out a message.

ALLOSAURUS	BIRD HIP	FOSSIL	PLANT-EATER
APATOSAURUS	COELURUS	JURASSIC	PLATED
ARMORED	DINOSAUR	MEAT-EATER	SAUROPOD
ARCHAEOPTERYX	DIPLODOCUS	PALEONTOLOGIST	STEGOSAURUS

```
S D B U R L I S S O F I S M N
G U I T H I S P E R I O T E T
J D R U A S O N I D S H E A S
U A D U L D L O S E W S G T I
R E H A A S O U C R O V O E G
A E I R E S R P D O M U S A O
S C P H O U O F O M N O A T L
S R T H L A M T E R R I U E O
I C A E A N D E A A U U R R T
C R O O D E T A L P P A U E N
A C N D R A I N S C A A S M O
E X Y R E T P O E A H C R A E
T O T H D I P L O D O C U S L
R E T A E T N A L P E D E S A
E R A L L O S A U R U S T S P
```

Hidden message:

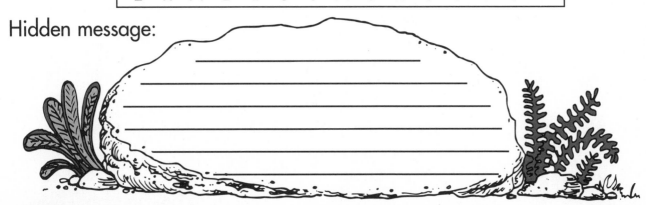

 Dinosaurs   **37**   © 2007 School Specialty Publishing

Name:_____

Words About Time

In telling time, the hours between 12:00 midnight and 12:00 noon are **a.m.** hours. The hours between 12:00 noon and 12:00 midnight are **p.m.** hours.

Directions: Draw a line to match the times that are the same.

Example:

7:30 in the morning   7:30 a.m.
half-past seven a.m.
seven thirty in the morning

9:00 in the evening   9:00 p.m.
nine o'clock at night

1. six o'clock in the evening   8:00 a.m.

2. 3:30 a.m.   six o'clock in the morning

3. 4:15 p.m.   6:00 p.m.

4. eight o'clock in the morning   eleven o'clock in the evening

5. quarter past five in the evening   three thirty in the morning

6. 11:00 p.m.   four fifteen in the evening

7. 6:00 a.m.   5:15 p.m.

UNIT 2

Telling Time

38

Name:_____

Words That Are Pronouns

Some pronouns show ownership. **My**, **our**, **your**, **his**, **her**, **its**, and **their** are called possessive pronouns.
Example: **his** hat, **her** shoes, **our** dog

You can use the following pronouns by themselves, without a noun: **mine**, **yours**, **ours**, **his**, **hers**, **theirs**, **its**.
Example: That is **mine**.

Directions: Rewrite each sentence replacing the bold words with a pronoun. The first one is done for you.

1. **My dog's** bowl is brown.

   Its bowl is brown.

2. That is **Lisa's** book.

   _____

3. This is **my pencil**.

   _____

4. This hat is **your hat**.

   _____

5. Fifi is **Kevin's** cat.

   _____

6. That beautiful house is **our home**.

   _____

7. **The gerbil's** cage is too small.

   _____

Name:_____

Words That Are Conjunctions

Or, **and**, and **but** are called **conjunctions**. This means that they join words or sentences. Use **or** with a choice. Use **and** with similar ideas. Use **but** with **opposite** ideas.

Examples: Is that a skunk **or** a cat? It has black fur **and** a white stripe. It is pretty, **but** it smells bad.

Directions: Rewrite the sentences using **or**, **and**, or **but** to join each pair of sentences.

1. The skunk has a small head. The skunk has small ears.

_____

2. The skunk has short legs. Skunks can move quickly.

_____

3. Skunks sleep in hollow trees. Skunks sleep underground.

_____

4. Skunks are chased by animals. Skunks do not run away.

_____

5. Skunks sleep during the day. Skunks hunt at night.

_____

Words That Are Conjunctions

And, **but**, and **or** are conjunctions. They join two sentences into one longer one.

Use **and** when the sentences are about the same noun or verb.
Example: Tom is in my class, **and** he lives near me.

Use **but** if the second sentence says something different from the first.
Example: Julie walks to school with me, **but** today she is sick.

Use **or** if each sentence names a different thing you could do.
Example: We could go to my house, **or** we could go to yours.

Directions: Rewrite the sentences using **and**, **but**, or **or** to join the two sentences.

1. Those socks usually cost a lot. This pack of ten socks is cheaper.

_____

_____

2. The kangaroo has a pouch. It lives in Australia.

_____

_____

3. The zookeeper can start work early. She can stay late.

_____

_____

Name:_____

UNIT 2

People Words

Directions: Use the words in the Word Bank to complete the puzzle about people.

Across

3. A server
4. Someone who finishes school
8. A teacher's boss

Word Bank

author

clerk

graduate

niece

passenger

principal

ruler

waiter

Down

1. A writer
2. A rider
5. A king or queen
6. Nephew and _____
7. A store worker

People Words

42

© 2007 School Specialty Publishing

Name:_____

Words About Dinosaurs

Directions: Read about dinosaurs. Then, answer the questions.

Dinosaurs are a group of animals that lived millions of years ago. Some were the largest animals that have ever lived on land. There are none alive today. They became **extinct**, or died off, millions of years ago. This was before people lived on Earth. Many scientists have ideas, but no one can know for sure exactly what happened to the dinosaurs.

1. Why is it not possible to know what caused all the dinosaurs to die?

   _____

2. Circle the main idea:
   The dinosaurs died when a comet hit Earth and caused a big fire.
   There are many ideas about what killed the dinosaurs, but no one knows for sure.

3. What does **extinct** mean?

   _____

   _____

4. Who are the people with ideas about what happened to dinosaurs?

   _____

Name:_____

UNIT 2

Words About Dinosaurs

Directions: Read about dinosaurs. Then, answer the questions.

Like snakes, dinosaurs may have been cold-blooded. Cold-blooded animals cannot keep themselves warm. Because of this, dinosaurs were likely not very active when it was cold. When the sun grew warm, the dinosaurs likely became active. The sun warmed the dinosaurs and gave them the energy they needed to move about.

1. Why would dinosaurs have been inactive when it was cold?

_____

_____

2. What time of day would dinosaurs have been most active?

_____

_____

3. What time of day would dinosaurs have been least active?

_____

_____

4. Why did dinosaurs need the sun?

_____

_____

Name:_____

Words About Reptiles

Directions: Read the statements about snakes. Write **fact** if the statement can be proven. Write **opinion** if the statement expresses a belief that cannot be proven.

1. _____ It is easy to take care of snakes.

2. _____ Snakes do not shed fur all over the house.

3. _____ Mom does not want to feed a snake.

4. _____ My sister is afraid of snakes.

5. _____ Snakes do not need to go for walks.

6. _____ Snakes are cold-blooded.

7. _____ Snakes need a heat lamp at all times.

8. _____ Snake

Directions: Write your opinion about snakes.

_____

_____

_____

_____

_____

Reptiles

45

Name:_____

Words About Time

UNIT 2

Directions: Read each sentence. Then, choose the best word or phrase to replace the underlined word. Circle the letter next to the correct answer.

1. Tim was born near the end of the 1900s, the <u>century</u> before this one.
   a. 100-year period
   b. 10-year period
   c. weekend
   d. 1,000-year period

2. The paint needs to dry for a <u>day</u>.
   a. 2-hour period
   b. 24-hour period
   c. weekend
   d. 1-hour period

3. Clothing styles change about every <u>decade</u>.
   a. 100-year period
   b. year
   c. 10-year period
   d. minute

4. I will see you one <u>week</u> from now.
   a. 2-day period
   b. 7-day period
   c. 10-minute period
   d. 10-day period

Name:_____

Words That Are Conjunctions

Words that combine sentences or ideas, such as **and**, **but**, **or**, **because**, **when**, **after**, and **so**, are called **conjunctions**.

Examples: I played the drums, **and** Sue played the clarinet.
She likes bananas, **but** I do not.
We could play music **or** just enjoy the silence.
I needed the book, **because** I had to write a report.
He gave me the book **when** I asked for it.
I asked her to eat lunch **after** she finished the test.
You wanted my bike **so** you could ride it.

Using different conjunctions can affect the meaning of a sentence.
Example: He gave me the book **when** I asked for it.
He gave me the book **after** I asked for it.

Directions: Choose the best conjunction to combine each pair of sentences. Write the new sentence on the line. The first one is done for you.

1. I like my hair curly. Mom likes my hair straight.

I like my hair curly, but Mom likes it straight.

2. I can remember what she looks like. I can't remember her name.

_____

3. We will have to wash the dishes. We won't have clean plates for dinner.

_____

4. The yellow flowers are blooming. The red flowers are not.

_____

5. I like banana cream pie. I like chocolate donuts.

_____

Name:_____

Words That Are Conjunctions

If and **when** can be conjunctions, too.

Directions: Rewrite the sentences using **if** or **when** to join the two sentences.

Example: The apples will need to be washed.
The apples are dirty.

<u>The apples will need to be</u>

<u>washed if they are dirty.</u>

1. The size of the crowd grew. It grew when the game began.

_____

_____

2. Be careful driving in the fog. The fog is thick.

_____

_____

3. Pack your suitcase. Do it when you wake up in the morning.

_____

_____

UNIT 2

Name:_____

Words That Are Conjunctions

Other words that can join sentences are **when**, **after**, and **because**.

Examples: **When** we got there, the show had already started.
After I finished my homework, I watched TV.
You can't go by yourself, **because** you are too young.

Directions: Use the joining words in the balloons to rewrite the sentences.

1.  The keeper opened the door. The bear got out.

   _____
   _____

2.  I didn't buy the tickets. They cost too much.

   _____
   _____

3. 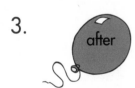 The kangaroo ate lunch. It took a nap.

   _____
   _____

4.  The door opened. The crowd rushed in.

   _____
   _____

5.  I cut the bread. Everyone had a slice.

   _____
   _____

 Conjunctions   **49**   © 2007 School Specialty Publishing

UNIT 2

Name:_____

People Words

Directions: Use the people words from the Word Bank to write about each picture.

Word Bank			
teenagers	toddler	adult	boy

1. _____
   _____

2. _____
   _____

3. _____
   _____

4. _____
   _____

Name:_____

Words About Reptiles

Snakes are a kind of **reptile**. A reptile is a cold-blooded animal with a skeleton inside its body and dry scales or hard plates on its skin. There are many kinds of snakes, in all sizes and colors. Pythons can be as long as a bus. Corn snakes are red and white, just like a candycane. Milk snakes are gentle and shy. They are usually tri-color, with rings of red, black, and white. Garter snakes have yellow stripes on brown or black. Garter snakes are very common, so they may be in your own backyard!

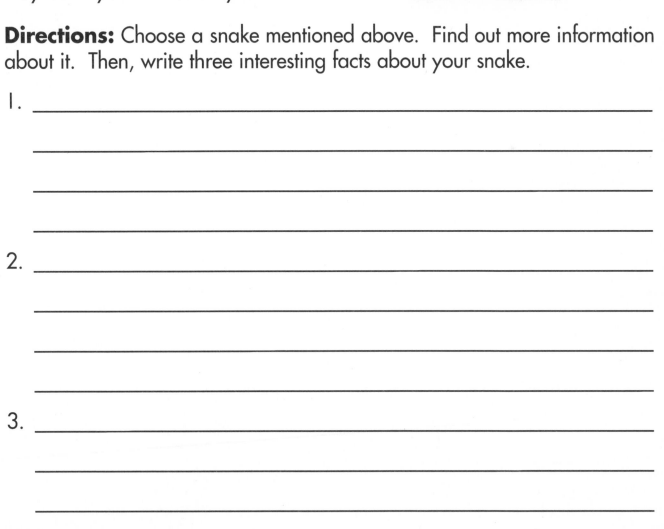

Directions: Choose a snake mentioned above. Find out more information about it. Then, write three interesting facts about your snake.

1. _____

_____

_____

_____

2. _____

_____

_____

_____

3. _____

_____

_____

_____

Name:_____

Words About Reptiles

Directions: Read about the rainforest lizard. Then, answer the questions.

The **rainforest lizard** is a reptile. It grows to be as large as a dog! It has scales on its skin. It has a very wide mouth. It has spikes sticking out of the top of its head. It looks scary, but don't be afraid! This lizard eats mostly weeds. Snakes and birds eat these lizards. Some people in the rainforest eat them, too!

1. What is the size of the rainforest lizard?

_____

2. Where do its scales grow?

_____

3. Which kind of food does the lizard eat?

_____

4. What animals eat these lizards?

_____

5. Would you like to see this lizard? Why or why not?

_____

Name:_____

Words About Reptiles

Directions: The five snakes described are held in the cages below. Use the descriptions and the clues under the cages to write each snake's name on the correct cage.

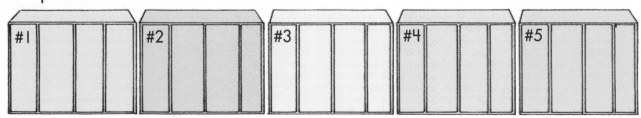

The King Cobra is the longest poisonous snake in the world. One of these snakes measured almost 19 feet long. It comes from southeast Asia and the Philippines.

The Gaboon Viper, a very poisonous snake, has the longest fangs of all snakes (nearly 2 inches). It comes from tropical Africa.

The Reticulated Python is the longest snake of all. One specimen measured 32 feet 9 1/2 inches. It comes from southeast Asia, Indonesia, and the Philippines. It crushes its prey to death.

The Black Mamba, the fastest-moving land snake, can move at speeds of 10–12 m.p.h. It lives in the eastern part of tropical Africa.

The Anaconda is almost twice as heavy as a reticulated python of the same length. One anaconda that was almost 28 feet long weighed nearly 500 pounds.

#1   #2   #3   #4   #5

Clues:
• The snake in cage #5 moves the fastest on land.
• The longest snake of all is between the snake that comes from tropical Africa and the longest poisonous snake.
• The very heavy snake is to the left of the longest poisonous snake.

Name:_____

Unit 2 Review

Directions: Read each sentence. Write the pronoun on the line that takes the place of each underlined noun or nouns.

1. <u>My friend and I</u> like to play together after school.   _____

2. <u>The children's</u> cat chased the lizard.   _____

3. <u>The Brontosaurus</u> was a giant dinosaur that weighed almost 40 tons.   _____

4. <u>My mother</u> gets up at six o'clock in the morning to get ready for work.   _____

5. <u>The teenagers</u> like to go to the movies on Friday night.   _____

6. That brand new bike belongs to <u>Catherine</u>.   _____

7. Spot is <u>Steven's</u> dog.   _____

8. <u>The paleontologist</u> wrote about her findings in a science journal.   _____

9. <u>Julia and William</u> have to go to bed at eight o'clock on school nights.   _____

Directions: Complete each sentence.

1. The girl is tall and athletic, but her sister is _____.

2. We should eat fruits and vegetables, because _____.

3. I got in trouble when _____.

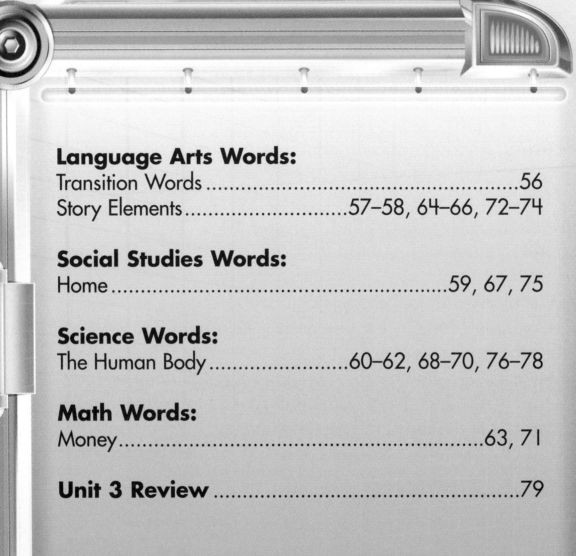

Name:_____

Transition Words

In some paragraphs, the order or sequence of the sentences is very important. **Transition words**, such as **first**, **next**, **after**, **then**, **finally**, and **last**, offer clues to help show the sequence of the sentences.

Directions: Read the story. Then, circle the transition words.

My family is entering the bake-off contest at the local fair. My dad thinks that we have the best apple pie recipe. Our friends agree.

First, dad takes us to the apple orchard to choose the ripest apples. Next, we go home to prepare the pie. After we wash and slice the apples, we mix in the rest of the ingredients. Then, while we make the crust, we wait for the oven to preheat. Finally, we add the apples in the crust. We bake the pie until it is cooked to perfection. Last, we take our apple pie to the fair and keep our fingers crossed that we win the blue ribbon!

Name:_____

Story Words

The **main idea** of a story is what the story is about. Story **details** are the characters and the events that make up the story.

Directions: Read each main idea sentence. Then, read the detail sentences that follow. Draw a ✓ on the line beside each detail that supports the main idea.

Example: Niagara Falls is a favorite vacation spot.
_✓_ There are so many cars and buses that it is hard to get around.
_____ My little brother gets sick when we go camping.
_✓_ You can see people there from all over the world.

1. Hummingbirds are interesting birds to watch.

_____ They look like tiny helicopters as they move around the flowers.

_____ One second they are "drinking" from the flower; the next, they are gone!

_____ It is important to provide birdseed for the winter for our feathered friends.

2. Boys and girls look forward to Valentine's Day parties at school.

_____ For days, children try to choose the perfect valentine for each friend.

_____ The school program is next Tuesday.

_____ Just thinking about frosted, heart-shaped cookies makes me hungry!

Name:_____

Story Words

All short stories have a plot, a setting, a theme, and characters.

The **plot** is what the story is about.
The **characters** are the people or animals in the story.
The **setting** is where and when the story occurs.
The **theme** is the message or idea of the story.

Directions: Use the diagram to plan a story that you would like to write.

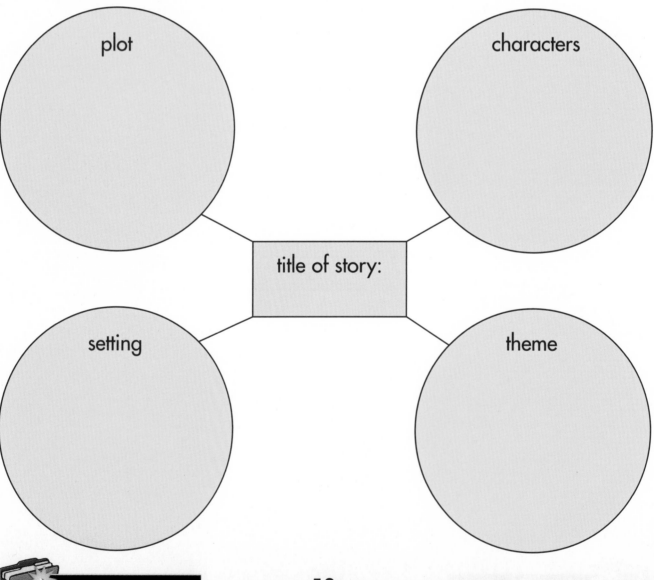

Name:_____

Words Around the House

Word Bank				
cabinet	curtains	cushion	drawer	mirror
quilt	sofa	sweep	towel	trash

Directions: Write a word from the Word Bank to fit each clue. The letters in the boxes will reveal the name of some of the noisiest things in people's homes.

1. Garbage

2. Thirsty cloth

3. Bed covering

4. Cupboard

5. You do it with a broom.

6. Couch pillow

7. I can see myself in it.

8. Window coverings

9. A home for socks

10. Couch

Directions: Imagine that you are a prince or a princess. On a separate sheet of paper, describe a room in your palace. Use the words in the Word Bank.

Home

59

UNIT 3

Words About the Human Body

Directions: Read about the human body. Then, use the bold words to finish the sentences below.

What gives you your **shape**? Like a house's frame, your body also has a frame. It is called your **skeleton**. Your skeleton is made of more than two hundred bones.

Your skeleton helps your body move. It does this by giving your **muscles** a place to attach. Your skeleton also **protects** the soft organs inside your body from injury.

Each bone has a hard, outer layer of **calcium**. Inside is a soft, **spongy** layer that looks like a honeycomb. The hollow spaces in the honeycomb are filled with **marrow**. Every minute, millions of **blood** cells die. But you don't need to worry. The bone marrow works like a little factory, making new blood cells for you.

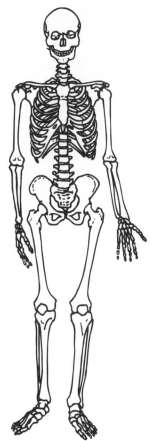

1. Your skeleton __ __ __ __ __ __ __ __ your soft organs.

2. Bone __ __ __ __ __ __ makes new blood cells.

3. Inside the bone is a soft, __ __ __ __ __ __ layer.

4. Millions of __ __ __ __ __ cells die every minute.

5. The hard, outer layer of bone is made of __ __ __ __ __ __ __.

6. More than two hundred bones make up your __ __ __ __ __ __ __ __.

7. Your skeleton is a place for __ __ __ __ __ __ __ to attach.

8. Your skeleton gives your body its __ __ __ __ __.

Name:_____

Words About the Human Body

Directions: Read about the human body. Then, use the bold words to answer the clues to complete the puzzle.

Your body is like an amazing **machine**. Every minute, your heart pumps six quarts of blood. Your brain sends thousands of **messages** to other parts of your body. The messages travel along the nerves at more than 100 miles an hour! Your **lungs** fill with air. Your **ears** hear **sounds**. Your eyes see **pictures**. And you thought you were just sitting here reading! Your body is always very **busy**, even when you sleep.

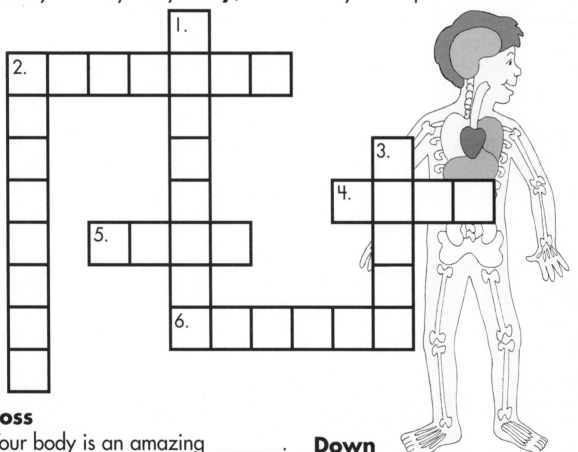

Across

2. Your body is an amazing _____.
4. Even when you sleep, your body is always _____.
5. You hear with these.
6. This is what you hear.

Down

1. Your eyes see these.
2. Your brain sends thousands of these to other parts of the body.
3. These fill with air.

Human Body

61

Words About the Human Body

Directions: Read about your lungs. Then, answer the questions.

Imagine millions of teeny, tiny balloons joined together. That is what your **lungs** are like. When you breathe, the air goes to your two lungs. One lung is located on each side of your chest. The heart is located between the two lungs. The lungs are soft, spongy, and delicate. That is why there are bones around the lungs. These bones are called the **rib cage**. The rib cage protects the lungs so they can do their job. The

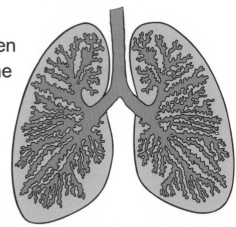

lungs bring **oxygen** into the body. They also take waste out of the body. This waste is called **carbon dioxide**. We could not live without our lungs!

1. Circle the main idea:

   The lungs are spongy and located in the chest. They are like small balloons.

   The lungs bring in oxygen and take out carbon dioxide. We could not live without our lungs.

2. What is the name of the bones around your lungs? _____

3. What is located between the lungs? _____

4. What goes into your lungs when you breathe? _____

5. Why are there bones around your lungs? _____

UNIT 3

Name:_____

Words About the Human Body

Directions: Read about the human body. Then, use the bold words to answer the clues to complete the puzzle.

Your body is like an amazing **machine**. Every minute, your heart pumps six quarts of blood. Your brain sends thousands of **messages** to other parts of your body. The messages travel along the nerves at more than 100 miles an hour! Your **lungs** fill with air. Your **ears** hear **sounds**. Your eyes see **pictures**. And you thought you were just sitting here reading! Your body is always very **busy**, even when you sleep.

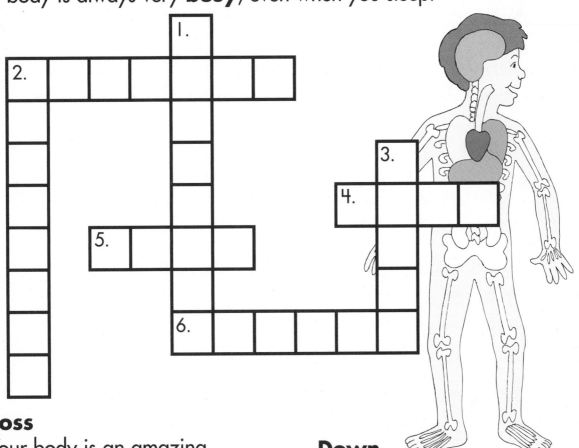

Across

2. Your body is an amazing _____.
4. Even when you sleep, your body is always _____.
5. You hear with these.
6. This is what you hear.

Down

1. Your eyes see these.
2. Your brain sends thousands of these to other parts of the body.
3. These fill with air.

Words About the Human Body

Directions: Read about your lungs. Then, answer the questions.

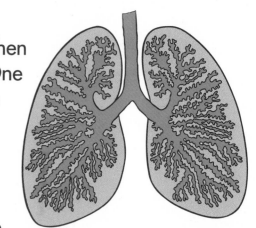

Imagine millions of teeny, tiny balloons joined together. That is what your **lungs** are like. When you breathe, the air goes to your two lungs. One lung is located on each side of your chest. The heart is located between the two lungs. The lungs are soft, spongy, and delicate. That is why there are bones around the lungs. These bones are called the **rib cage**. The rib cage protects the lungs so they can do their job. The lungs bring **oxygen** into the body. They also take waste out of the body. This waste is called **carbon dioxide**. We could not live without our lungs!

1. Circle the main idea:

   The lungs are spongy and located in the chest. They are like small balloons.

   The lungs bring in oxygen and take out carbon dioxide. We could not live without our lungs.

2. What is the name of the bones around your lungs? _____

3. What is located between the lungs? _____

4. What goes into your lungs when you breathe? _____

5. Why are there bones around your lungs? _____

UNIT 3

Name:_____

Money Words

Directions: Circle the letter beside the answer that correctly completes each sentence.

1. One quarter equals
   a. twenty-five pennies
   b. fifty cents
   c. five dollars
   d. twenty-five dimes

2. A half dollar equals
   a. five nickels
   b. two quarters
   c. five quarters
   d. twenty dimes

3. One ten-dollar bill equals
   a. one hundred dimes
   b. five dollars
   c. two five-dollar bills
   d. ten quarters

4. Two dimes are worth less than
   a. two nickels
   b. one quarter
   c. fifteen pennies
   d. three nickels

5. George Washington is pictured on a
   a. nickel
   b. five-dollar bill
   c. dollar bill
   d. penny

UNIT 3

Name:_____

Story Words

The **main idea** of a story is what the story is about. Story **details** are the characters and the events that make up the story.

Directions: Read the story about spiders. Then, answer the questions about the main idea and story details.

Many people think spiders are insects, but they are not. Spiders are the same size as insects, and they look like insects in some ways. But there are three ways to tell a spider from an insect. Insects have six legs, and spiders have eight legs. Insects have antennae, but spiders do not. An insect's body is divided into three parts; a spider's body is divided into only two parts.

1. The main idea of this story is:

Spiders are like insects.

Spiders are like insects in some ways, but they are not insects.

2. What are three ways to tell a spider from an insect?

a) _____

b) _____

c) _____

Circle the correct answer.

3. Spiders are the same size as insects.   True   False

Name:_____

Story Words

A good story contains these story elements:

Characters: the people, animals, or objects in the story
Setting: where and when the story takes place
Plot: the sequence of events
Conclusion: what happens in the end

Directions: Read the story. Then, answer the questions.

Ann and Tony are in line to go on the roller coaster. Ann is glad. She has never been on such a big ride before. She bites her lip, because she is nervous. Tony says he does not want to go with her. Ann does not want to go alone. She is not happy, but she steps out of the line with Tony. Then, Tony changes his mind. "I'll go with you," he says. Ann is glad her friend will go, too.

1. Who are the characters in the story? _____

2. What is the setting? _____

3. What is the plot? _____

_____

_____

4. What is the conclusion? _____

Name:_____

Story Words

The end of a story should bring all the parts of the story together and provide a satisfying conclusion. The elements of a story ending include:

The climax – the most thrilling part of the story where the problem is either solved or the plot thickens.

The resolution – how the characters solve the story problem.

The conclusion – what happens to the characters in the end.

Directions: Choose your favorite story. Think about its climax, resolution, and conclusion. Write why you think the ending is good, or write another ending for the story.

_____

_____

_____

_____

_____

Name:_____

Words Around the House

UNIT 3

Word Bank			
cabinet	curtains	cushion	drawer
quilt	sofa	sweep	towel

Directions: Write the word from the Word Bank that best completes each group.

1. cupboard, shelves, closet,

_____

2. pillow, pad, soft, _____

3. living room, couch, long,

_____

4. broom, clean, brush,

_____

5. bed, blanket, warm,

_____

6. bath, shower, drying,

_____

7. window, drapes, cloth,

_____

8. dresser, socks, slide, _____

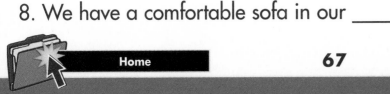

Directions: Choose the word that best completes each sentence. Write the correct letter on the line.

1. You use a towel when you are _____ .

2. To sweep the floor you need a _____ .

3. In a kitchen drawer we keep _____ .

4. Flowered curtains cover my bedroom _____ .

5. This cabinet has four _____ .

6. A cushion is soft like a _____ .

7. There is a warm quilt on my _____ .

8. We have a comfortable sofa in our _____ .

a. pillow

b. shelves

c. windows

d. broom

e. bed

f. living room

g. wet

h. forks

Name:_____

Words About the Human Body

Directions: Use the diagram to number the sentences below in the correct order from 1 to 8 to show what happens when you swallow a bite of food.

UNIT 3

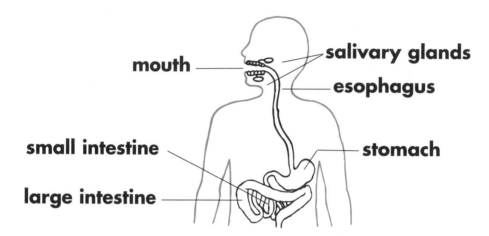

mouth —

salivary glands

esophagus

small intestine

stomach

large intestine

___ While your teeth are breaking the food into tiny pieces, saliva is making the food softer.

___ Whatever the body cannot use goes into the large intestine.

___ While the food is in your stomach, more juices help to dissolve it.

___ When the food in your mouth is soft enough, you swallow it.

___ When the food has dissolved in your stomach, it goes to your small intestine.

___ As you swallow your food, it moves down the esophagus to your stomach.

___ You use your teeth to take a bite out of a sandwich.

___ While the food is in your small intestine, the body absorbs whatever it needs.

Name:_____

Words About the Human Body

Directions: Read about the functions of blood in the human body. Then, use the bold words to complete the sentences below.

If you could look at a drop of your blood under a microscope, you would see some odd-shaped cells floating around in a liquid called **plasma**. These are the **white blood cells**. White blood cells are "soldiers" that fight germs which cause disease.

red blood cell

platelet

white blood cell

You would also see many smaller, saucer-shaped cells called **red blood cells**. Red blood cells give your blood its red color. They also have the important job of carrying **oxygen** to all of the cells in your body.

Blood **platelets** go to work when you have a cut. They form a plug, called a clot, that stops the bleeding.

Blood travels throughout your whole body. It goes to the **lungs** to pick up oxygen and to the intestines to pick up digested food. It carries the oxygen and **food** nutrients to all parts of your **body**. It also takes away carbon dioxide and other waste products.

1. Red blood cells carry __ __ __ __ __ __.

2. The blood gets oxygen from your __ __ __ __ __.

3. Blood carries __ __ __ __ nutrients from the intestines.

4. __ __ __ __ __ blood cells fight germs.

5. Blood travels to all parts of your __ __ __ __.

6. The liquid part of the blood is called __ __ __ __ __ __.

7. __ __ __ blood cells give blood its color.

8. __ __ __ __ __ __ __ __ __ form blood clots.

Name:_____

Words About the Human Body

Directions: Read about the circulatory system. Then, complete the activities.

Blood travels through three kinds of tubes. **Arteries** carry oxygen-rich blood from your heart to other parts of your body. Blood vessels called **veins** carry carbon dioxide-rich blood back to your heart. **Capillaries** are tiny vessels that connect arteries and veins. Capillaries take carbon dioxide from the cells and give the cells oxygen. Capillaries are fifty times thinner than a hair. They are so small that the blood cells must line up one at a time to travel through them.

Your heart, blood, arteries, veins, and capillaries work as a team. This team is called your **circulatory system**.

1. Name three kinds of blood vessels.

   a. _____

   b. _____

   c. _____

veins

arteries

2. The picture shows your circulatory system.

   • Color the veins **blue**.
   • Color the arteries **red**.
   • Color the heart **brown**.

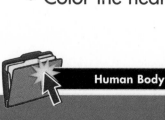

Name:_____

Money Words

Directions: Figure out which coins you need to make each amount. Then, color the coins.

Money	Quarters	Dimes	Nickels	Pennies
76¢	1	5		1
45¢				
98¢				
40¢				
84¢				
62¢				
31¢				
$1.42				
$1.98				

Name:_____

Story Words

Directions: Read the story. Then, answer the questions.

On Saturday, Tracy and her parents were watching television at home. Snow began falling around noon. Wow! It was really coming down. They turned off the television and looked out the window. The snow looked like a white blanket. They decided to put on their coats and go outside. All of the neighbors came out to see the snow. Tracy saw her friend, Jim. They built a snowman together. It was a great day!

1. Who are the characters of the story? _____

2. Where and when does the story take place? _____

_____

3. What is the plot? _____

_____

4. What is conclusion? _____

_____

UNIT 3

Story Words

A **concluding sentence** ties the story together.

Directions: Read each story. Then, choose the correct concluding sentence for the story. Write the sentence on the line.

1. Corn on the Cob

Corn on the cob used to be my favorite food. That is, until I lost my four front teeth. For one whole year, I had to sit and watch everyone else eat my favorite food without me. Mom gave me creamed corn, but it just wasn't the same. When my teeth finally came in, Dad said he had a surprise for me. I thought I was going to get a bike or a new CD player or something. I was just as happy to get what I did.

a. He gave me a new pair of shoes!

b. He gave me all the corn on the cob I could eat!

c. He gave me a new eraser!

---

2. A Train Ride

When our family took its first train ride, my sister brought along a big box. She would not tell anyone what she had in it. In the middle of the trip, we heard a sound coming from the box. "Okay, Jan, now you have to open the box," said Mom. When she opened the box, we were surprised.

a. I would like to take a train ride every year.

b. Trains move faster than I thought they would.

c. She had brought her new gerbil along for the ride.

Name:_____

UNIT 3

Story Words

Word Bank						
plot	events	character	setting	read	sentence	time

Directions: Write a word from the Word Bank to fit each clue. The letters in the boxes will reveal the name of things you read.

1. The time and place a story takes place

   ☐ _ _ _ _ _ _

2. The person or animal the story is about

   _ _ _ _ _ _ ☐ _ _

3. What the story is about

   _ _ ☐ _

4. What you do with a story

   ☐ _ _ _

5. The setting is the place and _____ .

   _ ☐ _ _

6. The concluding _____ ties the story together.

   _ ☐ _ _ _ _ _

7. The things that happen in a story

   _ _ _ _ _ ☐

Words Around the House

Directions: Read each sentence. Then, choose the best word or phrase to replace the underlined word. Circle the letter beside the correct answer.

1. We keep plates, cups, and glasses in the <u>cabinet</u> near the sink.
   - a. dresser
   - b. cupboard
   - c. refrigerator
   - d. bookcase

2. I opened the window <u>curtains</u> so I could see outside.
   - a. doors
   - b. locks
   - c. cloth coverings
   - d. wooden frames

3. I lay on the couch with my head on a soft <u>cushion</u>.
   - a. pillow
   - b. stuffed animal
   - c. blanket
   - d. warm sweater

4. We keep knives, forks, and spoons in a kitchen <u>drawer</u>.
   - a. closet for coats and jackets
   - b. shelf behind a glass door
   - c. closet for mop and brooms
   - d. box that slides in and out

Name:_____

Words About the Human Body

UNIT 3

Directions: Read about muscles. Then, use the bold words to complete the puzzle.

Muscles are tissues that move parts of the body. Each set of muscles has a **job** to do. The names of muscles have to do with the jobs they perform. The muscles that pull your forearms down are called **triceps**. Tri means "three." The triceps have three parts of muscle working together. The muscles that pull your forearms up are called **biceps**. Bi means "two." The biceps have two parts of muscle working together. Each set of muscles has a certain job to do. Muscles in the front of the foot pull your **toes** up. Muscles on the back of the thighs bend your **knees**.

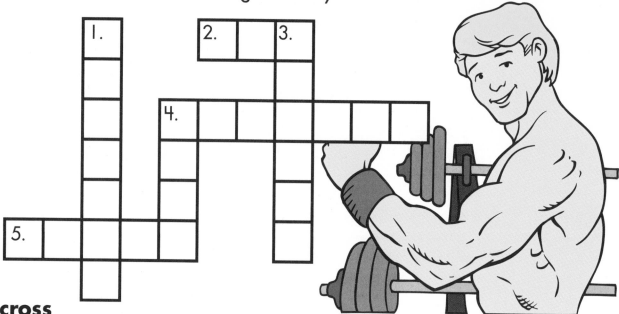

Across
2. Each set of muscles has a certain _____ to do.
4. These muscles pull your forearms down.
5. Muscles on the back of the thighs bend these.
Down
1. Without these, you would be a "bag of bones."
3. These muscles pull your forearms up.
4. Muscles on the front of your foot pull these up.

Words About the Human Body

Directions: Use the drawing of the tooth to complete the sentences.

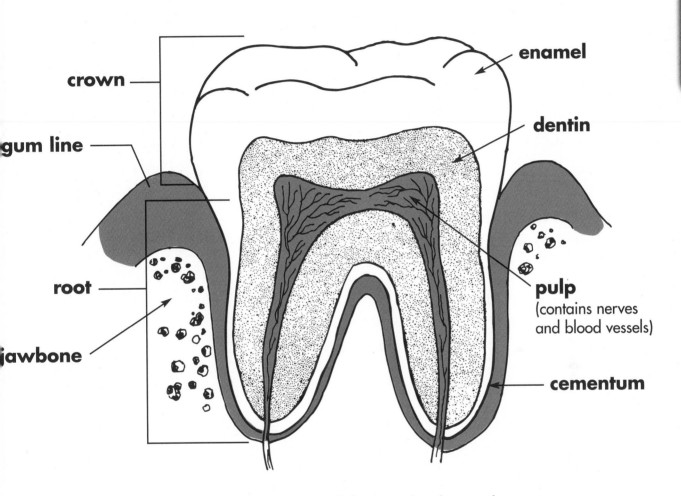

crown

enamel

gum line

dentin

root

pulp
(contains nerves
and blood vessels)

jawbone

cementum

1. The _____ is the part of the tooth above the _____.

2. The _____ of the tooth grows into the _____.

3. The outer covering of the crown is called _____.

4. The majority of the tooth is made of _____.

5. Any pain is transmitted to the brain through nerves in the _____.

6. _____ covers the dentin in the root.

Name:_____

Words About the Human Body

Directions: Read about your heart. Then, answer the questions.

Make your hand into a fist. Now, look at it. That is about the size of your **heart**, the muscle that pumps blood through your body! Your heart works all the time. Right now it is beating about 90 times a minute. When you run, it beats around 150 times a minute.

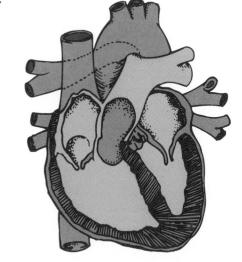

Inside, your heart has four spaces. The two spaces on the top are called **atria**. This is where blood is pumped into the heart. The two spaces on the bottom are called **ventricles**. This is where blood is pumped out of the heart. The blood is pumped to every part of your body. How? Open and close your fist. See how it tightens and loosens? The heart muscle tightens and loosens, too. This is how it pumps blood.

1. How often does your heart work? _____

2. How fast does it beat when you are sitting? _____

3. How fast does it beat when you are running? _____

4. How many spaces are inside your heart? _____

5. What are the heart's upper spaces called? What are the lower spaces called?

_____   _____

UNIT 3

Name:_____

Unit 3 Review

UNIT 3

Directions: Write the letter of the description on the right that best matches the word(s) on the left.

____ 1. details

____ 2. capillaries

____ 3. conclusion

____ 4. ears

____ 5. first, next, last

____ 6. esophagus

____ 7. oxygen

____ 8. tri

____ 9. quarter

____ 10. atria

____ 11. skeleton

____ 12. crown

____ 13. plot

____ 14. quilt

a. twenty-five cents

b. the human body's frame

c. three

d. bed covering

e. the sequence of events in a story

f. the part of the tooth you can see

g. tiny vessels that connect arteries and veins

h. the characters and events that make up a story

i. the tube that connects your mouth to your stomach

j. the end of a story

k. the heart's upper spaces

l. transition words

m. what red blood cells carry

n. the body part that allows you to hear sounds

UNIT 4

Name:_____

Genre Words

A **genre** is a category people use to organize different kinds of books. Everything you read can be classified in a specific genre.

Fiction is a genre. A fiction book is about things that are made up or are not true. Nonfiction is also a genre. A **nonfiction** book is about things that have really happened or are true. Books can be classified into more types within these two categories.

Mystery — a book that has clues that lead to solving a problem or mystery

Biography — a book about a real person's life

Poetry — a book that has a collection of poems, which may or may not rhyme

Fantasy — a book about things that cannot really happen

Sports — a book about different sports or sport figures

Travel — a book about going to other places

Directions: Read the titles. Then, write **biography**, **fantasy**, **mystery**, **poetry**, **sports**, or **travel** next to each title.

1. *Marty Frye, Private Eye*   _____

2. *Yoga Activities for Kids*   _____

3. *The Chronicles of Narnia*   _____

4. *A Sightseer's Guide to New York City*   _____

5. *Silly Verse for Kids*   _____

6. *100 Americans Who Shaped American History*   _____

 Genres

81

Name:_____

Genre Words

UNIT 4

Directions: Each genre listed below is nonfiction, which means it is about things that have really happened. Read the description for each genre. Then, draw a line to match each genre to the correct title.

An **autobiography** is the story of a person's life written by that person.

Ben Franklin and His First Kite

A **biography** is the story of a person's life written by another person.

My Story: In My Own Words

An **informational passage** gives information about a subject.

Heavy Rains Blamed for Flooding in the South

Name:_____

Genre Words

Directions: Read each passage. Then, choose the genre that best describes it. Write **autobiography**, **biography**, or **informational passage** on the line.

Americans began playing baseball on informal teams, using local rules, in the early 1800s. By the 1860s, baseball was being described as America's "national pastime." Alexander Cartwright invented the modern baseball field in 1845. He and members of his baseball club came up with the first rules and regulations for the modern game of baseball. The first recorded baseball game occurred in 1846 in New Jersey.

_____

Ted Williams was born on August 30, 1918 in San Diego, California. He made his major league debut with the Boston Red Sox at the age of 21. His batting records earned him the nickname, "The Splendid Splinter." He was an All-Star hitter who earned 2 MVP awards. His accomplishments on the field led to his induction in the Baseball Hall of Fame in 1966. Ted Williams died on July 5, 2002, in Inverness, Florida.

_____

Although people consider me a legendary baseball player, I am most proud of the time I served my country as a Marine Corps pilot during World War II and the Korean War. During the Korean War, John Glenn and I served in the same unit. I missed nearly five full seasons of baseball due to my military service. While these absences limited my career baseball totals, I will never regret my time in the Marines.

_____

  83 © 2007 School Specialty Publishing

UNIT 4

Name:_____

Words About the United States

Directions: Read about Delaware and Hawaii. Then, fill in the chart.

Fifty states make up the United States of America. Delaware became the first state on December 7, 1787. Hawaii became the fiftieth state on August 21, 1959.

Delaware is the second smallest state. Its nickname is First State. It is located on the east coast next to the Atlantic Ocean. The capital city of Delaware is Dover. The main industry is manufacturing.

Hawaii, nicknamed the Aloha State, actually consists of over 100 islands in the Pacific Ocean. Only three states are smaller than Hawaii. Honolulu is the capital city, located on the island of Oahu. Tourism is Hawaii's most important industry.

	Delaware	**Hawaii**
Date it became a state		
Nearby ocean		
Main industry		
Capital city		
Size of state		
Nickname		
Would you like to visit?		

Name:_____

Words About Nutrition

Vitamins are natural or human-made substances that our bodies need to grow and to stay healthy. We can get all of the vitamins we need by eating a well-balanced diet.

Directions: Using different colors, guide the Vita-Men on the left through the mazes to find out the jobs they do.

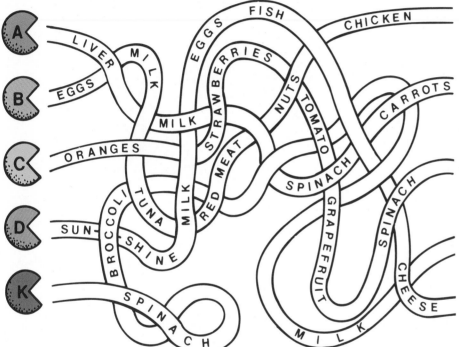

I help release energy from other nutrients.
Vitamin____

I help your eyes see at night and keep your skin healthy.
Vitamin____

I help heal cuts, scrapes, and scratches.
Vitamin____

I give you good, healthy blood.
Vitamin____

I help build strong bones and teeth.
Vitamin____

UNIT 4

Directions: Use the mazes to write the food sources for each vitamin.

Vitamin A	Vitamin B	Vitamin C	Vitamin D	Vitamin K

Words About Nutrition

UNIT 4

The food you eat must be digested before your body can use it. Digested food is changed into nutrients that help your body grow and give you energy.

Directions: Use the Word Bank to unscramble the names of the six nutrient groups.

Word Bank
proteins
vitamins
minerals
carbohydrates
water
fats

1. netroips _____

2. ralmenis _____

3. afts _____

4. ratew _____

5. timnivas _____

6. droracbaytesh_____

Directions: Write each nutrient name from the Word Bank on the line that best describes the job that it does for your body.

Needed: Nutrient to Deliver Food and Waste	Wanted: Muscle Builder and Body Repair Worker	Wanted: Nutrient to Store Energy
_____	_____	_____
Needed: Quick Energy Supplier	Needed: Growth and Good Health Helper	Needed: Nutrients for Many Jobs
_____	_____	_____

Name:_____

Words About Nutrition

Directions: A nutritious diet helps your body fight diseases. Write the foods from the Word Bank in the correct category.

Word Bank

tomatoes	bread	eggs	milk	potatoes
oranges	sugar	fish	cereal	green beans
chicken	margarine	cheese	noodles	rice
	apples	red meat	butter	

Carbohydrates

_____   _____

_____   _____

_____   _____

_____   _____

Proteins

_____   _____

_____   _____

_____   _____

_____   _____

Fats

_____   _____

_____   _____

Minerals

_____   _____

_____   _____

Directions: Write what you ate yesterday in each group. Did you get enough servings of each?

Dairy Group
(2–3 servings a day)

_____   _____

Meat & Protein Group
(2–3 servings a day)

_____   _____

Grain Group
(6–11 servings a day)

_____   _____

_____   _____

Fruit & Vegetable Group
(5–9 servings a day)

_____   _____

_____   _____

Fraction Words

A **fraction** is a part of a whole.

Directions: Read each fraction problem. Then, solve it. Write your answer as a fraction.

1. Fred played the ring-toss game. He tossed 27 rings. One-third of the rings landed on the ground. What fraction of rings landed on the bottles?

   Answer: _____

2. Charlotte worked at the refreshment stand. She served 30 glasses of lemonade, 15 glasses of milk, and 45 glasses of water. What fraction of people ordered water that day?

   Answer: _____

3. A book of tickets for rides contains 24 tickets. Mr. Dell gave one-fourth of the tickets to his son. What fraction of tickets does he have left?

   Answer: _____

4. A hot dog and soda costs $3.00. At the end of the day, Mrs. Ross sold the hot dog and soda for $1.50. What fraction of the original cost did people have to pay?

   Answer: _____

5. Lenny had a dozen yellow, red, and green balloons. Half of them were yellow. One-fourth were green. What fraction of the balloons were red?

   Answer: _____

Name:_____

Genre Words

Fiction writing is a story that has been invented. The story might be about things that could really happen (realistic) or about things that couldn't possibly happen (fantasy). **Nonfiction** writing is based on facts. It usually gives information about people, places, or things. A person can often tell while reading whether a story or book is fiction or nonfiction.

Directions: Read the paragraphs. Decide whether each paragraph is fiction or nonfiction. Circle the letter **F** for fiction or the letter **N** for nonfiction.

1. "Do not be afraid, little flowers," said the oak. "Close your yellow eyes in sleep and trust in me. You have made me glad many a time with your sweetness. Now I will take care that the winter shall do you no harm." **F N**

2. The whole team watched as the ball soared over the outfield fence. The game was over! It was hard to walk off the field and face parents, friends, and each other. It had been a long season. Now, they would have to settle for second place. **F N**

3. Be careful when you remove the dish from the microwave. It will be very hot, so take care not to get burned by the dish or the hot steam. If time permits, leave the dish in the microwave for 2 or 3 minutes to avoid getting burned. It is a good idea to use a potholder, too. **F N**

UNIT 4

Name:_____

Genre Words

Something that is **real** could actually happen. Something that is **fantasy** is not real. It could not happen.

Examples: **Real:** Pigs can wallow in mud.
Fantasy: Pigs can fly.

Directions: Read each sentence. Then, write **real** or **fantasy** on the line next to each one.

1. Lightning flashed across the sky during the storm. _____

2. We will fly by your house on our rocket-powered skates. _____

3. My mother uses a wheelbarrow to move dirt to her garden. _____

4. I have to wear boots and a coat when it is cold outside. _____

5. A caterpillar goes through four changes as it becomes a butterfly. _____

6. The mermaid left the water and walked along the beach. _____

7. The alien blasted off in his spaceship. _____

8. Leaves change their colors in autumn. _____

9. The tree spoke to me as I walked past it on my way to school. _____

10. We go to the beach when it is hot. _____

Genres

90

Name:_____

Genre Words

Directions: Read about fiction and nonfiction books. Then, look at each different type of book listed. Write **F** if the book is fiction. Write **NF** if the book is nonfiction.

UNIT 4

There are many kinds of books. Some books have make-believe stories about princesses and dragons. Some books contain poetry and nursery rhymes, like Mother Goose. These are **fiction**.

Some books contain facts about space and plants. And still other books have stories about famous people in history like Abraham Lincoln. These are **nonfiction**.

_____ 1. dictionary entry about horses

_____ 2. history of sports

_____ 3. riddles and jokes

_____ 4. true life story of a president

_____ 5. Aesop's fables

_____ 6. an encyclopedia entry about clouds

_____ 7. story about a talking puppet

_____ 8. nursery rhyme

_____ 9. story about a panda that talks to zoo visitors

_____ 10. story about the first space flight

Name:_____

Words About the United States

In 1803, President Thomas Jefferson sent Meriwether Lewis and William Clark to find a water route to the Pacific and explore the uncharted West. They began their journey along the Missouri river from their St. Louis-area camp. As they traveled, Clark spent most of his time on a boat, charting the course and making maps. Meanwhile, Lewis was often ashore, studying the rock formations, soil, animals, and plants along the way. Lewis and Clark encountered many interesting things: over 300 species unknown to science, nearly 50 Indian tribes, and the Rockies. They journeyed all the way to Fort Clatsop, which sits on the border between Oregon and Washington. After nearly two and half years, Lewis and Clark returned to St. Louis on September 23, 1806.

Directions: Color the states that Lewis and Clark traveled through on their expedition. Then, choose a state and do research to find out what Lewis and Clark discovered there.

Name:_____

Words About Nutrition

Carbohydrates are the main source of quick energy. Foods with lots of sugar and starch are rich in carbohydrates. You get carbohydrates from many foods like spaghetti, bread, cake, and candy.

Directions: Write a word from the Word Bank to complete each sentence and learn more about carbohydrates.

1. Carbohydrates are the __ __ __ __ __ foods to be digested.

2. __ __ __ __ __ __ __ __ are changed to sugars.

3. Sugar gives us __ __ __ __ __ __ .

4. Leftover sugar is stored as __ __ __ .

Word Bank

fat

first

starches

energy

Directions: Fill in the plate with carbohydrate-rich foods. Find pictures of these foods in magazines. Cut them out and glue them on the plate.

Name:_____

Words About Nutrition

Directions: Read about snack foods. Then, take the snacker's survey.

Do you have a bad case of the munchies, crunchies, or nibbles? Some snack foods can be healthy for you, while others are not. Foods that are lower on the food pyramid are usually much better for you because they contain smaller amounts of fat.

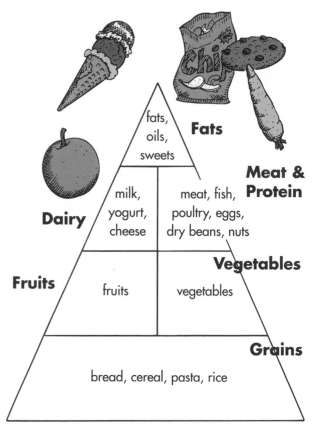

Snacker's Survey

Write the food group to which each snack belongs. Then, using a scale of 1–10, with 1 being the lowest, give each snack a taste score and a nutrition score.

Snack	Food group	Taste score	Nutrition score
Apple			
Cheese			
Cookie			
Potato Chips			
Orange			
Carrot			
Cake			
Candy Bar			
Bagel			
Beef Jerky			
Popcorn			
Pretzels			

Nutrition

94

UNIT 4

Name:_____

Words About Nutrition

Fat is a white or yellow oily substance found in some parts of animals or plants. Our bodies need some fat to stay healthy.

Directions: Many of the foods we eat contain fat. Try this fat test on several foods.

Materials Needed

6" x 6" pieces of brown paper bags (one per person)
6 containers each containing 1/4 cup of the following:
    water, oil, peanut butter, soft cheese,
    orange juice, soft margarine
6 toothpicks (one in each container)

Directions:

- Predict which foods contain fat on the chart below.
- Use the toothpick from each container to make a spot on your bag. Be careful to use small amounts of each item so they won't run together.
- Wait several minutes and check the spots. Those with fat will leave a greasy spot. Record your observations.

Name of Food	I Predict . . .		I Observed . . .	
	Fat	**No Fat**	**Fat**	**No Fat**

1. Which food seemed to have the most fat? Why? _____

2. Which food surprised you? _____

3. Which of the foods do you eat often? _____

4. What could you eat instead of the fatty foods? _____

Name:_____

Fraction Words

Directions: Color the number of items that show each fraction.

1. Color **one-third** of the cookies.

2. Color **one-fourth** of the dog treats.

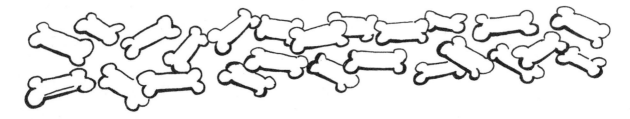

3. Color **one-fifth** of the pepperoni.

4. Color **one-half** of the books.

Name:_____

Genre Words

Directions: Read each sentence about books. The
book titles are in italics. Decide what type of book each
title is. Then, on the line, write **mystery**, **biography**,
poetry, **fantasy**, **sports**, or **travel**.

1. I read aloud to my sister from the book
   Read-Aloud Rhymes for the Very Young.   _____

2. *The Secret of Shadow Ranch* features my
   favorite detective, Nancy Drew.   _____

3. I will lend you my copy of *A Wrinkle in Time.*   _____

4. Mom bought us *Games You Can Play in the Car*
   to keep us busy on our road trip.   _____

5. I like baseball, so my dad bought me the
   book *The Story of Jackie Robinson.*   _____

6. *Kids in Sports* is a great book about child athletes.   _____

7. *Harry Potter and the Sorcerer's Stone* is one
   of the top-selling books of all time.   _____

8. *The Last Flight of Amelia Earhart* is an
   interesting story about aviation.   _____

9. I borrowed *The Case of the Treasure Hunt*
   from the library.   _____

10. My dad bought me *A Complete Handbook to Soccer*
    to help me with my game.   _____

UNIT 4

Name:_____

Genre Words

A **mystery** story usually has lots of suspense and exciting events. At the end, you get to find out "who did it"!

Directions: Follow these directions to make a mystery cube:

1. Cut a 12 x 16 1/2-inch piece of cardboard.

2. Draw the outline of the cube as shown below.

3. Cut out the shape.

4. Measure three 4-inch segments horizontally. Draw a dotted line between each segment.

5. Measure three 4-inch segments and one 4 1/2-inch segment vertically. Draw a dotted line between each segment.

6. Fold along the dotted lines.

7. Carefully tape the edges with clear tape.

8. Tuck the flap into the top of the cube.

9. Write the following on your cube:

Top:	Title
Right side:	Characters
Left side:	Where the story takes place
Front:	What is the mystery?
Back:	Three clues that help solve the mystery
Bottom:	Author's name
Inside top:	Solution to the mystery

10. Place some items inside the cube that symbolize the mystery or how it was solved.

11. Illustrate or decorate the cube.

Front

Left Side | Bottom | Right Side

Back

Top

Genre Words

An **autobiography** is the story of your life written by you! An outline can help you to organize details about your life.

Directions: Use the outline to write information about your life.

I. My Early Years

    A. Birthdate _____ Place _____

    B. Favorite activities _____

    C. Family members _____

    D. Things I learned _____

    E. First school _____

II. My Present

    A. School grade _____

    B. Friends _____

    C. Favorite subjects _____

    D. Sports or hobbies _____

    E. Family fun _____

III. My Future

    A. Middle school/High school _____

    B. College _____

    C. Ambitions _____

    D. Places I would like to see _____

    E. Things I would like to accomplish _____

    _____

Name:_____

Words About the United States

Directions: Study the map of the United States. Then, fill in the circle beside each correct answer.

1. Which state is a peninsula?

   (A) Nevada

   (B) Florida

   (C) Washington

   (D) Georgia

2. Which state is farthest north?

   (A) Texas

   (B) Arizona

   (C) New York

   (D) Kansas

3. Which state is on the West Coast?

   (A) California

   (B) North Carolina

   (C) Utah

   (D) Minnesota

4. Which state is east of Nebraska?

   (A) Oregon

   (B) Mississippi

   (C) Idaho

   (D) New Mexico

Name:_____

Words About Nutrition

Nutritious food is not dull, boring food. Angelo's pizza is very nutritious. It has food from all six food groups.

Directions: Draw a line to match each ingredient with its food group. Then, with an adult's help, follow the recipe to make the pizza.

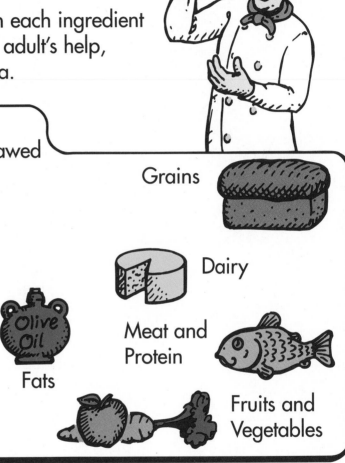

Angelo's Pizza Supreme
1 loaf frozen bread dough, thawed
Mozzarella cheese (shredded)
hamburger (cooked)
pepperoni (sliced)
anchovies
sausage (cooked)
vegetable oil
pizza sauce (6 oz. can)
tomatoes (chopped)
onion (chopped)
green pepper (chopped)
mushrooms (sliced)
olives (sliced)

Grains

Dairy

Meat and Protein

Fats

Fruits and Vegetables

Press thawed bread dough onto a greased pizza tin. Prick with a fork and brush with oil. Bake at 400° until light brown (about 10 minutes). Cover crust with tomato sauce, cheese, and other ingredients. Bake at 400° until cheese is melted.

UNIT 4

Name:_____

Words About Nutrition

Directions: Write the letter of each of the fruits and vegetables under the correct plant part.

Directions: Circle the vegetables that are the seeds of the plant.

pea pod	cabbage	carrot	string bean
cucumber	avocado	broccoli	green pepper
spinach	zucchini	potato	turnip

Name:_____

Words About Nutrition

Directions: Read about calcium. Then, try the experiment.

The **skeleton** is a framework of 206 bones that has three main jobs: to hold up your body, to protect your inner organs, and to produce new blood cells inside the bones. It is important to keep our bones healthy. The outer part of a bone contains calcium. Calcium keeps our bones strong. What would happen if our bones lacked calcium?

Materials Needed:
1 chicken bone
1 glass jar with a lid
1 cup vinegar

Directions:
1. Clean the chicken bone.
2. Place the bone in the jar and cover it with vinegar.
3. Cover the jar tightly.
4. Let the jar sit for two weeks.

After two weeks:

How has the chicken bone changed? _____

_____

_____

What would happen to your body without calcium? _____

_____

_____

Name:_____

Unit 4 Review

Directions: Unscramble the letters of words you have learned in this unit. Use the Word Bank if you need help.

Word Bank			
sports	energy	cereal	genre
nutrition	vegetables	fractions	biography
fantasy	vitamins	expedition	Delaware

1. gereny _____

2. sfaynat _____

3. edexitonpi _____

4. sitavmin _____

5. grene _____

6. laceer _____

7. ewlaread _____

8. norunitit _____

9. storps _____

10. giopyahrb _____

11. sonticarf _____

12. beglestave _____

UNIT 4

Name:_____

Words That Are Sounds

Onomatopoeia is the use of words that sound like the noises they represent. These words can make writing more interesting to read.

Example: The bees **buzzed** around my head in an angry swarm. The door made a loud **bang** when it closed.

Directions: Write a sentence for each word. Then, draw a picture to illustrate one of your sentences.

1. chugged _____

2. snap _____

3. hiss _____

4. splash _____

5. boom _____

6. splat _____

7. thump _____

8. pop _____

Name:_____

Words That Are Sounds

Animal noises are another example of onomatopoeia.

Directions: Write the noise that each animal makes.

Name:_____

Figures of Speech

An **idiom** is a figure of speech. An idiom means something different than what the words actually say.

Directions: Read each story. Then, put an **X** in front of the best example of the idiom in bold type.

1. I was really frustrated on Monday. First, my alarm clock broke, and I overslept. Next, my mom drove over a nail. We got a flat tire, and I was late for school. The **last straw** was when I forgot to bring my lunch to school. It was a horrible day!

_____ The last straw is when there are no more straws for your soda pop.

_____ The last straw is when a person is pushed to his or her limit and feels angry or frustrated.

_____ The last straw is when the farmer runs out of straw for the barn.

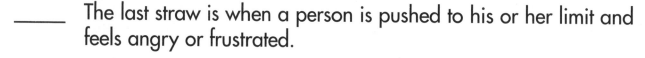

2. Matt decided to change his bad habits and **turn over a new leaf**. From now on, he was going to stop watching T.V. and study more.

_____ Matt will go leaf collecting tomorrow.

_____ Matt will rake leaves instead of watch T.V.

_____ Matt will change what he is doing and start fresh to make things different and better.

Name:_____

Words About U.S. Presidents

Directions: Use the Word Bank to find and circle the names of U. S. presidents in the puzzle. Look across, down, diagonally, and backward.

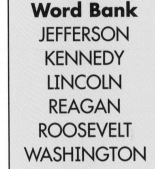

N	R	K	L	E	A	L	R	H	R	I	W
S	O	E	N	O	X	I	G	J	O	N	D
K	C	T	A	G	N	W	V	M	O	M	C
E	H	T	G	L	O	C	O	S	S	V	R
N	R	L	N	N	J	N	R	H	E	S	E
N	O	F	I	O	I	E	C	I	V	R	V
E	O	E	X	N	F	H	F	O	E	Y	O
D	S	V	D	F	C	T	S	F	L	U	A
Y	L	N	E	Y	S	O	P	A	T	N	H
T	E	J	H	R	H	N	L	I	W	E	O
K	N	G	R	E	A	G	A	N	X	C	O

Word Bank
JEFFERSON
KENNEDY
LINCOLN
REAGAN
ROOSEVELT
WASHINGTON

Directions: Write the correct name from the Word Bank under each description.

1. He was America's first elected president.

— — — — — — — — — —

2. The teddy bear was named for this president.

— — — — — — — — —

3. This president wrote the Declaration of Independence.

— — — — — — — — —

4. He was the youngest man to be elected President.

— — — — — — —

5. This president led the Union through the Civil War.

— — — — — — —

6. This president was a former movie star.

— — — — — —

Name:_____

Words About Plants

Directions: Use the words in the Word Bank to complete the puzzle about plants.

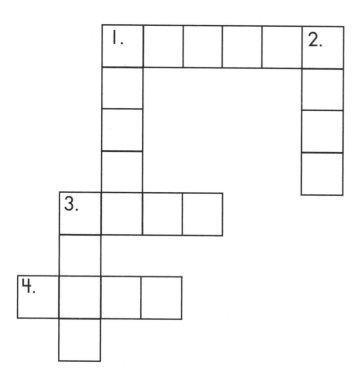

Word Bank
stem
root
leaf
flower
fruit
seed

Across
1. I often have bright colors, but my real job is to make seeds.
3. I carry water from the roots to the leaves and food back to the roots.
4. I collect energy from the sun to make food for the plant.

Down
1. I often taste delicious, but my job is to hold and protect the seeds.
2. I hold the plant tight like an anchor but also collect water and minerals from the soil.
3. Someday a new plant will grow from me.

UNIT 5

Name:_____

Words About Plants

Directions: Plants give us all the fruits, vegetables, grains, spices, and herbs we eat. Use the picture of the garden to write the fruits and vegetables under the correct plant part that can be eaten.

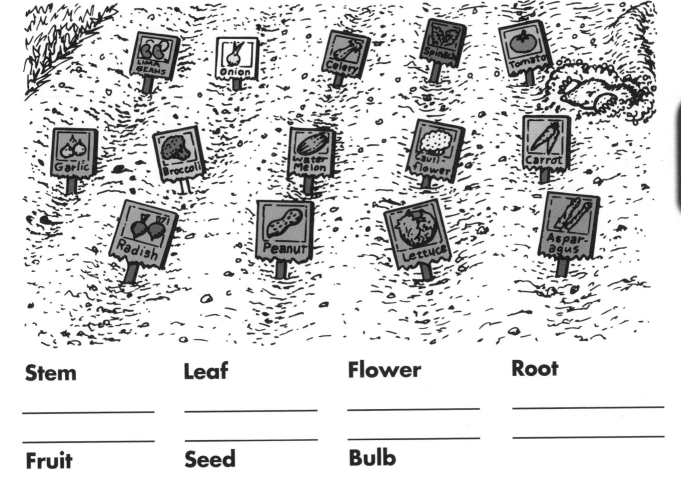

Stem	Leaf	Flower	Root
_____	_____	_____	_____
_____	_____	_____	_____

Fruit	Seed	Bulb
_____	_____	_____
_____	_____	_____

Directions: On a separate sheet of paper, make a chart like the one below. Complete the chart with as many kinds of fruits and vegetables you can name.

Vegetable or Fruit	Root	Stem	Leaf	Flower	Bulb	Fruit	Seed
kiwi						✓	

Plants

111

Name:_____

Words About Plants

Directions: Read about leaves. Then, use the bold words to complete the sentences. Use the numbered letters to answer the mystery question.

Leaves work like little factories making food for the plant, using a **green** material called **chlorophyll**. In each leaf, chlorophyll is like a little "green machine," changing **water** and air into food. Like most machines, chlorophyll needs energy to work. The green machine gets its energy from **sunlight**. This process is called **photosynthesis**. Without sunlight, the **leaves** could not make food.

1. Food-making material in leaves is called __ __ __ __ __ __ __ __ __ __ __ .
                                                          3   1 2 7

2. Plants make food from air and __ __ __ __ __ .
                                          4

3. The green machine gets its energy from __ __ __ __ __ __ __ __ .
                                                  8   9

4. Food is made in the plant's __ __ __ __ __ __ .
                                            6

5. The color of chlorophyll is __ __ __ __ __ .
                                      5

Mystery Question

What is the scientific name for the process of making food with the help of light?

__ __ __ __ __ __ __ __ __ __ __ __ __ __
1 2 3 4 3 6 7 8 4 2 5 6 9 6

Name:_____

Measurement Words

Look at the units used to measure length, width, and distance.

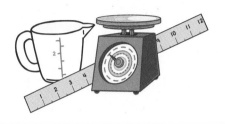

12 inches   = 1 foot
3 feet   = 1 yard
5,280 feet = 1 mile

Different units are used to measure weight.

16 ounces   = 1 pound
2,000 pounds = 1 ton

Directions: Reach each question. Circle the best estimate.

1. How long is a football field?   a. 100 feet   b. 100 yards

2. How long is a pencil?   a. 6 inches   b. 10 inches

3. How far is it between two cities?   a. 100 yards   b. 100 miles

4. How wide is your bedroom door?   a. 3 feet   b. 3 yards

5. How long is a book?   a. 12 inches   b. 2 feet

6. How long is your bed?   a. 15 feet   b. 5 feet

7. How heavy is your backpack?   a. 50 pounds   b. 5 pounds

8. How long is a crayon?   a. 4 inches   b. 10 inches

9. How heavy is the average dog?   a. 25 pounds   b. 25 tons

10. How long is your arm?   a. 1 1/2 feet   b. 1 1/2 yards

11. How heavy is a can of soda?   a. 12 ounces   b. 2 pounds

Directions: Look around your house and estimate the length, width, and weight of various items. Use a ruler and scale to measure each item to see how close your estimate was.

Measurement: Length

Name:_____

Figures of Speech

An **idiom** is a colorful way of saying something ordinary. The words in an idiom do not mean exactly what they say. The words are read in a figurative way, not a literal one.

Directions: Read each idiom. Draw a picture of its literal meaning. Then, draw a line to match the idiom to its meaning.

Jump on the bandwagon! ●   ● She doesn't eat very much.

She eats like a bird. ●   ● Keep the secret.

Don't cry over spilled milk! ●   ● Make sure you don't miss an opportunity.

Don't let the cat out of the bag! ●   ● Get involved!

You are the apple of my eye. ●   ● Don't worry about things that have already happened.

Don't miss the boat. ●   ● I think you are special.

UNIT 5

Name:_____

Figures of Speech

Directions: Read each sentence. Then, write the letter of the phrase that tells what the speaker really means.

UNIT 5

He says:	**What he means is:**
_____ 1. It's "raining cats and dogs."	a. don't eat very much
_____ 2. I remember when you were "knee-high to a grasshopper."	b. make me very happy
	c. robbed the bank
_____ 3. You "eat like a bird."	
_____ 4. He "held up the bank."	d. very small
_____ 5. You "light up my life!"	
	e. pouring hard
_____ 6. Which way should I turn "at the fork in the road?"	
	f. was hoarse
_____ 7. The speaker "had a frog in her throat."	g. where the road splits

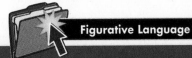

Name:_____

Figures of Speech

You can make sentences more interesting by using figures of speech. The following are four popular kinds of figures of speech.

Personification—gives human characteristics to things
   Example: The sun smiled down on me.

Hyperbole—great exaggeration
   Example: She was so frightened that she said
                    she would never sleep again.

Simile—compares two unlike things using **like** or **as**
   Example: He runs as fast as the wind.

Metaphor—suggests a comparison of two unlike things
   Example: The empty field was a desert.

Directions: Read each sentence. Identify the figure of speech used. Write **personification**, **hyperbole**, **simile**, or **metaphor** on the line.

1. The leaves danced in the wind.   _personification_

2. He was an angel during class.   _____

3. I have heard that story at least one hundred times. _____

4. After playing in the snow, her hands were as cold as ice. _____

5. The old car groaned as it went up the steep hill. _____

6. I was not at work yesterday, because I was as sick as a dog. _____

7. She is a graceful swan.   _____

8. He was so hungry he could eat a horse.   _____

9. The storm slept for two days.   _____

10. He said she was as pretty as a picture.   _____

Name:_____

Words About Leaders

Directions: Circle the correct answer to finish each sentence.

1. The leader of a school is a
    a. principal
    b. student
    c. police officer
    d. firefighter

2. The leader of the United States is a
    a. mayor
    b. governor
    c. president
    d. senator

3. The leader of England is a
    a. president
    b. prime minister
    c. princess
    d. prince

4. The leader of a family is often a
    a. parent
    b. sister
    c. brother
    d. cousin

5. Leaders are usually
    a. responsible
    b. hard working
    c. good with people
    d. all of the above

UNIT 5

Name:_____

Words About Flowers

Flowers are beautiful to look at and pleasant to smell, but they also have a very important job. Most plants make seeds inside the flower.

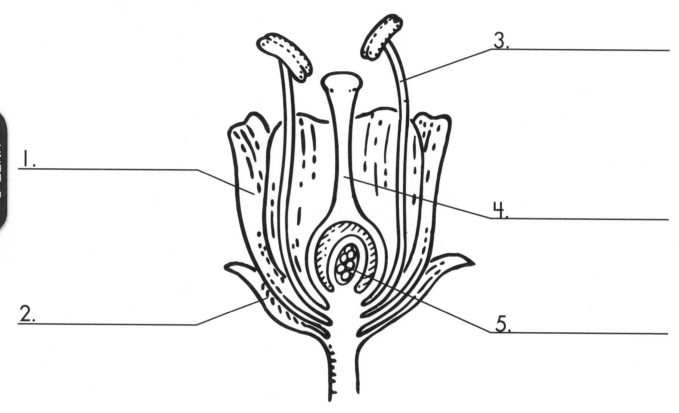

3.

1.

2.

4.

5.

Directions: Use the chart to color and label each flower part.

Flower part	Description	Color
pistil	A large center stalk, often shaped like a vase.	yellow
stamen	A tall, thin stalk with a knobbed tip. It holds grains of pollen.	brown
petal	Brightly colored and sweet-smelling leaves.	red
sepal	Small leaf-like part at the base of the flower.	green
ovary	Ball-shaped part at the base of the pistil. This is where the seeds develop.	blue

Plants

UNIT 5

Name:_____

Words About Plants

Directions: Read about dangerous plants. Then, write the correct words on the lines to complete the sentences.

You may have been warned about some plants. Poison ivy and poison oak are two examples of plants to be careful around. The itching and burning some people get from touching or even being around these plants is enough to make them extra careful. Have you ever walked through a field and felt like you had been stung? You probably touched the stinging nettle. This plant with jagged edges should be avoided.

Other plants can be more dangerous. You should not pick and eat any berries, seeds, or nuts without first checking to make sure they are safe. You could get very sick or even die if you ate from one of these poisonous plants. Rhubarb and cherries are two common pie-making ingredients, but never eat the leaves of the rhubarb plant. Also, cherry leaves and branches have poison in them.

1. You should not pick and eat any _____ , _____ or _____ without first making sure they are safe.

2. _____ and _____ might make your skin itch and burn.

3. If you touched a stinging nettle plant, you would

_____

_____

Plants

Name:_____

Words About Trees

Directions: Read about trees. Then, answer the questions.

Have you ever seen a tree that has been cut down? If so, you may have seen many circles in the trunk. These are called the **annual rings**. You can tell how old a tree is by counting these rings.

Trees have rings because they grow a new layer of wood every year. The new layer grows right below the bark. In a year when there is a lot of rain and sunlight, the tree grows faster; the annual ring that year will be thick. When there is not much rain or sunlight, the tree grows slower and the ring is thin.

1. The annual ring of a tree tells how big the tree is.
   True   False

2. Each year, a new layer of wood grows on top of the bark.
   True   False

3. In a year with lots of rain and sunlight, the annual ring that year will be thick.
   True   False

4. Trees grow faster when there is more rain and sunlight.
   True   False

5. How old was the tree on this page? _____

UNIT 5

Name:_____

Measurement Words

Directions: Read about two different kinds of measurement. Then, answer the questions.

Perimeter is the distance around a shape. To find the perimeter, measure the length of all of the sides of the shape and add them together. Each shape, even the funny looking ones, has a perimeter. If the sides of a shape are all the same length, you can multiply one length by the number of sides. You can measure perimeter in inches, feet, yards, and miles. You can also measure it in centimeters, meters, and kilometers.

The number of square units covering a space is called **area**. A square unit is a way to measure. It is a perfect square with all of the sides the same length. For instance, a square inch is like a piece of space that is 1 inch on each side. You can sometimes find area by counting the square units. If you want to find the area of a rectangle, multiply the length times the width. Area is calculated in square units. That means that if you are measuring area in inches, the result is inches squared, or in^2.

1. What is the definition of perimeter?

   _____

   _____

2. You have a unit that is 2 inches by 4 inches. Is this a square unit? Why or why not?

   _____

   _____

3. What is a perfect square?

   _____

   _____

4. Find the perimeter and area of the figure.

   perimeter = _____

   area = _____

   5 meters

   3 meters

Measurement: Length

Name:_____

Foreign Words

Directions: Many foreign words have worked their way into the English language. Read each foreign word. Then, write the letter of the word or phrase that defines it. Use a dictionary if you need help.

1. ____ au revoir (French)   a. a lobby or entryway

2. ____ Gesundheit (German)   b. a flat bread made from corn or flour

3. ____ crepe (French)   c. thin sticks used for eating

4. ____ tortilla (Spanish)   d. a married woman

5. ____ pita (Greek)   e. a dip made with avocado

6. ____ chopsticks (Asian)   f. a scarf worn on the head

7. ____ oui (French)   g. fabric wrapped to wear as a skirt

8. ____ sarong (Malaysian)   h. a friend

9. ____ amigo (Spanish)   i. yes

10. ____ rendezvous (French)   j. a rich layer cake

11. ____ babushka (Russian)   k. a meeting place

12. ____ lasagna (Italian)   l. a flat hat

13. ____ madam (French)   m. good-bye

14. ____ guacamole (Spanish)   n. a dish made with long, flat noodles

15. ____ Torte (German)   o. a thin cloth or pancake

16. ____ foyer (French)   p. round bread with a pocket

17. ____ beret (French)   q. "Good health!" to someone
                                     who sneezes

Name:_____

Foreign Words

Directions: The words in the Word Bank mean **hello** or **good-bye** in different languages. Write each word in the correct column.

Word Bank
Hola (Spanish)
Au revoir (French)
Arrivederci (Italian)
Adiós (Spanish)
Sayonara (Japanese)
Bonjour (French)
Guten tag (German)
Buon giorno (Italian)

Hello	Good-bye
1. _____	1. _____
2. _____	2. _____
3. _____	3. _____
4. _____	4. _____

Name:_____

Foreign Words

Directions: Match the words with their meanings.

_____ 1. éclair (France)

_____ 2. piñata (Mexico)

_____ 3. quiche (France)

_____ 4. chow mein (China)

_____ 5. limone (Italy)

_____ 6. pesto (Italy)

_____ 7. cannoli (Italy)

_____ 8. sushi (Japan)

_____ 9. flamenco (Spain)

_____ 10. croissant (France)

_____ 11. burrito (Spanish)

a. sauce made of basil, parmesan cheese, and pine nuts

b. horn-shaped bread

c. type of dance

d. decorated container filled with candy

e. lemon

f. cold, cooked rice wrapped in seaweed

g. pastry filled with custard

h. fried noodle dish

i. an unsweetened custard pie

j. a deep fried tube of pastry filled with cheese

k. a flour tortilla rolled or folded around a filling

UNIT 5

Name:_____

Words About U.S. Presidents

Directions: Read about Thomas Jefferson. Then, answer the questions.

Thomas Jefferson was the third president of the United States. He was also an inventor. That means he created things that had never been made before. Thomas Jefferson had many inventions. He built a chair that rotated in circles. He created a rotating music stand. He also made a walking stick that unfolded into a chair. Thomas Jefferson even invented a new kind of plow for farming.

1. The main idea is: (Circle one)
   Thomas Jefferson was very busy when he was president.
   Thomas Jefferson was a president and an inventor.

2. What do we call a person who has new ideas and makes things that no one else has made before? _____

3. What are three of Thomas Jefferson's inventions?

   a) _____

   b) _____

   c) _____

UNIT 5

Name:_____

Words About Trees

What is the largest plant growing near your home? It is probably a tree. It may be a maple, oak, pine, or palm. All trees have many of the same parts as the plants that grow in your garden—only much larger.

Directions: The riddles below tell about the jobs of the tree parts. Use the tree parts listed in the Word Bank to solve each riddle. Then, label the parts of the tree.

Word Bank
seed
trunk
leaves
roots
bark

1. Green and flat
   Or needle-like,
   We make food by day
   And rest at night.

   _____

2. From roots to branches,
   Short or long,
   My tough wood
   Keeps me tall and strong.

   _____

3. Scattered by wind
   When breezes blow,
   I'll make a new tree
   When I sprout and grow.

   _____

4. Thin-like hair,
   Or thick and round,
   We hold the tree
   Firmly in the ground.

   _____

5. Rough or smooth,
   A very tough cover,
   I keep out insects,
   Fire, and weather.

   _____

Name:_____

Words About Trees

Directions: Read about trees. Then, answer the questions.

Each year, as the hours of daylight grow shorter and colder weather comes, many types of trees lose their leaves. The falling of the leaves is so regular and amazing that the entire autumn season is called "fall."

The trees that lose their leaves are known as **deciduous** (dee-SID-you-us) trees. The word means "falling down." The leaves on these trees are wide, not like the needle-shaped leaves on pine and other **evergreen** trees. Trees lose water through their leaves, and wide leaves lose more water than the ones that look like needles. Water is very important to a tree. Because there is less water in the winter, the tree must drop its leaves to stay alive.

1. In what season do deciduous trees lose their leaves? _____

2. What are the trees that do not lose their leaves called?

_____

Directions: Circle the correct answer.

3. Deciduous trees have needle-shaped leaves.   True   False

4. Trees drop their leaves to save water.   True   False

UNIT 5

Name:_____

Words About Plants

Directions: Use the words in the Word Bank to complete the puzzle about plants.

Across
4. Deep-growing type of root
6. Beautiful, seed-making part of plant
7. Brightly colored "leafy" parts of the flower
9. Large part of seed that supplies food
10. Sweet food made by the leaves

Down
1. Making food with the help of light
2. Green food-making material in a leaf
3. Plant's "food factory"
5. Plant's anchor
8. What plants get their energy from

Word Bank

| petals | cotyledon | root | flower | leaf |
| sugar | chlorophyll | sun | photosynthesis | tap |

Name:_____

Unit 5 Review

Directions: Finish the story. Use words from the Word Bank.

Word Bank			
seeds	inches	roots	flower
fruit	light	water	area

Today, I am going to turn over a new leaf. My mom says that I am lazy and need a hobby to keep me busy. I am going to try gardening. I love to be outside, and I'm excited to learn about plants and how to take care of them.

First, I have to plan out how big I want my garden to be.

_____

_____

_____

_____

_____

_____

UNIT 5

Name:_____

Words That Are Antonyms

Antonyms are words that have opposite meanings.

Example: neat — sloppy

Directions: Cut out each frog. Then, glue each frog to the lily pad with its antonym.

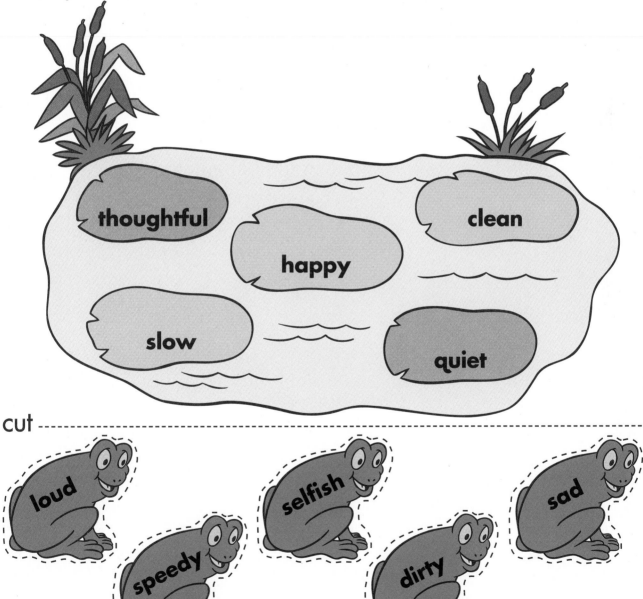

thoughtful

happy

clean

slow

quiet

cut -

loud

speedy

selfish

dirty

sad

Page left blank for cutting activity.

Name:_____

Words That Are Synonyms

Synonyms are words that mean almost the same thing.

Example: sick — ill

Directions: Use the words from the Word Bank to complete the sentences.

Word Bank				
glad	fast	noisy	filthy	angry

1. When I am mad, I could also say I am _____ .

2. To be _____ is the same as being happy.

3. After playing outside, I thought I was dirty, but Mom said I was _____ !

4. I tried not to be too loud, but I couldn't help being a little _____ .

5. If you're too _____ , or speedy, you may not do a careful job.

Think of another pair of synonyms. Write the words on the lines

_____   _____

UNIT 6

Name:_____

Words About the Statue of Liberty

Directions: Read about the Statue of Liberty. Then, use the bold words to complete the puzzle. Color the picture.

The **Statue of Liberty** is the statue of a woman holding a burning **torch**. There are 25 windows in her **crown** that serve as an observation deck for visitors. Visitors ride ferries to visit the statue, because it is surrounded by **water** in the **New York** Harbor. F.A. Bartholdi designed the statue. **France** presented it as a gift to the United States in 1886. To people all around the world, the statue is a symbol of **freedom**.

Across
1. The Statue of Liberty is a symbol of _____ .
3. The statue is located in the state of _____ .
4. There are 25 windows in Lady Liberty's _____ .

Down
1. _____ gave the statue to the United States as a gift.
2. She carries a _____ in her right hand.
5. Liberty Island is surrounded by _____ .

Name:_____

Space Words

Directions: Read about the sun's core. Then, use the bold words to complete the sentences.

If we could travel from the sun's **core**, or center, to the surface, we would be at the **photosphere**, which is the surface part of the sun seen from Earth. The flashes of light that scientists have seen on the surface of the sun are called **flares**. The dark patches are called **sunspots**. Sometimes, eruptions of gas, called **prominences**, can also be seen during a solar eclipse. Just above the sun's surface is a layer of bright gases called the **chromosphere**. The **corona**, the region beyond the chromosphere, consists of white concentric circles of light that radiate from the sun.

1. The _____ is the surface part of the sun that we can see.

2. The _____ is the layer of bright gases above the sun's surface.

3. The _____ consists of white concentric circles of light.

4. _____ can be seen during a solar eclipse.

5. The flashes of light on the sun's surface are _____ .

6. The sun's center is also known as its _____ .

7. The dark patches that sometimes appear on the sun are _____ .

Name:_____

Space Words

Directions: Unscramble each space word. Use the numbers below the letters to tell you what order the letters belong in.

1. _____

i	r	t	b	o
4	2	5	3	1

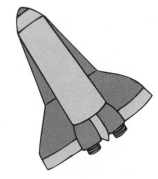

2. _____

u	t	o	n	c	w	d	n	o
3	5	7	9	1	8	6	4	2

4. _____

u	l	e	f
2	4	3	1

3. _____

a	t	s	r	a	t	n	o	u
7	9	2	4	1	3	6	5	8

5. _____

t	e	h	t	s	u	l
5	7	2	4	1	3	6

Directions: Write a space word beside each definition. Use the words that you unscrambled above.

1. A member of the team that flies a spaceship.

_____

2. A rocket-powered spaceship that travels between Earth and space.

_____

3. The material, such as gas, used for power.

_____

4. The seconds just before take-off.

_____

5. The path of a spaceship as it goes around Earth.

_____

UNIT 6

Name:_____

Space Words

On a clear night, you can see about two thousand stars in the sky. Scientists use giant telescopes to see billions of stars.

Stars in groups form pictures called **constellations**. People have been able to recognize these constellations for hundreds of years. Ancient people named many constellations for animals, heroes, and mythical creatures. We still use many of these names.

We can see some constellations every night of the year. Others change with the seasons.

Since all stars are constantly moving, these same constellations that we now see will be changed thousands of years from now.

Connect the stars to form the constellation called the Little Dipper.

Directions: Read about constellations. Then, complete the activities. There may be more than one correct answer

Write:
Stars in groups form pictures called _____ .

telescopes   constellations

Check:
Ancient people named many constellations for:

☐ animals   ☐ heroes   ☐ oceans   ☐ mythical creatures

Circle Yes or No:
Some constellations can be seen every night.   **Yes   No**
Some constellations change with the seasons.   **Yes   No**
In thousands of years, all constellations will be the same.   **Yes   No**

Name:_____

Geometric Shape Words

Directions: Read about geometric shapes. Then, follow the instructions.

Your kitchen is full of shapes.

You drink from **cylinders**. Color the glass. Then, draw two foods that come in cylinders.

You put your food in a **hemisphere**.
Color the bowl.

You eat **spheres**, **cubes**, **triangular prisms**, and **rectangular prisms.** Color the grapes, cheese, cake, and candy bar. Then, draw one other food that shares each shape.

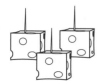

CHOCOLATE BAR

Name:_____

Words That Are Antonyms

Directions: Write each word from the Word Bank on the correct "antonym ant."

Word Bank					
careful	save	sour	fat	dirty	pretty
cry	far	poor	under	winter	low

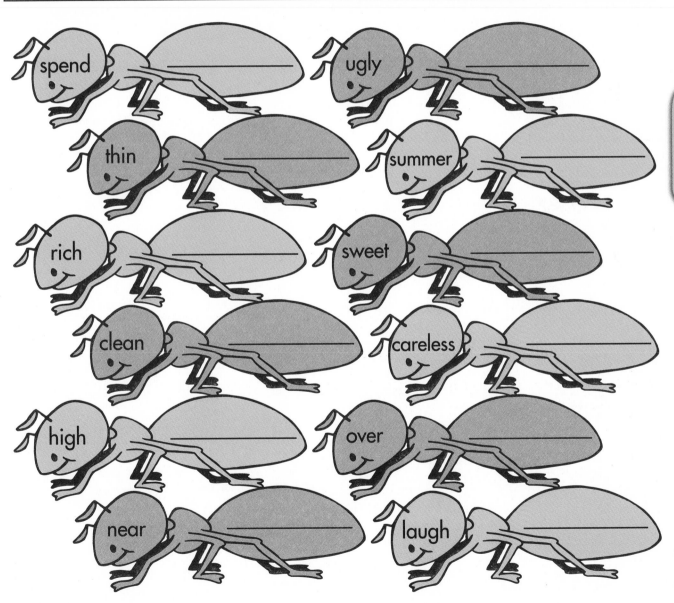

spend _____

ugly _____

thin _____

summer _____

rich _____

sweet _____

clean _____

careless _____

high _____

over _____

near _____

laugh _____

Name:_____

Words That Are Synonyms

Directions: Circle a synonym for the underlined word in each row below. Then, write another synonym from the Word Bank on the line.

Word Bank		
assist	rich	daring
processed	same	easy

1. <u>prosperous</u>   mansion   wealthy   _____

2. <u>simple</u>   plain   plan   _____

3. <u>artificial</u>   flavor   fake   _____

4. <u>bold</u>   brave   warrior   _____

5. <u>uniform</u>   soldier   attire   _____

6. <u>support</u>   help   bridge   _____

Name:_____

Words That Are Synonyms

Directions: Read the words on the kite tails. Choose a synonym for each word from the Word Bank. Then, write it on the correct tailpiece.

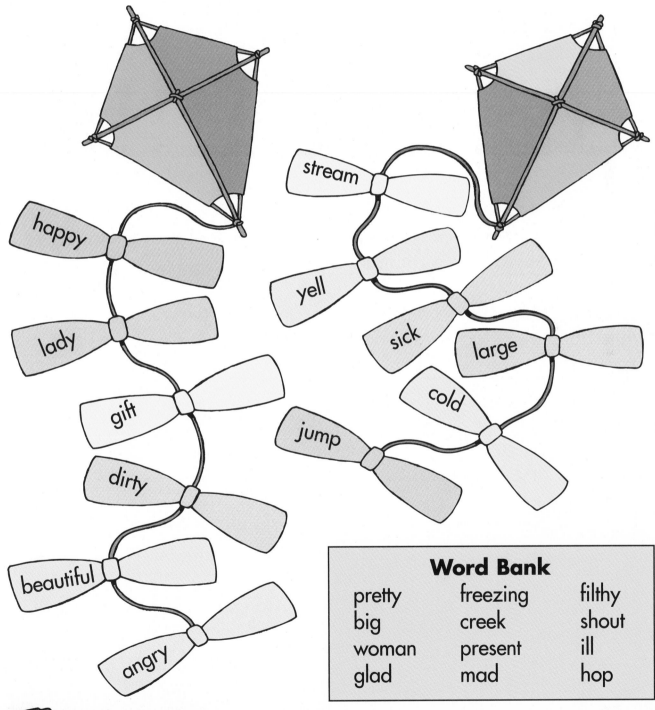

happy

lady

gift

dirty

beautiful

angry

stream

yell

sick

cold

large

jump

Word Bank

pretty	freezing	filthy
big	creek	shout
woman	present	ill
glad	mad	hop

Name:_____

Words About the White House

UNIT 6

The **White House** has been the home of every president in United States history except George Washington. However, George Washington chose the site and approved the construction of the home in 1792.

Directions: Use the Word Bank to find and circle the words about the White House. Look across and down.

Word Bank

president
Washington
oval
white
house
government
office

v	s	e	v	o	a	v	b	o	p
l	o	h	i	f	b	m	t	u	i
t	v	i	s	f	t	s	x	h	c
w	a	s	h	i	n	g	t	o	n
n	l	t	m	c	e	s	c	u	l
g	h	r	o	e	s	e	z	s	m
k	e	y	r	w	h	i	t	e	s
d	p	r	e	s	i	d	e	n	t
g	o	v	e	r	n	m	e	n	t

Name:_____

Space Words

Planets vary greatly in size. Look at the list of planets and their diameters.

Planet	Diameter (in miles)
Mercury	3,000
Venus	7,500
Earth	7,900
Mars	4,200
Jupiter	88,700
Saturn	74,600
Uranus	31,600
Neptune	30,200

Directions: Write the names of the planets in size order starting with the planet that has the largest diameter. Then, color the picture.

1. _____

2. _____

3. _____

4. _____

5. _____

6. _____

7. _____

8. _____

Name:_____

Space Words

Directions: Read about our solar system. Then, complete the activities. There may be more than one correct answer.

Our **solar system** is made up of the sun and all the objects that go around, or **orbit**, the sun.

The sun is the only star in our solar system. It gives heat and light to the eight planets in the solar system. The planets and their moons all orbit the sun.

The time it takes for each planet to orbit the sun is called a **year**. A year on Earth is 365 days. Planets closer to the sun have shorter years. Their orbit is shorter. Planets farther from the sun take longer to orbit, so their years are longer.

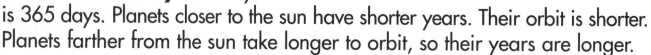

Sun

Draw the eight planets around the sun.

Underline:

The solar system is: the sun without the planets.
                         the sun and all the objects that orbit it.

Check:

The Sun

☐ is the center of our solar system
☐ is the only star in our solar system.
☐ is a planet in our solar system.
☐ gives heat and light to our solar system.

Write:

A _____ is the time it takes for a planet to orbit the sun.
   month   year

Match:

Planets closer to the sun . . .   have a longer year.
Planets farther from the sun . . .   have a shorter year.

Space

144

UNIT 6

Name:_____

Space Words

Directions: Read about the Milky Way. Then, complete the activities. There may be more than one correct answer.

The **Milky Way** galaxy is made up of our solar system as well as many other stars and solar systems. There are over 100 billion stars in the Milky Way!

The Milky Way is shaped much like a record. The outer part spins around the center.

The Milky Way is always spinning slowly through space. It is so large that it would take 200 million years for the galaxy to turn one complete time.

Many stars in the Milky Way are in clusters. Some star clusters contain up to one million stars!

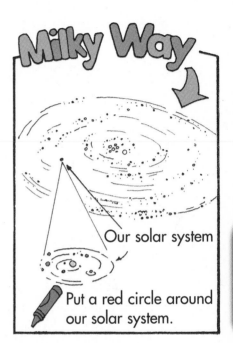

Our solar system

Put a red circle around our solar system.

UNIT 6

Check:

The Milky Way galaxy is made up of

☐ Earth.
☐ no Sun.
☐ our solar system.
☐ 100 billion stars.

Circle Yes or No:

The Milky Way is shaped like a pencil.	**Yes**	**No**
The Milky Way is always slowly moving in space.	**Yes**	**No**
Many stars in the Milky Way are in clusters.	**Yes**	**No**
Some star clusters have one million stars.	**Yes**	**No**

Circle:

It would take   200
                    90   million years for the galaxy to spin once.
                    600

Underline:

Which object is the Milky Way shaped much like?

 record    ruler

Name:_____

Geometric Shape Words

Objects are **congruent** if they are the same size and shape.

These cones are congruent: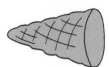

Objects are **similar** if they have the same shape, but are not the same size.

A grapefruit and a grape are similar because they are both spheres. They are not congruent because they are not the same size.

Directions: Circle **similar** or **congruent** to describe each set of items.

1.

similar   congruent

4.

similar   congruent

2.

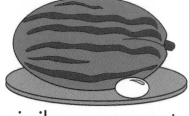

similar   congruent

5.

similar   congruent

3.

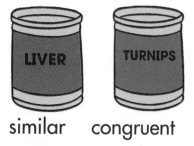

similar   congruent

6.

similar   congruent

UNIT 6

Name:_____

Words That Are Antonyms

Word Bank			
allow	blossom	bud	capture
forbid	release	tender	tough

Directions: Use the words in the Word Bank to write each antonym pair.

1. tender _____

2. capture _____

3. bud _____

4. allow _____

Directions: Use the word pairs from items 1–4. Complete the sentences by writing an antonym pair.

5. To _____ an animal means to catch it. To _____ an animal means to let it go.

6. School rules _____ us to yell on the playground. But the rules _____ us to yell in class.

7. A flower _____'s petals are tightly closed. A _____'s petals are open.

8. It is easy to chew _____ meat. But _____ meat is hard to chew.

Name:_____

Words That Are Antonyms

Directions: Write a word from the Word Bank to complete each sentence.

Word Bank					
open	right	light	full	late	below
hard	clean	slow	quiet	old	nice

1. My car was dirty, but now it is _____ .

2. Sometimes my cat is naughty, and sometimes she's _____ .

3. The sign said, "Closed," but the door was _____ .

4. Is the glass half empty or half _____ ?

5. I bought new shoes, but I like my _____ ones better.

6. Skating is easy for me, but _____ for my brother.

7. The sky is dark at night and _____ during the day.

8. I like a noisy house, but my mother likes a _____ one.

9. My friend says I'm wrong, but I say I'm _____ .

10. Jason is a fast runner, but Adam is a _____ runner.

11. We were supposed to be early, but we were _____ .

12. A roof is above a house, and a basement is _____ it.

UNIT 6

Name:_____

Words That Are Synonyms

Directions: Read each sentence. Write a synonym from the Word Bank that can take the place of the underlined word.

Word Bank		
runs	throw	dress
quilt	ribbon	

1. My friend and I like to toss the ball.

_____

2. The mouse scurries across the kitchen floor.

_____

3. I decorated each package with a pretty bow.

_____

4. He likes to sleep with the blanket his mother made for him.

_____

5. Her gown is beautiful.

_____

Synonyms

149

UNIT 6

Name:_____

Words About the American Flag

Directions: How much do you know about the American flag? Write a sentence using each of the words or phrases from the Word Bank.

Word Bank			
stars	stripes	pledge	red, white, and blue
American	parade	fifty	thirteen

1. _____

2. _____

3. _____

4. _____

5. _____

6. _____

7. _____

8. _____

UNIT 6

Name:_____

Space Words

Directions: Read about Venus. Then, complete the activities. There may be more than one correct answer.

Venus is the nearest planet to Earth. Because it is the easiest planet to see in the sky, it has been called the **Morning Star** and **Evening Star**. The Romans named Venus after their goddess of love and beauty.

Venus is covered with thick clouds. The sun's heat is trapped by the clouds. The temperature on Venus is nearly 900 degrees! Space probes can report information about the planet to scientists. But they can last only a few hours on Venus because of the high temperature.

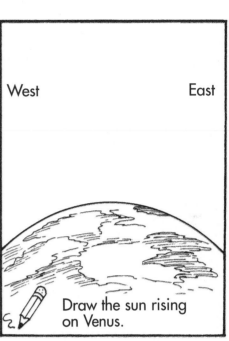

West   East

Draw the sun rising on Venus.

Venus turns in the opposite direction from Earth. So, on Venus, the sun rises in the west and sets in the east!

Circle:
Venus is the farthest planet to Earth.
              nearest

Check:
It is called the ☐ Evening Sun
                 ☐ Morning Star   because it is so easy to see.
                 ☐ Evening Star

Circle:

The Romans named Venus for their:

goddess of love and beauty   god of light   goddess of truth

Circle Yes or No:
Half of Venus is frozen with ice and snow.   **Yes   No**
On Venus, the sun rises in the east and sets in the west.   **Yes   No**

UNIT 6

Name:_____

Space Words

Directions: Read about Saturn. Then, complete the activities. There may be more than one correct answer.

Saturn is a planet famous for its rings. The rings are made of billions of tiny pieces of ice and dust. They are very wide and very thin. If you look at the rings from the side, they are almost too thin to be seen.

Draw 22 moons around Saturn!

Saturn is the second largest planet in our solar system. It is so big that 758 Earths could fit inside it!

Saturn is covered by clouds. Strong, fast winds move the clouds quickly across the planet.

Saturn has 22 moons! Its largest moon is called **Titan**.

Circle:
Saturn is most famous for its

spots.　　　rings.

Write:
Saturn's rings are made of _____ and _____ .

mud　　ice　　　dust　　moons

Check:
Saturn's rings are
☐ red, yellow, and purple.
☐ wide, but thin.

Underline:

is the second largest planet in our solar system.
is big enough to hold 758 Earths inside it.
is farther from the sun than any other planet.
is covered by fast, strong winds.
has a moon called Titan.

Name:_____

Space Words

Directions: Read about Pluto. Then, complete the activities. There may be more than one correct answer.

Pluto is a dwarf planet. It is farther from the sun than the eight planets of our solar system.

If you could stand on Pluto, the sun would look just like a bright, distant star in the sky. Pluto is so far away that it gets little of the sun's heat. That is why it is freezing cold on Pluto.

Some scientists think that Pluto was once one of Neptune's moons that escaped from orbit and drifted into space. Others believe it has always been a planet in our solar system.

Pluto is so far away from the sun that it takes 247 Earth years just to orbit the sun once!

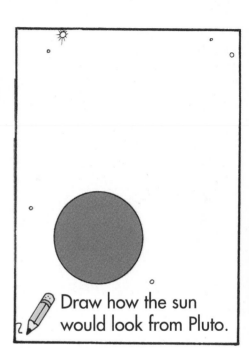

Draw how the sun would look from Pluto.

UNIT 6

Circle:

Pluto is a   dwarf   planet.
                planet.

Pluto is   closer to   the sun than any of the planets of our solar system.
Check:
          farther from

Pluto Facts

☐ On Pluto, the sun looks like a bright star.
☐ Pluto gets very little of the sun's heat.
☐ Pluto has very hot weather.
☐ Pluto takes 247 Earth years to orbit the sun.

Circle:

Some scientists believe that Pluto was once Neptune's   sun.
                                                    moon.

Name:_____

Unit 6 Review

Directions: Read each sentence. Look at the bold word. Write its antonym on the line to correct the sentence.

1. If you run **slow**, you will win the race. _____

2. The **sweet** candy made my lips pucker. _____

3. She was too **healthy** to go to work. _____

4. Some constellations can be seen every **day**. _____

5. If I **spend** my money, I know I will have enough for a new bike. _____

6. The Milky Way is always spinning **quickly** though space. _____

7. We were told to be **loud** in the library. _____

8. It was **hot** enough for me to wear a coat. _____

9. The girls are so **different** that you would think they were sisters. _____

10. He is so **poor** that he owns three restaurants. _____

11. Her **cowardly** deeds brought her great fame. _____

12. Pluto, the dwarf planet, is the **closest** planet from the sun. _____

13. The Statue of Liberty carries a torch in her **left** hand. _____

14. The flower was so **ugly** that it won first prize in the gardening show. _____

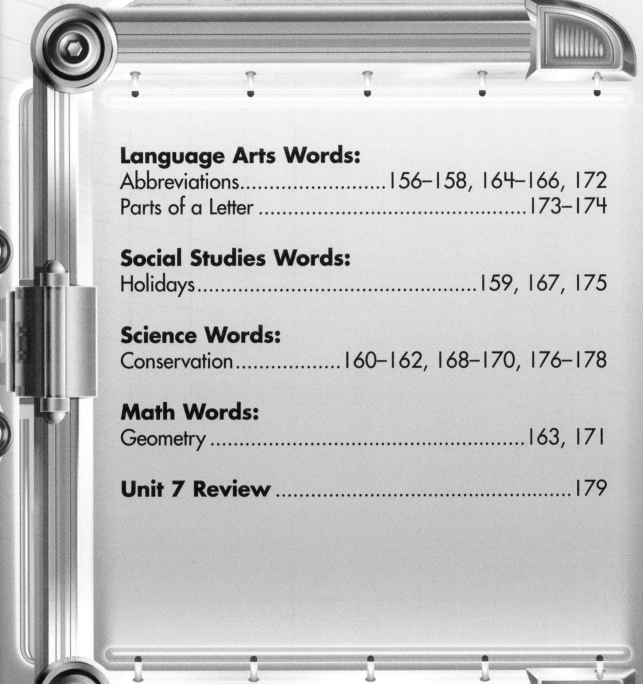

Name:_____

Words That Are Abbreviations

An **abbreviation** is the general term for the shortened form of a word of phrase used in writing.

An **acronym** is a kind of abbreviation in which a word is formed by putting together the first letters or parts of a series of words in a longer phrase.

Example: SCUBA
Self **C**ontained **U**nderwater **B**reathing **A**pparatus

Directions: Write acronyms that you know. Then, write what they stand for. The first one is done for you.

1. ___DARE___   ___Drug Abuse Resistance Education___

2. _____   _____

3. _____   _____

4. _____   _____

5. _____   _____

6. _____   _____

7. _____   _____

8. _____   _____

9. _____   _____

Name:_____

Words That Are Abbreviations

Initialism is a kind of abbreviation formed from the first (initial) letter or series of letters of several words. Each letter is pronounced individually. **TV**, **AM**, and **PM** are examples of initialism.

Directions: Initialism is used often when referring to computers and technology words. Use the Word Bank to complete each sentence with the correct initialism.

Word Bank					
TV	PC	CD	URL	DVD	www

UNIT 7

1. Let's listen to my classic rock _____ .

2. We can watch movies on my _____ player.

3. I watch cartoons on _____ every Saturday morning.

4. My new _____ has computer games and Internet access.

5. The "World Wide Web" is commonly referred to as _____ .

6. My teacher wants me to list the _____ of each website I used.

Words That Are Abbreviations

Some abbreviations are formed by using the first and second or first and last letters of a word.

Examples: **Dr.**   -   doctor
                St.   -   street

Some abbreviations are formed with the first and last letters of a word as well as letters in between.

Example: **Blvd.** -   boulevard

Directions: Rewrite each sentence by spelling out each bold abbreviation.

1. **Mr.** Stevens is out today.

   _____

2. The car turned onto Front **St.**

   _____

3. We need to find **Dr.** Hamilton.

   _____

4. Franklin **Ave.** crosses Stuart **Blvd.**

   _____

Name:_____

Holiday Words

Thanksgiving is a holiday in the United States held on the fourth Thursday in November. On Thanksgiving, Americans remember the good harvest of the Pilgrims in 1621 and show thanks for what they have now.

Directions: Use the Word Bank to find and circle the hidden Thanksgiving words in the puzzle. Look across and down. Then, color the picture.

f	l	t	r	i	b	e	x	v
i	h	u	n	t	q	x	h	p
s	x	r	c	o	r	n	a	i
h	w	k	h	a	n	t	r	l
o	c	e	a	n	g	y	v	g
M	a	y	f	l	o	w	e	r
v	g	o	b	b	l	e	s	i
d	i	n	n	e	r	v	t	m
r	d	o	n	a	t	i	v	e

Word Bank

ocean	gobble	corn	fish
Pilgrim	Mayflower	native	tribe
harvest	turkey	hunt	dinner

Name:_____

Conservation Words

To **conserve** is to keep safe from loss, destruction, or waste. In order to take care of our planet, we must conserve the materials and resources that we take from the planet. April 22 is designated as Earth Day, a day to remember how important it is to be good to our planet.

Directions: Make a poster to celebrate Earth Day or to inspire others to conserve resources. Use words from the Word Bank on your poster. Use the space below to plan out your poster.

UNIT 7

Word Bank

polluting	Earth	solar	creatures	conserve
energy	clean	reduce	reuse	recycle

STOP POLLUTING
MOTHER EARTH!

Let's use more windmills, electric cars, and <u>solar</u> power!

All living <u>creatures</u> need clean air.

Conservation

160

Name:_____

Conservation Words

To **recycle** is to put through a process that allows used things to be reused.

What do you throw away every day? What could you do with these things? You could change an old greeting card into a new card. You could make a puppet with an old paper bag. Old buttons make great refrigerator magnets. You can plant seeds in plastic cups. Cardboard tubes make perfect rockets. So, use your imagination!

Directions: Write a sentence to tell what you could do to reuse each item.

1. A cardboard tube _____

2. Buttons _____

3. An old greeting card _____

4. Paper bag _____

5. Plastic cups _____

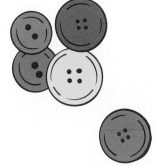

Conservation

Name:_____

Conservation Words

Directions: Circle the letter of the word or phrase that means the same as the underlined word.

1. Riding a bike saves energy and <u>reduces</u> pollution.
   a. decreases
   b. cleans
   c. increases
   d. eliminates

2. This house runs on <u>solar</u> power instead of gas or electricity.
   a. from the phone company
   b. from Mars
   c. from the sun
   d. from water

3. We try to <u>reuse</u> paper at school.
   a. write on
   b. use again
   c. put away
   d. throw away

4. In the morning, we <u>carpool</u> to school.
   a. share the ride
   b. ride a bike
   c. walk
   d. go for a swim

5. We need more laws against <u>polluting</u> our air and water.
   a. dirtying
   b. cleaning
   c. protecting
   d. studying

Conservation

162

Name:_____

Geometry Words

Geometry is the branch of mathematics that has to do with **points**, **lines**, and **shapes**.

A **line** goes on and on in both directions. It has no end points.

 Line CD

A **segment** is part of a line. It has two endpoints.

 Segment AB

A **ray** has a line segment with only one endpoint. It goes on and on in the other direction.

 Ray EF

An **angle** has two rays with the same end point.

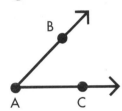 Angle BAC

Directions: Write the name for each figure. The first one is done for you.

1.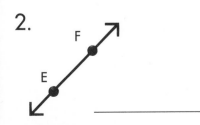
   Line MN

2.
   _____

3.
   _____

4.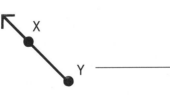
   _____

5.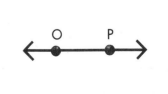
   _____

6.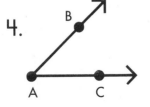
   _____

UNIT 7

Words That Are Abbreviated

An **abbreviation** is the shortened form of a word. Most abbreviations begin with a capital letter and end with a period. Look at the abbreviations in the box.

Mr.	Mister	St.	Street
Mrs.	Missus	Ave.	Avenue
Dr.	Doctor	Blvd.	Boulevard
A.M.	before noon	Rd.	Road
P.M.	after noon		

Days of the week: Sun. Mon. Tues. Wed. Thurs. Fri. Sat.
Months of the year: Jan. Feb. Mar. Apr. Aug. Sept. Oct. Nov. Dec.

Directions: Write the abbreviation for each word.

1. street _____

2. road _____

3. missus _____

4. before noon _____

5. doctor _____

6. mister _____

7. October _____

8. March _____

9. Tuesday _____

10. avenue _____

11. Friday _____

12. August _____

Directions: Rewrite each sentence using abbreviations.

1. On Monday at 9:00 before noon, Mister Jones had a meeting.

_____

2. In December, Doctor Carlson saw Missus Zuckerman.

_____

3. One Tuesday in August, Mister Wood went to the park.

Name:_____

Words That Are Abbreviated

A person's title is often abbreviated. Look at the abbreviations and their meanings.

Full Title	Abbreviation	Definition
Mister	Mr.	title for a man
Missus	Mrs.	title for a married woman
Doctor	Dr.	title for someone with a doctoral degree
Junior	Jr.	a son with the same first, middle, and last name as his father

Directions: Draw a line through each word that could be abbreviated. Then, write the abbreviation above the word. The first one is done for you.

1. Liz, should I call your mother ~~Missus~~ ^{Mrs.} Marks or ~~Doctor~~ ^{Dr.} Marks?

2. Doctor Martin Luther King, Junior, was a great man.

3. Our neighbor's name is Mister Samuels.

4. I have an appointment with Doctor Garza.

5. My mom likes to be called Missus Reed.

Abbreviations

UNIT 7

Name:_____

Words That Are Abbreviated

Sometimes, measurement words are abbreviated. Read the abbreviations in the box.

oz.	ounce(s)
lb./lbs.	pound/pounds
in.	inch(es)
ft.	foot or feet

Directions: Rewrite each sentence without abbreviations. Some sentences have more than one abbreviation.

1. I weigh 73 lbs.

_____

2. My height is 4 ft., 5 in.

_____

3. My baby sister is 21 in. long.

_____

4. She weighs only 7 lbs., 6 oz.

_____

5. Our dad is 77 in. tall. That is over 6 ft!

_____

UNIT 7

Name:_____

Holiday Words

Directions: Use the words in the Word Bank to complete the puzzle about holidays.

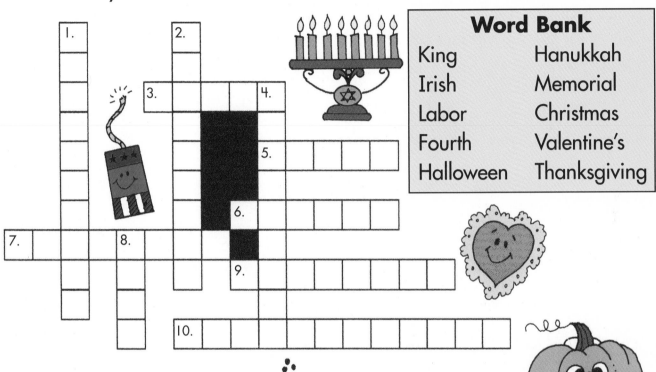

Word Bank

King	Hanukkah
Irish	Memorial
Labor	Christmas
Fourth	Valentine's
Halloween	Thanksgiving

Across

3. St. Patrick's Day is an _____ holiday.
5. _____ Day is the first Monday in September.
6. The _____ of July is Independence Day.
7. _____ is a Jewish holiday.
9. _____ Day is a day of remembrance.

10. _____ Day began with Pilgrims and Indians.

Down

1. Hearts are all around on _____ Day.
2. _____ is celebrated in December.
4. _____ is a time to trick-or-treat.
8. Martin Luther _____ , Jr., is honored in January.

UNIT 7

Name:_____

Conservation Words

The things we throw away affect the environment. Things that are biodegradable will eventually break down and become part of the earth. Things that are not biodegradable stay with us forever as litter. Check out what is, or is not, biodegradable with this long-term activity. Find an adult to help you.

You will need: a trowel, apple cores, large lettuce leaves, a plastic wrapper, Styrofoam cups, craft sticks, markers

Directions:

1. Find a spot where it is all right to dig four holes. Dig all about the same size—2 inches deep by 3 inches square.

2. Put the apple cores, lettuce leaves, plastic wrapper, and Styrofoam cups in their respective holes and cover them with dirt.

3. Write the name of each item on a craft stick. Put each craft stick in the ground to mark the spots.

4. In a month, go back and dig up the items. Discuss with an adult what you discover.

UNIT 7

Name:_____

Conservation Words

Directions: Many people devote their lives to helping the earth. Here are some job titles those people have. Can you think of others?

solid waste technician
air pollution inspector
sewage plant worker
pollution scientist
city planner
park ranger
forest ranger

geologist
ecologist
forester
oceanographer
marine biologist
forest naturalist
conservationist

_____ _____

_____ _____

Select from the list above a career about which you would like to learn. Write a report about it. If someone in the community holds one of those jobs, you should write the person to ask for an interview and/or on-site visit, or ask if they might send information about their job. You may also learn about environmental careers from reference books or by obtaining material from one of the organizations below.

Air and Waste Management Association
One Gateway Center, 3rd Floor
Pittsburgh, PA 15222

American Forests
1516 P Street NW, P.O. Box 2000
Washington, D.C. 20005

American Geological Institute
4220 King Street
Alexandria, VA 22302

American Institute of Architects
1735 New York Avenue NW
Washington, D.C. 20006

American Water Works Association
6666 W. Quincy Avenue
Denver, CO 80235

Conservation Fund
1800 N. Kent Street, Suite 1120
Arlington, VA 22209

Conservation Words

Many places in your community do things to help the environment.

aquarium	national park	library
science museum	landfill	recycling center

Directions: Visit one of the places listed above. After your trip, write a list of what this place is doing to protect the environment. Also, write ways that you can help.

_____

_____

_____

_____

_____

_____

UNIT 7

Name:_____

Geometry Words

A **triangle** is a figure with three sides and three angles. The angles of a triangle always add up to 180 degrees.

Triangles are organized sometimes by the characteristics of their sides.

An **isosceles triangle** has two equal sides. A **scalene triangle** has no equal sides. An **equilateral triangle** has three equal sides.

Directions: Write the name of each triangle.

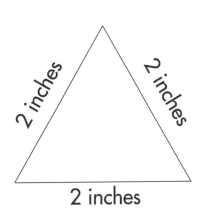

2 inches   2 inches

2 inches

_____

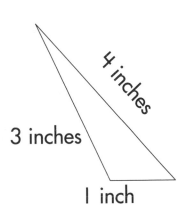

3 inches   4 inches

1 inch

_____

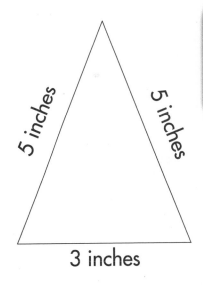

5 inches   5 inches

3 inches

_____

Words That Are Abbreviated

Recipes sometimes contain abbreviations. Look at the common abbreviations in the box.

c.	cup
tsp.	teaspoon
tbsp.	tablespoon
min.	minute
hr.	hour

Directions: Read the recipe. Circle the abbreviations. With the help of an adult, try the recipe!

Peanut Butter Balls

Ingredients:
1 c. creamy peanut butter
1 c. honey
2 c. powdered milk
2 tbsp. chocolate chips

Get a large bowl and a big, strong spoon. Put all of the ingredients in the bowl. Mix them together for 5 min. Roll the mixture into balls. Arrange the balls on a plate. Chill them in the refrigerator for 1 hr. Enjoy!

UNIT 7

Names for the Parts of a Letter

Directions: Read about the parts of a letter.

123 Main Street
Plainsville, NY 41698
January 30, 2007

Dear Frank,
   Our class just went on a field trip to the aviation museum. I know how much you like airplanes, so it reminded me of you. I saw an open cockpit biplane like the ones used in World War I. Wouldn't it be cool to ride in one of those?
   I hope you are having fun in school. Does your class take any field trips?

Your friend,
Jack

Heading:
This can be your address and the date, or just the date. It starts halfway across the page.

Greeting:
It is the opening of the letter. It usually starts with **Dear**. Then, add the person's name and a comma. It starts on the left side of the page.

Body:
This is the main part of the letter. Each paragraph has its own main idea. Each new paragraph is indented.

Closing:
It is the ending of the letter. It usually says good-bye with phrases like **Your friend**, **Your grandson**, or **Love**. The first letter in the first word is capitalized, and a comma follows the phrase.

Signature:
Write your name. It goes below the closing.

UNIT 7

Name:

Names for the Parts of a Letter

Directions: Label the parts of a letter. Then, write a letter to a friend or relative about your favorite holiday.

My Name Here
5th Street
Ashland, Oh 44805

Friend
Main Street
Columbus, Oh 43210

Name:_____

Holiday Words

Directions: Use the Word Bank to write the correct holiday to complete each sentence.

Word Bank
Valentine's Day   Halloween
The Fourth of July   Thanksgiving   St. Patrick's Day

1. _____ takes place on October 31. Children celebrate this holiday by dressing up in costumes and going from house to house begging for treats.

2. _____ takes place on March 17. It is a day to celebrate the patron saint of Ireland.

3. _____ takes place on February 14. It is a day to celebrate love and friendship.

4. _____ is also called Independence Day. It is a day that Americans celebrate the signing of the Declaration of Independence from England in 1776.

5. _____ is held on the fourth Thursday of November. On this day, Americans remember the good harvest of the Pilgrims in 1621 and show thanks for what they have now.

UNIT 7

Name:_____

Conservation Words

When you **recycle**, you find a way to use something again. With an adult, follow the directions to make recycled paper.

You will need: newspaper, a blender or beater, a bowl, a dishpan (or large, deep pan), a piece of window screen, paper towels, sections of the newspaper, pens, a measuring cup, a large board, water, tape.

Put tape around the edges of the screen. Then, follow the directions. An adult should work with you on the activity after the first soaking (step #1).

Directions:

1. Tear enough old paper into tiny pieces to fill six cups. Put the pieces in a pan. Cover the paper with water. Soak this overnight.

2. Blend or beat a small handful of the soaked paper with two or three cups of water. Add water if blending or beating is too difficult. Empty the pulp into a large bowl. Continue making small batches of pulp.

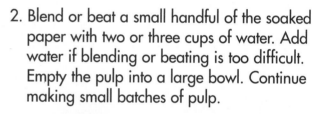

3. Add enough water to the pan so that when you stir the mixture with your fingers, you cannot feel the pulp.

4. Tilt the screen and slide it to the bottom of the pan. Using your fingers, spread the pulp evenly over the screen. Let it settle a minute.

5. Open a section of newspaper to its center. Cover one side of it with paper towels.

paper towels

newspaper

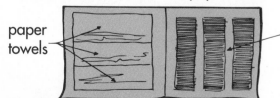

6. Lift the screen straight up over the pan. Let it drain.

screen

pan

UNIT 7

Name:_____

Conservation Words

7. Place the screen with the pulp onto the side of newspaper without towels. Close the paper making sure the towels are over the screen.

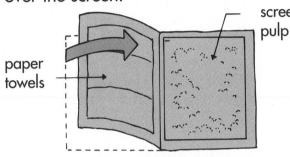

paper towels

screen with pulp

8. Carefully flip the entire newspaper section so that the screen is on top of the pulp.

9. Put the board on top of the newspaper. Press on the board to squeeze out the excess water.

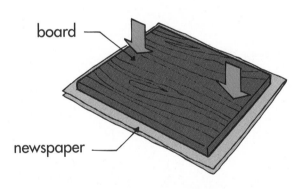

board

newspaper

10. Open the newspaper. Remove the screen. Carefully remove the paper towel with the pulp on it to a dry piece of newspaper. Let the pulp dry.

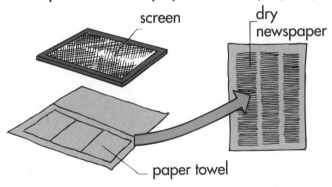

screen

dry newspaper

paper towel

11. When dry, carefully peel the pulp away from the paper towel.

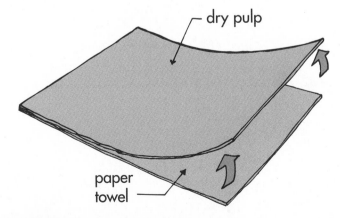

dry pulp

paper towel

12. Write a message about recycling on the paper you made.

RECYCLE OLD PAPER

SAVE A TREE

UNIT 7

Name:_____

Conservation Words

Directions: Draw a line to match each conservation word with its definition.

1. landfill

to put through a process that allows used things to be reused

2. biodegradable

able to be broken down by the action of living organisms such as bacteria

3. pollute

an artificial substance that can be formed into many materials and products

4. litter

full of or covered with living plants, trees, and grass

5. plastic

to make messy by scattering rubbish or other objects

6. recycle

a place to dispose of garbage and rubbish

7. green

everything that surrounds a living thing and affects its growth and health

8. environment

to make something dirty or harmful by mixing in or adding waste material

Name:_____

Unit 7 Review

Directions: Write a letter to your local state representative. Write five things that you would like your representative to do to preserve the environment in your community.

Remember the parts of a letter, abbreviations, and conservation words that you have learned in this unit.

_____

_____

_____

_____

_____

_____

_____

_____

_____

_____

_____

UNIT 7

UNIT 8

Name:_____

Classifying Words

Classifying means putting similar things into groups.

Directions: Write each word from the Word Bank on the correct line.

Word Bank				
baby	donkey	whale	family	fox
uncle	goose	grandfather	kangaroo	policeman

people   **animals**

_____

_____

_____

_____

_____

_____

_____

_____

_____

UNIT 8

Name:_____

Classifying Words

Directions: Read the three words in each box. Then, add one more word that is like the others.

1. cars trucks		6. cows pigs	
airplanes _____		chickens _____	
2. bread bagels		7. pens pencils	
muffins _____		paints _____	
3. square triangle		8. violets tulips	
rectangle _____		iris _____	
4. milk yogurt		9. mom dad	
cheese _____		sister _____	
5. merry-go-round swings		10. snowpants boots	
sandbox _____		jacket _____	

Challenge: Can you write the theme of each group?

1. _____
2. _____
3. _____
4. _____
5. _____

6. _____
7. _____
8. _____
9. _____
10. _____

UNIT 8

Name:_____

Classifying Words

Directions: The words in each box form a group. Choose the word from the Word Bank that describes each group. Then, write it on the line.

Word Bank
clothes   family   noises   colors   flowers
fruits   animals   coins   toys

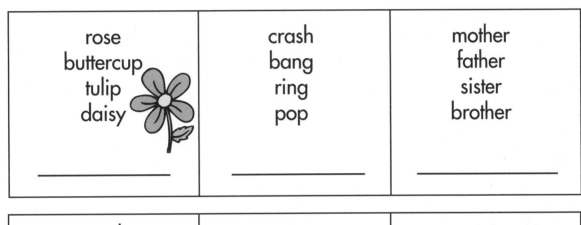

rose buttercup tulip daisy	crash bang ring pop	mother father sister brother
_____	_____	_____

puzzle wagon blocks doll	green purple blue red	grapes orange apple plum
_____	_____	_____

shirt socks dress coat	dime penny nickel quarter	dog horse elephant moose
_____	_____	_____

UNIT 8

Name:_____

Words About Canada

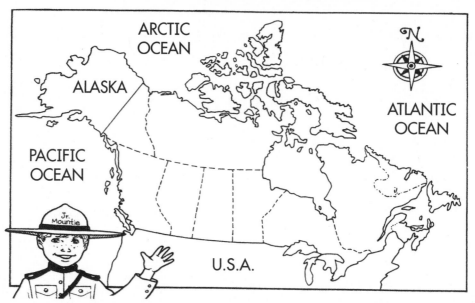

Directions: Unlike the United States, Canada is not divided into states. Follow the directions to label the ten provinces and two territories that make up Canada.

1. The Yukon Territory is connected to Alaska. The Northwest Territory is the large area to its east. Label them.
2. British Columbia is south of Yukon. Label the province and color it yellow.
3. East of British Columbia is Alberta. Label it and color it red.
4. The province between Alberta and Manitoba is called Saskatchewan. This is where Big Foot supposedly lives. Draw him there and label the provinces.
5. Winnipeg is a city in Manitoba. Label the city and color the province brown.
6. The province north of the Great Lakes is Ontario. Color it orange.
7. The largest province is Quebec. Label the province and color it green.
8. New Brunswick borders Quebec on the southeast, and Nova Scotia is attached to it. Label them and color them purple.
9. Nestled above the two provinces is Prince Edward Island. Color this province black.
10. The last province is Newfoundland. This province borders Quebec and includes the large island near it. Label both parts.

UNIT 8

Name:_____

Weather Words

Directions: Read about lightning. Then, complete the activities. There may be more than one correct answer.

Clouds are made of many water droplets. All of these droplets together contain a large electrical charge. Sometimes these clouds set off a large spark of electricity called **lightning**. Lightning travels very fast. When it cuts through the air, it causes the air to move violently. The sound the air makes is called **thunder**.

Lightning takes various forms. Some lightning looks like a zigzag in the sky. **Sheet lightning** spreads and lights the sky. **Ball lightning** looks like a ball of fire.

Underline:
Lightning is a flash of light
1. caused by sunshine.
2. caused by electricity in the sky.

Circle Yes or No:

	Yes	No
Sometimes clouds set off a huge spark of electricity.	**Yes**	**No**
Lightning is caused by dry weather.	**Yes**	**No**
Lightning travels very fast.	**Yes**	**No**
Lightning can cause thunder.	**Yes**	**No**

Unscramble and write in the puzzle above:

1. _____
   l a b l
   3 2 1 4

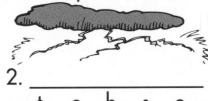

2. _____
   t e h s e
   5 3 2 1 4

3. _____
   g a i z g z
   3 5 2 1 6 4

UNIT 8

Weather Words

Directions: Read about hurricanes. Then, complete the activities. There may be more than one correct answer.

A **hurricane** is a powerful storm that forms over some parts of an ocean. A hurricane can be several hundred miles wide.

A hurricane has two main parts: the **eye** and the **wall cloud**. The eye is the center of the storm. In the eye, the weather is calm. The storm around the eye is called the wall cloud. It has strong winds and heavy rain. In some hurricanes, the wind can blow 150 miles an hour!

As the storm moves across the water, it causes giant waves in the ocean. As the storm moves over land, it can cause floods, destroy buildings, and kill people who have not taken shelter.

Circle:

A hurricane has two main parts: tornado   wall cloud   eye

Match:

The calm center of the hurricane.   wall cloud
The wind and rainstorm around the eye.   eye

Check:

A hurricane ☐ can be several hundred miles wide.
☐ can have winds that move 150 miles an hour.
☐ is a small storm.
☐ can cause giant waves in the ocean.
☐ can cause floods and hurt people.

Name:_____

Weather Words

Directions: Read about tornados. Then, complete the activities. There may be more than one correct answer.

Did you know that a tornado is the most violent windstorm on Earth? A **tornado** is a whirling, twisting storm that is shaped like a funnel.

A tornado usually occurs in the spring on a hot day. It begins with thunderclouds and thunder. A cloud becomes very dark. The bottom of the cloud begins to twist and form a funnel. Rain and lightning begin. The funnel cloud drops from the dark storm clouds. It moves down toward the ground.

A tornado is very dangerous. It can destroy almost everything in its path.

Circle:

A   thunder
       tornado   is the most violent windstorm on Earth.

Check:
Which words describe a tornado?
☐ whirling   ☐ twisting   ☐ icy   ☐ funnel-shaped   ☐ dangerous

Underline:
A funnel shape is:

Write and Circle:
A tornado usually occurs in the _____ on a   cool
                                                       hot   day.
                              autumn   spring

Write 1 - 2 - 3 below and in the picture above.
○ The funnel cloud drops down to the ground.
○ A tornado begins with dark thunder clouds.
○ The dark clouds begin to twist and form a funnel.

UNIT 8

Name:_____

Number Words in Spanish

Directions: Draw a line to match the number words one through twenty from Spanish to English. The first one is done for you.

uno	six
siete	thirteen
catorce	eight
cuatro	eighteen
doce	one
dieciséis	fifteen
dos	seven
ocho	fourteen
dieciocho	two
seis	nineteen
diez	ten
diecisiete	seventeen
tres	three
quince	twenty
once	nine
cinco	twelve
trece	four
diecinueve	sixteen
nueve	eleven
veinte	five

UNIT 8

Name:_____

Classifying Words

Directions: After each sentence, write three words from the Word Bank that belong to the group described.

Word Bank

eagle	whistle	horn	frog
dime	wheel	throat	ball
sun	airplane	penny	marble
banana	balloon	dollar	heart
camel	grasshopper	horse	kangaroo
chipmunk	lemon	butterfly	mouth

1. These are things that can hop.

_____ _____ _____

2. These things all have wings.

_____ _____ _____

3. These are types of money.

_____ _____ _____

4. These are four-legged animals.

_____ _____ _____

5. These are parts of your body.

_____ _____ _____

6. These things are yellow.

_____ _____ _____

7. These things can roll.

_____ _____ _____

8. These are things you can blow.

_____ _____ _____

Classifying

189

UNIT 8

Name:_____

Classifying Words

Directions: Write the word from the Word Bank that tells what kinds of things are in each sentence.

Word Bank				
birds	toys	states	insects	women
men	numbers	animals	flowers	letters

1. A father, uncle, and king are all _____ .

2. Fred has a wagon, puzzles, and blocks. These are all _____ .

3. Iowa, Ohio, and Maine are all _____ .

4. A robin, woodpecker, and canary all have wings. They are kinds

   of _____ .

5. Squirrels, rabbits, and foxes all have tails

   and are kinds of _____ .

6. Roses, daisies, and violets smell sweet. These

   are kinds of _____ .

7. A, B, C, and D are all _____ . You use them to spell words.

8. Bees, ladybugs, and beetles are kinds of _____ .

9. A mother, aunt, and queen are all _____ .

10. Seven, thirty, and nineteen are all _____ .

190

Name:_____

Classifying Words

Directions: Write a word from the Word Bank to complete each sentence. If the word names an article of clothing, write **1** on the line in front of the sentence. If it names food, write **2** on the line. If it names an animal, write **3** on the line. If the word names furniture, write **4** on the line.

Word Bank				
jacket	chair	shirt	owl	mice
bed	cheese	dress	bread	chocolate

_____ 1. Danny tucked his _____ into his pants.

_____ 2. _____ is my favorite kind of candy.

_____ 3. The wise old _____ sat in the tree and said, "Who-o-o."

_____ 4. I can't sit on the _____ because it has a broken leg.

_____ 5. Don't forget to wear your _____ because it is chilly today.

_____ 6. Will you please buy a loaf of _____ at the store?

_____ 7. She wore a very pretty _____ to the dance.

_____ 8. The cat chased the _____ in the barn.

_____ 9. I was so sleepy that I went to _____ early.

_____ 10. We put _____ in the mouse trap to help catch the mice.

Classifying

191

UNIT 8

Name:_____

Words About Canada

Canada is located north of the United States on the continent of North America. Canada's largest province, **Quebec**, is unique because most of its inhabitants speak French. The people there have long been referred to as French-Canadians.

Montreal is Quebec's most famous city and is often called the "Heart of French Canada." By day or night, it is an exciting city with fine universities, the National Hockey League (Montreal Canadiens), incredible museums, and the one-of-a-kind Cirque du Soleil.

Cirque du Soleil means "Circus of the Sun." This circus is unique because it has only human performers and no animals. Quebec funds a school called the École Nationale de Cirque. With an enrollment of 20 youngsters, the school provides an academic education while the students learn the arts of the big top on the trapeze, stilts, trampoline, and tightrope.

Directions: Imagine that you are a student at the school. On a separate sheet of paper, write about what a typical day is like for you. Then, draw a picture of yourself performing.

Circus

192

UNIT 8

Name:_____

Weather Words

Wind is the air as it moves naturally over the surface of the earth. You probably already know of the dangerous aspects of wind. Hurricanes and tornadoes cause property damage, topple down trees, and knock down electric wires and telephone wires.

Think of some of the helpful aspects of wind. Wind can create energy with windmills, cool you off on a hot day, move sailboats, dry wet areas, transport seeds, etc.

Directions: Divide a large sheet of paper in half. Label one side **Destructive Wind Forces** and the other side **Helpful Wind Forces**. Cut out newspaper articles and draw pictures to show the effects of wind. Glue each article and picture on the correct side of the paper.

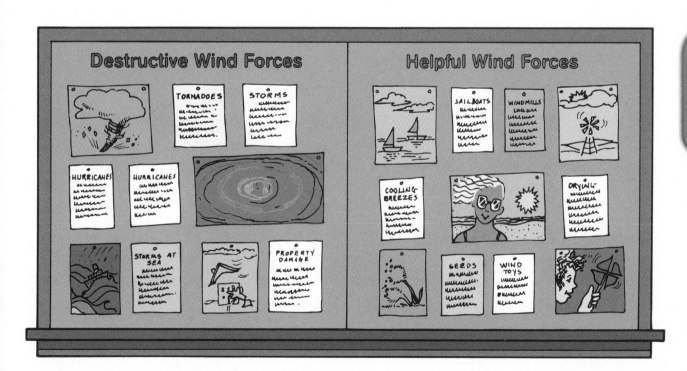

Name:_____

Weather Words

The three major types of clouds are **cirrus**, **cumulus**, and **stratus**. You can become more familiar with these types of clouds when you do this project.

You will need: cotton balls, dryer lint or gray flannel, glue, poster board (11 inches x 18 inches), a pencil, crayons, markers, white paint, paintbrushes, and glitter.

Directions: Use a pencil to divide the poster board into six sections. Use the top sections to simulate the three major types of clouds by following the directions below.

1. **Cirrus Clouds**—high, white clouds with a feathery appearance. To create this type of cloud, paint white streaks at the very top of your poster board and sprinkle glitter sparingly while the paint is still wet to represent the ice that may be present in these high clouds.

2. **Cumulus Clouds**—puffy, white, low clouds with flat bottoms. In the second top box, glue cotton balls of various sizes approximately 1/3 of the way down the poster board.

3. **Stratus Clouds**—wide, often gray, low clouds that can drip snow flurries and drizzle. Glue dryer lint or gray flannel across the top of the third top box covering the length of the box.

After each of the three major cloud types is completed, draw pictures in the box underneath each cloud. The pictures should show activities you could do if you were to observe that particular type of cloud on any given day.

UNIT 8

Name:_____

Weather Words

An **idiom** means something different than what the words actually say. Many idiomatic expressions contain weather words.

Example:
Ray has his **head in the clouds.**

This expression means that Ray is not paying attention.

Directions: Read each idiom that uses weather words. Write what it means on the line.

1. raining cats and dogs _____

2. under the weather _____

3. fair-weather friend _____

4. come rain or shine _____

5. shoot the breeze _____

6. wet behind the ears _____

7. cold feet _____

8. cloud nine _____

9. steal someone's thunder _____

UNIT 8

Number Words in Spanish

Addition means **putting together** or adding two or more numbers to find the sum. For example, 3 + 5 = 8.

Más means **plus** in Spanish.

Directions: Add to solve the problems. Write the correct answer on the line.

Example: uno   más   tres   = ___4___
           1   +   3

1. siete más catorce = _____

2. cuatro más doce = _____

3. dieciséis más dos = _____

4. cinco más tres = _____

5. tres más diez = _____

6. nueve más veinte = _____

7. once más quince = _____

8. ocho más uno = _____

9. diez más seis = _____

UNIT 8

Name:_____

Words That Are Homophones

Homophones are words that sound alike but are spelled differently and have different meanings.

Directions: Underline the wrong homophone in each sentence. Then, write the correct homophone on the line.

1. How much do you think I way?   _____

2. My brother blue the car's horn loudly.   _____

3. She needed to so Mr. Rogers's torn shirt.   _____

4. The son shone through the curtains.   _____

5. Mom baked the cake with flower.   _____

6. My friend went on a plain to visit her aunt.   _____

7. She swept the stares.   _____

8. Mr. Rogers's shirt was bright read.   _____

9. The boy was stung by a be.   _____

10. We rode a Ferris wheel at the fare.   _____

Name:_____

Words That Are Homophones

Directions: On the line before each homophone, write the letter of the phrase that best defines its meaning.

_____ 1. hare

_____ 2. hair

_____ 3. peer

_____ 4. pier

_____ 5. doe

_____ 6. dough

_____ 7. bare

_____ 8. bear

_____ 9. dew

_____ 10. due

_____ 11. nose

_____ 12. knows

_____ 13. prey

_____ 14. pray

_____ 15. tail

_____ 16. tale

A. any creature hunted for food

B. a mass of unbaked bread

C. a body part used to smell

D. something that is owed

E. the end of an animal's body

F. an animal related to the rabbit

G. a large, furry animal with a short tail

H. to look closely; to gaze

I. to beg for or ask for by prayer

J. a female deer, hare, or rabbit

K. a platform built out over water

L. a story

M. naked; without any covering

N. growth that covers the scalp of a person or the body of a mammal

O. understands; to be certain of something

P. water droplets

UNIT 8

Name:_____

Words That Are Homophones

Directions: Circle the words that are not used correctly. Use the Word Bank to write the correct word above the circled word. The first one is done for you.

Word Bank								
road	see	one	be	so	I	brakes	piece	there
wait	not	some	hour	would	no	deer	you	heard

Jake and his family were getting close to Grandpa's. It had taken them

hour
nearly an (our) to get their, but Jake knew it was worth it. In his mind, he

could already sea the pond and could almost feel the cool water. It had

been sew hot this summer in the apartment.

"Wood ewe like a peace of my apple, Jake?" asked his big sister Clare.

"Eye can't eat any more."

"Know, thank you," Jake replied. "I still have sum of my fruit left."

Suddenly, Dad slammed on the breaks.

"Did you see that dear on the rode? I

always herd that if you see won, there

might bee more."

"Good thinking, Dad. I'm glad you are

a safe driver. We're knot very far from

Grandpa's now. I can't weight!"

UNIT 8

Name:_____

Words About North America

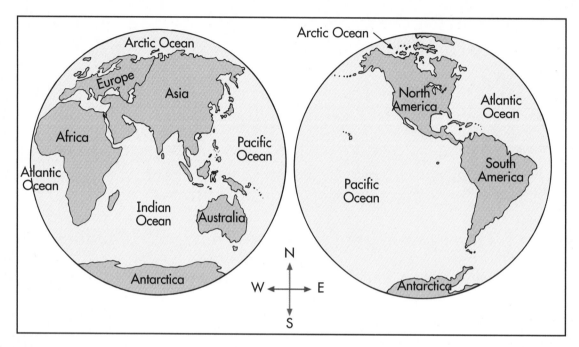

Directions: Fill in the circle beside the answer that best completes each sentence.

1. The United States is a
   - Ⓐ   continent.
   - Ⓑ   country.
   - Ⓒ   hemisphere.
   - Ⓓ   state.

2. Mexico is in the continent of
   - Ⓐ   South America.
   - Ⓑ   North America.
   - Ⓒ   Africa.
   - Ⓓ   Europe.

Directions: Read each statement. Decide whether it is true or false. Then, fill in the correct circle.

3. Canada is in the continent of North America.

   Ⓐ True   Ⓑ False

4. The United States is in the continent of South America.

   Ⓐ True   Ⓑ False

5. To travel from North America to Antarctica, you need to cross the Indian Ocean.

   Ⓐ True   Ⓑ False

Weather Words

Directions: Word webs are a good way to classify weather words. Look at the groups below. Add more words in each group.

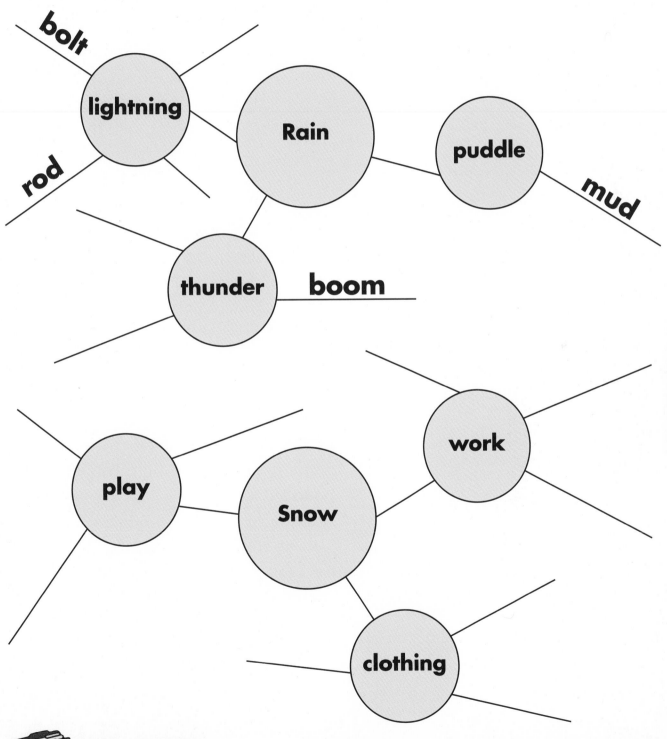

Name:_____

Weather Words

Directions: Does color have anything to do with temperature? Try this experiment to find out.

You will need:

2 identical glasses
one 9" x 12" sheet of
　　black paper
one 9" x 12" sheet of
　　white paper
masking tape
a pencil
a pen
an outside thermometer
water
scissors

Directions:

Wrap one glass with black paper and one with white paper. Tape the paper closed. Cut off the excess paper. Fill each glass with the same amount of water. Set both glasses in a sunny spot. Leave them there for at least an hour. Then, put the thermometer into each glass and record the temperature of each on the Cool Color chart. Also, write on the chart what you concluded from this experiment. Do this experiment at least two more times to verify your conclusion. Try other colors to see if there is any difference.

Note: The water in the jar wrapped with black paper should be warmer because the black paper absorbs more heat than the white.

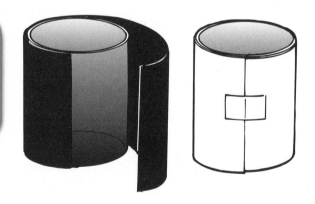

Cool Color Chart			
Paper Color	Time	Temperature	Conclusion

UNIT 8

Name: _____

Weather Words

Directions: Use the weather words from the Word Bank to complete the sentences.

Word Bank				
sunny	temperature	foggy	puddles	rainy
windy	rainbow	cloudy	lightning	snowy

1. Sometimes, the school closes on very _____ days.

2. I will wait for a _____ day so I can use my new umbrella.

3. Today is a _____ day, so I'm wearing sunglasses.

4. The day is _____ with a chance of showers.

5. The _____ flashed during the thunderstorm.

6. After it rains, I like to jump in _____ .

7. The _____ cooled down in the evening.

8. A colorful _____ appeared in the sky in the light rain.

9. This morning it was so _____ that the air was thick.

10. It was so _____ that I almost blew away!

Name:_____

Unit 8 Review

Directions: Read each word in the Word Bank. Then, write the word in the correct group.

Word Bank				
storm	nueve	mother	lightning	baby
territory	sister	sunny	clouds	twenty
trece	four	ocean	Canada	uncle
island	diez	temperature	father	continent

Family Words

_____

_____

_____

_____

Number Words

_____

_____

_____

_____

Weather Words

_____

_____

_____

_____

Geography Words

_____

_____

_____

_____

UNIT 8

Commonly Misused Words

The word **this** is an adjective that refers to things that are near. **This** always describes a singular noun. **Singular** means **one**.

Example: I will buy **this** coat.
(**Coat** is singular.)

The word **these** is also an adjective that refers to things that are near. **These** always describes a plural noun. **Plural** means **more than one thing**.

Example: I will buy **these** flowers.
(**Flowers** is a plural noun.)

Directions: Write **this** or **these** on each line to finish the sentence correctly. The first one is done for you.

1. ___this___ A cat with orange and black stripes sits on this/these fence.

2. _____ I will buy this/these gloves for my dad.

3. _____ She would like to try this/these new recipe.

4. _____ He said he would take this/these bag with him.

5. _____ This/These dresses look very expensive.

6. _____ The hen is sitting on this/these nest to keep its eggs warm.

7. _____ Would you like to taste this/these cookies?

8. _____ How long will it take to get this/these situation corrected?

9. _____ I would like to borrow this/these books from the library.

10. _____ Did you write this/these letters to me?

11. _____ He took this/these bus to school.

12. _____ Are you on this/these soccer team, too?

Name:_____

Commonly Misused Words

The word **can** means **am able to** or **to be able to**.

Example: I **can** do that for you.
           Can you do that for me?

The word **may** means **be allowed to** or **permitted to**. **May** is used to ask or give permission. **May** can also mean **might** or **perhaps**.

Example: **May** I be excused?
           You **may** sit here.

Directions: Write **can** or **may** on each line to finish the sentence correctly. The first one is done for you.

1. _Can_ Can/May you take this suit to the dry cleaner?
2. _____ Can/May you tell me how to get to the post office?
3. _____ I can/may be able to help you if I can get my own work finished.
4. _____ You can/may borrow this video.
5. _____ Can/May you help your little brother tie his shoes?
6. _____ Can/May I have a piece of cake?
7. _____ The baby can/may see his sister from his highchair.
8. _____ I can/may play outside after I do my chores.
9. _____ She can/may have a cold.
10. _____ The boy can/may swim.
11. _____ The casserole can/may be taken out of the oven in an hour.
12. _____ He is smart enough that he can/may solve the problem himself.
13. _____ I can/may have to go out of town tomorrow.
14. _____ Can/May I sit beside you?

UNIT 9

Name:_____

Words That Are Contractions

The word **your** shows possession.

Examples: Is that **your** book? I visited **your** class.

The word **you're** is a contraction for **you are**. A **contraction** is two words joined together as one. An **apostrophe** shows where letters have been left out.

Examples: **You're** doing well on that painting.
If **you're** going to pass the test, you should study.

Directions: Write **your** or **you're** on each line to finish the sentence correctly. The first one is done for you.

1. _____Your_____ Your/You're mom is very nice.

2. _____ Your/You're going to get in trouble when your parents see the broken lamp.

3. _____ Did your/you're friend buy that gift for you?

4. _____ How do your/you're brother and sister get along?

5. _____ Do you think your/you're going to finish this work on time?

6. _____ Why are your/you're cheeks so red?

7. _____ What is your/you're grandfather like?

8. _____ If your/you're going on the class trip, let me know.

9. _____ I thought your/you're art project was the best one.

10. _____ What is your/you're opinion?

11. _____ What is your/you're favorite color?

12. _____ Did your/you're team score the winning goal?

13. _____ Your/You're going to enjoy this performance.

14. _____ What are your/you're parents doing tonight?

UNIT 9

Name:_____

Words About Africa

Directions: Read about Africa. Then, answer the questions.

Africa is the second largest continent. South of Europe, Africa is between the Atlantic and Indian Oceans. It is in the Eastern Hemisphere.

Northern Africa is almost entirely covered by the **Sahara**, the largest desert in the world. Ancient Egypt, one of the first great civilizations, is located in northern Africa along the **Nile River**. The Nile is the longest river in the world.

Central Africa stretches from Senegal in the west to Tanzania in the east. The Rift Valley, in Kenya, Uganda, and Tanzania, is called the birthplace of humanity. It is here that the very earliest traces of our ancestors have been found, dating back to over four million years ago.

Southern Africa holds the country South Africa, which has three capitals, one for each main branch of its government. The capitals are Cape Town, Pretoria, and Bloemfontein.

1. How big is Africa compared to the other six continents of the world?

   _____

2. If you were a scientist, which part of Africa would you most like to visit? Why?

   _____

   _____

3. Compare what you know of Africa to North America, where we live.

   _____

   _____

   _____

UNIT 9

Name:_____

Words About Magnets

A **magnet** is an object that produces an invisible force that attracts, or draws near, iron or steel. Magnets are often made of iron or steel.

Directions: Gather some of the objects listed in the chart. Hold a small magnet next to these objects. Which objects will the magnet pull? Add some of your own objects to the list.

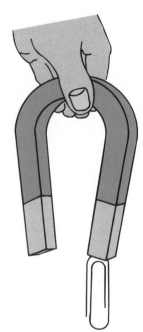

Object	Magnet Attracts	Magnet Does Not Attract
scissors		
wood ruler		
eraser		
paper clip		
thumbtack		
paper		
aluminum foil		

Directions: Magnets do not attract all metals. Find and circle the six metals in the word search. The metals listed up and down are attracted to magnets. The metals written across are not attracted. Write each metal in the correct group.

```
B N B R A S S X
Z I K L N T I A
A C O P P E R D
N K T R O E O S
T E K G N L N P
A L U M I N U M
```

Attracted to Magnets

_____

_____

_____

Not Attracted to Magnets

_____

_____

_____

Name:_____

Words About Magnets

All magnets are strongest at their **poles**. The poles are at opposite points of the magnet. They are referred to as the **north pole** and the **south pole**. Opposite poles attract each other. The north pole of one magnet attracts the south pole of another magnet. Matching poles repel, or push away from, each other. The north pole of one magnet repels the north pole of another magnet. The invisible force that attracts materials to magnets is called **magnetism**.

Directions: After each magnet word, write its meaning.

attract _____

repel _____

north pole _____

south pole _____

magnetism _____

Directions: Draw a picture below to show how the north and south poles of magnets attract each other.

UNIT 9

Name:_____

Words About Magnets

Some materials, such as wood and water, do not seem to respond to magnets. But actually, all materials respond to a magnetic force. Some just respond so weakly to the force that it is not observable in everyday life.

There are even certain materials that are not attracted to magnets. These metals include gold, silver, lead, zinc, copper, aluminum, and brass.

Directions: Use the Word Bank to unscramble the words about magnets.

Word Bank				
scissors	force	attract	repel	iron
steel	metals	poles	opposites	field

1. slope   _____

2. noir   _____

3. estel   _____

4. stalem   _____

5. cerof   _____

6. difel   _____

7. perel   _____

8. sopitopes   _____

9. scosrsis   _____

10. arttact   _____

Name:_____

Metric Words

Directions: Read about metric measurement. Then, answer the questions.

The **metric system** is one way we use to measure. The basic units of the metric system are **meters**, **liters**, and **grams**. Meters measure length. Liters measure volume. Grams measure weight. There are also smaller and larger measurements in the metric system. It is very easy to convert between larger and smaller units because the metric system is based on units of 10. Look at the graphic below. You can convert either higher or lower in the metric system by moving the decimal point. Each new unit has a different prefix. To move to a smaller unit, you go left on the graphic and move the decimal point to the right. To move to a larger unit, you go right on the graphic and move the decimal point to the left.

For example, you have 1 liter of paint and want to know how many milliliters you have. Simply move left. Milli- is three to the left of liters, so you move the decimal point right 3 spaces. One liter is equal to 1,000 milliliters.

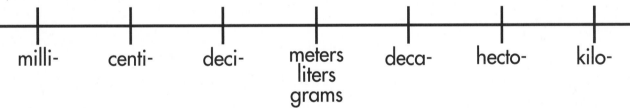

milli-   centi-   deci-   meters liters grams   deca-   hecto-   kilo-

1. What is the unit of volume in the metric system?

   _____

2. On what number is the metric system based?

   _____

3. When converting to a larger unit, in which direction do you move the decimal point?

   _____

4. 45 milliliters = _____ liters

5. 6.7 grams = _____ milligrams

6. 23 hectoliters = _____ milliliters

7. 528 meters = _____ kilometers

Commonly Misused Words

Use the word **good** to describe a noun. **Good** is an adjective.

Example: She is a **good** teacher.

Use the word **well** to tell or ask how something is done or to describe someone's health. **Well** is an adverb. It describes a verb.

Example: She is not feeling **well**.

Directions: Write **good** or **well** on each line to finish the sentence correctly. The first one is done for you.

1. ___good___ I could use a good/well book on how to fix bikes.

2. _____ She did good/well on her oral presentation.

3. _____ Do you feel good/well enough to go with us to the park?

4. _____ That television program about penguins was good/well.

5. _____ You should treat your family and friends good/well.

6. _____ The baby can walk good/well.

7. _____ Did you see how good/well he kicked the ball?

8. _____ You did a good/well job writing that report.

9. _____ Keep up the good/well work!

10. _____ Complaining too much is not a good/well thing to do.

11. _____ We went out to dinner, because I did good/well on my report card.

12. _____ The dog does those tricks good/well.

UNIT 9

Name:_____

Words That Are Contractions

The word **they're** is a contraction for **they are**.

Examples: **They're** our very best friends!
Ask them if **they're** coming over tomorrow.

The word **their** shows ownership.

Examples: **Their** dog is friendly.
It is **their** bicycle.

The word **there** shows place or direction.

Examples: Look over **there**. **There** it is.

Directions: Write **they're**, **their**, or **there** on each line to finish the sentence correctly. The first one is done for you.

1. __There__ They're/Their/There is the boy that has been teasing me.

2. _____ Who are they're/their/there parents?

3. _____ They're/Their/There cat keeps coming into our backyard.

4. _____ We're going over they're/their/there to play ball.

5. _____ Do you know what they're/their/there serving for dinner?

6. _____ I would like to know they're/their/there address so I can send a postcard.

7. _____ He has to be they're/their/there by seven o'clock.

8. _____ The clouds over they're/their/there look very dark.

9. _____ They're/their/there going to be here soon.

10. _____ The animals they're/their/there are fun to watch.

11. _____ She wants they're/their/there stay to be pleasant.

12. _____ They're/their/there meeting us here for lunch.

Commonly Misused Words

The word **sit** means to rest.

Examples: Please **sit** here!
Will you **sit** by me?

The word **set** means to put or place something.

Examples: **Set** your purse there.
Set the dishes on the table.

Directions: Write **sit** or **set** on each line to finish the sentence correctly. The first one is done for you.

1. _____sit_____ I would like you to sit/set beside me.

2. _____ You can sit/set your bag on the counter.

3. _____ He sit/set the dirty dishes in the sink.

4. _____ Please sit/set here and wait for the nurse.

5. _____ She sit/set her watch back an hour.

6. _____ Can you sit/set these papers on the desk?

7. _____ I would like to sit/set here with you, but I have to go.

8. _____ The farmer sit/set the food in the trough.

9. _____ Sit/Set the table, please.

10. _____ Instead of cleaning up the mess, he decided to sit/set down to rest.

11. _____ Sit/Set the blocks on top of each other.

12. _____ Sit/Set still!

Words About Japan

Directions: Follow the directions from 1 to 9 to complete the map of Japan.

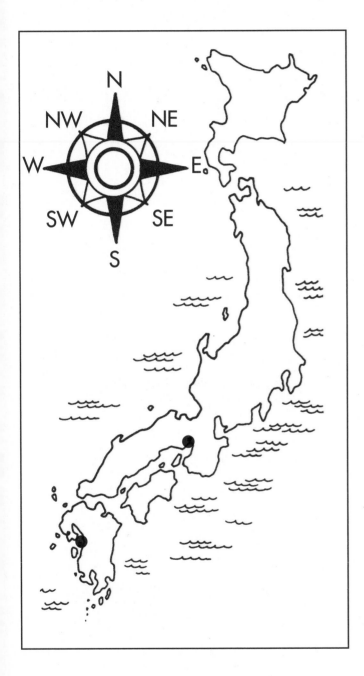

1. Label the islands in capital letters:
   KYUSHU-southernmost
   HOKKAIDO-northernmost
   HONSHU-south of Hokkaido
   SHIKOKU-north of Kyushu

2. Add a red (set a star) and label the capital city, Tokyo.

3. Draw a mountain at Mount Fuji's location.

4. Label **Nagasaki** (by the dot on Kyushu Island.)

5. Label the **Sea of Japan** and the **Pacific Ocean**. Add blue waves.

6. Label **Osaka** by the dot on Honshu Island.

7. Outline the islands in these colors:
   Hokkaido-orange
   Honshu-green
   Shikoku-red
   Kyushu-yellow

8. Along the northern edge of the box, label the map **JAPAN**, using a different color for each letter.

9. Draw the flag of Japan under the map.

UNIT 9

Name:_____

Words About Magnets

The ends of a magnet are called its **poles**. One pole is called the north-seeking pole or north pole; the other is the south-seeking pole, or south pole.

When the poles of two bar magnets are put near each other, they have a force that will either pull them together or push them apart. If the poles are **different**, then they will pull together, or **attract** each other. (One pole is a south pole and one pole is a north pole.) If the poles are the **same**, then they will push apart, or **repel** each other. (They are either both south poles or both north poles.) The push and pull force of a magnet is called **magnetism**.

Directions: Write attract or repel on each line to tell what happens when the magnets are brought toward each other.

1.

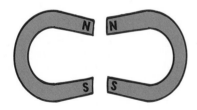

_____

3.

_____

2.

_____

4.

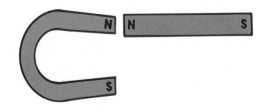

_____

Name:_____

Words About Magnets

Directions: Read about Earth and magnets. Then, follow the directions below to complete the map.

Earth is like a big magnet and has magnetic poles just like a magnet.

A **compass** is a free-turning magnet. Compasses that you buy are made with a thin magnet, called a **needle**, that turns freely inside a case. The case is made of a non-magnetic material. The north-seeking pole of the magnet is attracted toward Earth's magnetic north pole. The other end points to the magnetic south pole. A compass helps you find the directions north and south.

There is a **compass rose** in the bottom right corner of the map. The compass rose gives the eight compass directions: North (N), South (S), East (E), West (W), Northeast (NE), Southeast (SE), Southwest (SW), and Northwest (NW).

Directions:

1. Start at the star.
2. Go North 5 steps.
3. Go East 9 steps.
4. Go Southwest 4 steps.
5. Go East 2 steps.
6. Go South 2 steps.
7. Go Northeast 4 steps.
8. Draw an X to show your final location!

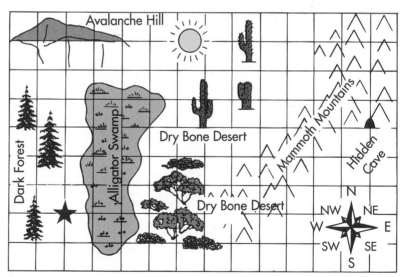

UNIT 9

Name:_____

Words About Magnets

Electromagnets are made of wire that is tightly wound around an iron core and connected to a source of electricity. When electricity flows through the wire, the iron core behaves like a permanent magnet. When the flow of electricity stops, the iron core is no longer magnetic. Electromagnets are some of the strongest magnets in the world.

Directions: You can find electromagnets all around your home. The words in the Word Bank name machines or devices that contain electromagnets. Use the Word Bank find and circle the hidden words. Look across and down.

Word Bank			
doorbell	motor	radio	refrigerator
stereo	tape recorder	telephone	television

```
T  D  O  O  R  B  E  L  L  T
E  T  A  B  E  K  J  S  R  A
L  X  O  L  F  V  R  E  L  P
E  S  T  E  R  E  O  T  R  E
V  A  E  L  I  T  H  O  N  R
I  M  L  O  G  U  A  R  B  E
S  P  E  R  E  N  O  G  L  C
I  X  P  L  R  K  A  M  I  O
O  R  H  R  A  D  I  O  T  R
N  R  O  L  T  U  P  R  O  D
B  A  N  M  O  T  O  R  K  E
S  H  E  L  R  M  U  S  L  R
```

Magnets

220

© 2007 School Specialty Publishing

Name:_____

Metric Words

Directions: Solve each metric problem. Write your answer on the line.

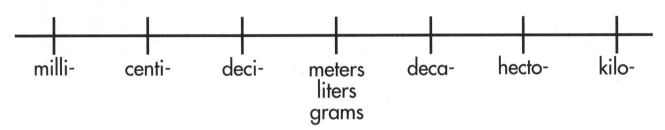

milli-   centi-   deci-   meters   deca-   hecto-   kilo-
                              liters
                              grams

1. Rafael wants to measure the hallway to find out how much room on the wall he has for his mural. What metric unit of measure should he use and why?

_____

_____

2. Elma has a 4-liter bottle of glue for refilling smaller bottles. The small bottles hold 200 milliliters. How many small bottles can she fill from the big one?

_____

3. Meg has a plastic art case that is 4 centimeters by 4 centimeters. She found a shell for a project she's making that is 34 millimeters long. Will it fit in her case?

_____

4. Rena made a woven mat that is 1.27 meters long. How long is it?

a. in centimeters _____

b. in decimeters _____

c. in millimeters _____

5. Shane knows that he needs 3,500 milliliters of paint to finish his project. Paint is sold in 1-liter bottles. How many bottles does he need to buy in order to have enough paint?

_____

6. Natasha is using glitter to decorate stars for the school play. Is the glitter measured in grams or meters?

_____

Name:_____

Words That Are Contractions

The word **its** shows ownership.

Examples: **Its** leaves have all turned green.
Its paw was injured.

The word **it's** is a contraction for **it is**.

Examples: **It's** better to be early than late.
It's not fair!

Directions: Write **its** or **it's** on each line to finish the sentence correctly. The first one is done for you.

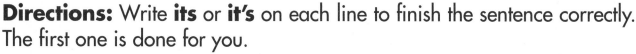

1. ___It's___ Its/It's never too late for ice cream!

2. _____ Its/It's eyes are already open.

3. _____ Its/It's your turn to wash the dishes!

4. _____ Its/It's cage was left open.

5. _____ Its/It's engine was beyond repair.

6. _____ Its/It's teeth were long and pointed.

7. _____ Did you see its/it's hind legs?

8. _____ Why do you think its/it's mine?

9. _____ Do you think its/it's the right color?

10. _____ Don't pet its/it's fur too hard!

11. _____ Its/It's from my Uncle Harry.

12. _____ Can you tell its/it's a surprise?

13. _____ Is its/it's stall always this clean?

14. _____ Its/It's not time to eat yet.

UNIT 9

Name:_____

Commonly Misused Words

The word **than** is used to show a difference.

Example: Your feet are bigger **than** mine.

The word **then** means next.

Example: Let's go to the end of the block. **Then**, I'll race you.

Directions: Write **than** or **then** on each line to finish the sentence correctly. The first one is done for you.

1. ___than___ You are much taller then/than I.

2. _____ If you invited me, than/then I would go.

3. _____ I was planning on going, and then/than I had a change of plans.

4. _____ This movie is funnier than/then the last one we saw.

5. _____ Read the story. Then/Than, answer the questions.

6. _____ I would rather play soccer then/than watch cartoons.

7. _____ I settled into the car, and then/than I put on my seatbelt.

8. _____ Today is a colder day than/then yesterday.

9. _____ First the leaves turned yellow. Then/Than, they fell off the tree.

10. _____ No season is more colorful then/than the fall.

Word Identification

223

UNIT 9

Name:_____

Words That Are Contractions

The word **who's** is a contraction meaning **who is**.

Example: **Who's** your teacher this year?

The word **whose** indicates possession.

Example: **Whose** book is this?

Directions: Write **who's** or **whose** on each line to finish the sentence correctly. The first one is done for you.

1. __Whose__ Whose/Who's responsibility is it to erase the board?

2. _____ Who's/Whose on your baseball team, Jake?

3. _____ This is the girl who's/whose a great dancer.

4. _____ Whose/Who's ready to answer the question?

5. _____ Anthony, whose/who's desk is across from mine, is very smart.

6. _____ Who's/Whose your best friend in school?

7. _____ Who's/Whose sitting at Sara's desk?

8. _____ Terrance, whose/who's mom owns a bakery, brought muffins today.

9. _____ I need to know whose/who's not going on the trip.

10. _____ Raoul, whose/who's absent today, is not going.

Name:_____

Words About Africa

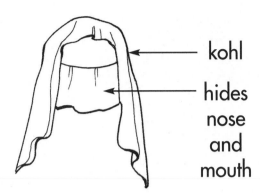

← kohl

— hides
nose
and
mouth

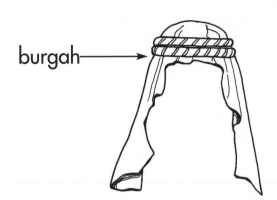

burgah →

Tunisia is located in northeastern Africa. Much of the land is desert, so the people must protect themselves from sun and blowing sand. For this reason, many children wear special head coverings like the ones pictured.

Directions: Finish the picture above by following the instructions.

1. Use pencil to draw a boy wearing the burgah.
2. Draw a girl wearing the kohl.
3. Draw a white robe on the boy.
4. Draw a black robe on the girl.
5. Draw desert sand under their feet.
6. Draw the blazing sun.
7. Draw a camel nearby.
8. Color the boy and the girl.

UNIT 9

Name:_____

Words About Magnets

Permanent magnets are the most familiar to us. The magnets on a refrigerator, for example, are permanent magnets. Once this type of material is magnetized, it never loses its level of magnetism.

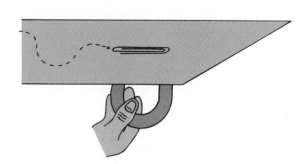

Permanent magnets may be stronger or weaker depending upon the materials from which they are made. Certain materials are easily magnetized, including iron, steel, nickel, cobalt, and ceramics.

You Will Need: 1 magnet, 2 needles or straight pins, and paper clips

Directions:
Hold a needle close to a pile of paper clips. The needle and the paper clips are not attracted to each other.

Now, stroke the magnet 50 times in one direction (not back and forth) across the needle.

Hold the needle close to the pile of paper clips again. Count the number of paper clips that are attracted to the needle.

Stroke the magnet 75 times in one direction across the second needle.

Hold this needle close to the pile of paper clips. Count the number of paper clips that are attracted to the needle.

1. Did you pick up more paper clips with the first or second needle?

_____

2. What do you think this means?

_____

_____

UNIT 9

Name:_____

Words About Magnets

Directions: Read about electromagnets. Then, answer the questions.

Some of the most powerful magnets are made with electricity. These magnets are called **electromagnets**. A strong magnet can be made by winding wire around an iron bar. As soon as the current from a battery is switched on, the bar becomes a strong electromagnet. The magnet can be switched off by stopping the flow of current.

Larry and Eddie each made an electromagnet. Only one of them worked.

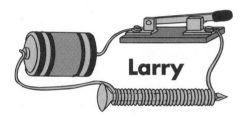

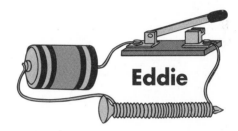

1. Whose electromagnet worked? _____

2. Why wouldn't the other electromagnet work? _____

_____

3. Electromagnets have many uses and can be found in many places. Write a sentence to tell how and where you use each electromagnet.

a. doorbell _____

b. radio _____

c. motor _____

d. television _____

e. telephone _____

f. refrigerator _____

UNIT 9

Name:_____

Words About Magnets

Directions: Write a word from the Word Bank to fit each clue. When you are finished, the letters in the squares will form a word that means "attracted to a magnet."

Word Bank			
paper clip	attract	locker	chain
refrigerator	nail	can	metal

1. It is shiny and can be melted. ☐ _ _ _ _

2. Soup is sold in it. _ ☐ _

3. Cold food is inside. _ _ _ _ _ _ ☐ _ _ _ _ _

4. A carpenter uses this. ☐ _ _ _

5. Where to store your coat in school _ _ _ _ ☐ _

6. To pull close _ _ ☐ _ _ _ _

7. Many metal links _ _ _ ☐ _

8. This holds papers together. _ _ _ _ _ ☐ _ _ _

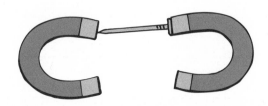

UNIT 9

Name:_____

Unit 9 Review

Directions: Write the letter of the definition in the right column that matches the word on the left.

1. _____ Sahara

2. _____ well

3. _____ may

4. _____ their

5. _____ attract

6. _____ Tokyo

7. _____ meters

8. _____ these

9. _____ compass

10. _____ electromagnets

11. _____ kohl

12. _____ you're

13. _____ Africa

14. _____ poles

a. a word that shows ownership

b. the capital of Japan

c. opposite points of a magnet

d. a head covering that hides the nose and mouth

e. an adjective that refers to things that are near

f. some of the strongest magnets in the world

g. the second largest continent

h. a free-turning magnet

i. a contraction of "you are"

j. an adverb used to describe a verb

k. a word that means be allowed to or permitted to

l. draw near

m. metric unit used to measure length

n. the largest desert in the world

UNIT 9

Name:_____

Words to Use Instead

It's easy to use certain words again and again. Try giving these "tired" words a break! Instead of a "wonderful" time, try using a different word.

Example: I had an **extraordinary** time at the party!
I had a **marvelous** time at the party!

Directions: Write three words that can replace the first.

1. nice   _____   _____   _____
2. beautiful _____   _____   _____
3. good   _____   _____   _____
4. many   _____   _____   _____

Directions: Write a paragraph about a class field trip. Use the words that you wrote above to make your paragraph interesting.

_____

_____

_____

_____

_____

_____

_____

Word Choice

231

Name:_____

Words to Use Instead

Specific words tell the reader more information than vague or unclear words. Read the examples in the box.

vivid verb:	The bubble broke. The bubble **burst**.
added names:	The teacher cried when she read the book. **Mrs. Brenner** cried when she read **The Invisible Man**.
specific word:	He saw something in the water. He saw a **jellyfish** in the water.

Directions: Read each sentence. Then, circle the revised sentence that makes it clearer. A hint after each sentence tells what kind of specific word is needed.

1. He stood by the fire and looked out at the snow. (name)
   a. The old man stood by the fire and looked out at the snow.
   b. Old Mr. Janski stood by the fire and looked out at the snow.

2. My friend broke the mirror in the bathroom. (vivid verb)
   a. Someone broke the bathroom mirror.
   b. My friend shattered the mirror in the bathroom.

3. The thief left some stuff in the safe. (specific word)
   a. The thief left some valuables in the safe.
   b. The thief left some diamonds in the safe.

4. A scientist looked through the microscope. (name and specific words)
   a. Dr. Singh, the famous chemist, looked through the microscope.
   b. The scientist looked through the old microscope.

UNIT 10

Words to Use Instead

Good writing helps the reader to see something in his or her mind. When writing, **don't tell** the reader about what is happening. **Show** the reader. Use words to paint a picture for the reader to see.

Examples: **tell:**   The meadow was pretty.

show: The alpine meadow glittered with the early morning dew. Tiny, white wildflowers bloomed among the meadow grass. The air was cool.

Directions: Read the sentences. Then, circle the letter of the sentence that shows the reader what is happening.

1. a. Trey ran all the way back to the school.
   b. He went back to school.
   c. Trey bolted three blocks back to school.

2. a. The bees flew around Beth's head.
   b. Thirty bees buzzed around Beth's head.
   c. There were lots of bees near Beth.

3. a. She stomped her feet and screamed at me.
   b. She was mad at me.
   c. She got mad and yelled at me.

4. a. The player was dirty.
   b. The player had mud on his clothes.
   c. The player's clothes were crusted with black dirt.

5. a. Rebbie was happy for her father.
   b. Rebbie smiled proudly at her father.
   c. Rebbie felt very happy for her dad.

Name:_____

Transportation Words

Directions: Read about "horseless carriages." Then, answer the questions.

Do you know how people traveled before cars? They rode horses! Often the horses were hooked up to wagons. Some horses were hooked up to carriages. Wagons were used to carry supplies. Carriages had covered tops. They were used to carry people. Both wagons and carriages were pulled by horses.

The first cars in the United States were invented shortly before the year 1900. These cars looked a lot like carriages. The seats were high off the ground. They had very thin wheels. The difference was that they were powered by engines. Carriages were pulled by horses. Still, they looked alike. People called the first cars "horseless carriages."

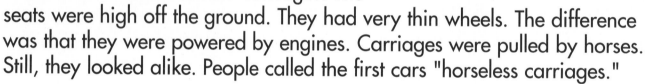

1. Write one way wagons and carriages were the same.

_____

2. When were the first cars invented?

_____

3. Why were the first cars called "horseless carriages"?

_____

4. What was the difference between a carriage and a "horseless carriage"?

_____

_____

UNIT 10

Name:_____

Words About Simple Machines

Look at the children in the picture. How are they moving their friends? A push or a pull on something is called a **force**. Forces can cause an object to move, slow down, speed up, change direction, or stop.

Directions: You use pushing and pulling forces to move objects. Write five ways that you use each of these forces.

Pushing Forces

1. _____
2. _____
3. _____
4. _____
5. _____

Pulling Forces

1. _____
2. _____
3. _____
4. _____
5. _____

Directions: It takes more force to move some objects than it does to move others. Circle the object in each picture that would take more force to move.

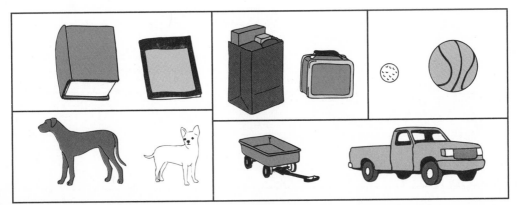

Simple Machines

235

UNIT 10

Words About Simple Machines

Simple machines have been used for hundreds of years. The castle builders in Europe did not have modern machines. But they did have some simple machines to help them make their castles.

Directions: Look carefully at the men building the castle. They are working hard, but their simple machines are missing. Use the Picture Bank to draw the missing machines.

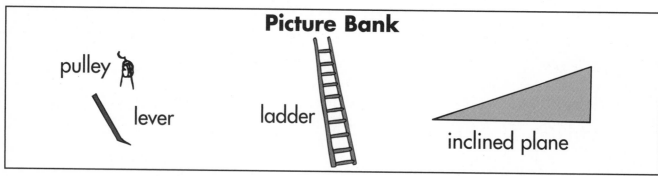

Picture Bank

pulley

lever

ladder

inclined plane

UNIT 10

Name:_____

Words About Simple Machines

Machines help to make work like pushing, pulling, and lifting easier. A machine is often made up of different parts that move, is sometimes big and complicated, and is other times small and simple.

Read the examples and definitions of some simple machines.

Lever—A hammer can be used as a kind of lever. This type of machine helps to move things with less force.

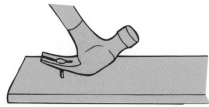

Wheel and axle—(such as those on a wagon or car) Wheels can be used to move things more easily from one place to another.

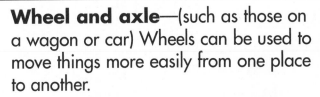

Pulley—A pulley can be used to hoist a flag or sail. Pulleys can be used to lift loads more easily.

Screw—Screws are typically used to hold things together. Sometimes screws are used to lift hinges such as the seat of a chair.

Wedge—An ax is an example of a kind of wedge. Wedges help cut or split things.

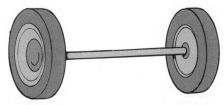

Inclined plane—A ramp up to a building is an example of an inclined plane. This type of simple machine can be used to move things from a lower place to a higher place and vice versa.

Directions: On another sheet of paper, make a collage of machines you use or see every day. Use books about machines, drawing paper, crayons, markers, magazines, and newspapers.

UNIT 10

Name:_____

Early Algebra Words

In math, there are some basic rules that always apply.

The **commutative property** says that you can add or multiply numbers in any order without changing the outcome.

Examples: 1 + 2 = 2 + 1   2 x 3 = 3 x 2

The **associative property** says that you can group numbers when adding or multiplying in any way without changing the outcome.

Examples: (5 + 6) + 1 = 5 + (6 + 1)   (4 x 2) x 3 = 4 x (2 x 3)

Directions: Look at the addition and multiplication problems. Decide which property each problem demonstrates. Then, write **commutative property** or **associative property** on the line.

1. 1 + 2 + 3 + 4 + 5 = 2 + 1 + 3 + 5 + 4   _____

2. 1 x 1 x 8 = 1 x 8 x 1   _____

3. 8 + 9 + (10 + 11) = 8 + (9 + 10) + 11   _____

4. 25,262 x (4,000,000 x 3) =
   (25,262 x 4,000,000) x 3   _____

UNIT 10

Name:_____

Words to Use Instead

Some verbs, such as **went** or **said**, are used too often. Changing an overused verb to an exciting or **vivid verb** can add more meaning to a sentence. It can also make your sentence more fun to read.

overused:	**vivid:**
went	skipped
went	zoomed
said	yelled
said	whispered

Directions: Circle a vivid verb to complete each sentence. Then, write it on the line.

1. A train _____ into the tunnel. (went, zoomed)

2. A person was _____ to the tracks. (strapped, tied)

3. She _____, "Help!" (said, cried)

4. I _____ across the sky. (streaked, flew)

5. The train _____ louder. (seemed, roared)

6. Its headlight _____ brightly. (burned, shone)

7. I _____ the girl just in time. (found, rescued)

8. I _____ her from the tracks. (got, pulled)

9. The train _____ past us. (went, thundered)

10. The girl _____, "You saved my life!" (shouted, said)

UNIT 10

Name:_____

Library Words

Reference books are books that tell basic facts. Usually, you cannot check them out from the library. **Dictionaries** and **encyclopedias** are reference books. A dictionary tells you about words. Encyclopedias give you other information, such as when the president was born, when the Civil War took place, and where Eskimos live. Encyclopedias usually come in sets of more than 20 books. Information is listed in alphabetical order, just like the words in a dictionary. There are other kinds of reference books, too, like books of maps called **atlases**. You likely will not need to read a reference book from cover to cover.

Directions: Draw a line from each sentence to the correct type of book. The first one is done for you.

1. I can tell you the definition of **divide**.

2. I can tell you when George Washington was born.

3. I can give you the correct spelling for many words.

4. I can tell you where Native Americans live.

5. I can tell you the names of many butterflies.

6. I can tell you what **modern** means.

7. I can give you the history of dinosaurs.

8. If you have to write a paper about Eskimos, I can help you.

UNIT 10

Name:_____

Library Words

Directions: Read about periodicals. Then, complete the activities.

Libraries have **periodicals**, such as **magazines** and **newspapers**. They are called periodicals because they are printed regularly within a set period of time. There are many kinds of magazines. Some discuss the news. Others cover fitness, cats, or other topics of special interest. Almost every city or town has a newspaper. Newspapers are usually printed daily, weekly, or even monthly. Newspapers cover what is happening in your town and in the world. They usually include sections on sports and entertainment. They present a lot of information.

1. Choose an interesting magazine.

   What is the name of the magazine? _____

   Write the titles of three articles in the magazine.

   _____

   _____

   _____

2. Now, look at a newspaper.

   What is the name of the newspaper? _____

   The title of a newspaper story is called a **headline**.

   Write two headlines from your local newspaper.

   _____

   _____

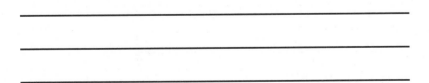

UNIT 10

Transportation Words

Directions: Read about the first trains. Then, answer the questions.

A train is a connected series of cars that moves along tracks. Trains have been around much longer than cars or trucks. The first train that Americans used came from England. The United States brought it back in 1829. Because it was light green, people nicknamed it "Grasshopper." Unlike a real grasshopper, this train was not fast. It traveled only 10 miles an hour.

In the same year, an American built another train. Compared to the Grasshopper, the American train was fast. It traveled 30 miles an hour. People were amazed. They called this train the "Rocket."

1. Where was the first train made that was used by the United States?

_____

2. What did people call this train?

_____

3. How fast did it travel?

_____

4. What year did the Grasshopper arrive in the United States?

_____

5. What American train was built that same year?

_____

UNIT 10

Name:_____

Words About Simple Machines

A doorknob is a simple machine you use every day. It is a **wheel-and-axle** machine. The wheel is connected to the axle. The axle is a center post. When the wheel moves, the axle does, too.

Opening a door by turning the axle with your fingers is very hard. But by turning the doorknob, which is the "wheel," you use much less force. The doorknob turns the axle for you. The doorknob makes it easy because it is much bigger than the axle. You turn the doorknob a greater distance, but with much less force.

Sometimes the "wheel" of a wheel-and-axle machine doesn't look like a wheel. But look at the path the doorknob makes when it is turned. The path makes a circle, just like a wheel.

Directions: Color only the wheels of the wheel-and-axle machines. Then, answer the questions.

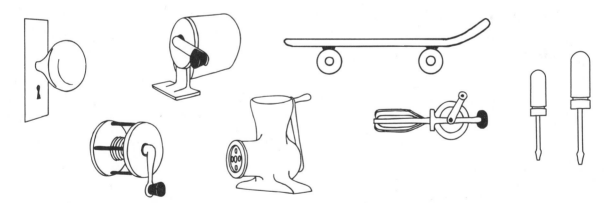

1. A screwdriver is a wheel and axle. What part of a screwdriver is the wheel? _____

2. What part of a screwdriver is the axle? _____

3. Which screwdriver has the largest wheel? _____

4. Which screwdriver would take the least amount of force to turn? _____

UNIT 10

Name:_____

Words About Simple Machines

An eggbeater has a special kind of wheel. It is called a **gear**. A gear is a wheel with teeth. The teeth allow one gear to turn another gear.

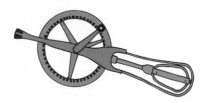

Gears are often used to increase or decrease speed. If the large gear turns one time, the small gear will turn two times.

Directions: You can find gears in many machines. Find and circle all of the machine words in the puzzle. Look across, down, and diagonally. Then, write only the machines that use gears.

```
S  T  K  N  Z  O  R  K  G
H  A  M  M  E  R  U  T  K
O  P  S  O  R  E  R  C  N
V  G  Z  V  F  A  O  T  S
E  B  O  I  C  L  G  X  Z
L  Z  N  E  C  B  Z  E  K
D  K  X  P  W  I  Y  G  L
C  K  T  R  U  C  K  G  K
R  R  M  O  X  Y  T  B  G
A  T  N  J  S  C  U  E  H
K  N  R  E  R  L  V  A  Z
E  G  S  C  Q  E  W  T  R
P  L  K  T  G  Z  T  E  S
Z  K  P  O  H  O  X  R  T
Z  U  T  R  A  M  P  N  P
```

Machines with Gears

_____

_____

_____

_____

_____

UNIT 10

Name:_____

Words About Simple Machines

Directions: Use the words in the Word Bank to complete the sentences.

Word Bank		
machine	easier	force
inclined	shorter	longer

Simple machines help people do work. In the picture above, the ramp makes the man's work a lot _____. The ramp is a simple _____ called an inclined plane.

An _____ plane makes work easier. It lessens the amount of force needed to move a load. By using the ramp, the man moves the barrel with much less force than if he tried to lift the barrel himself. With the ramp, the man moves the barrel a _____ distance, but with much less force. By just lifting the barrel onto the truck, he would move it a _____ distance, but he would need to use much more _____ .

Directions: People use ramps in many different places. They are especially useful for people in wheelchairs. Write the names of places where you have seen ramps in your community.

1. _____

2. _____

3. _____

© 2007 School Specialty Publishing

UNIT 10

Name:_____

Early Algebra Words

The **distributive property** is important when an addition problem is multiplied by something. According to this property, you can add first and then multiply the sum, or you can multiply first and then add together the products. You "distribute" the multiplication across the problem.

Examples: $3 \times (4 + 5) = (3 \times 4) + (3 \times 5)$

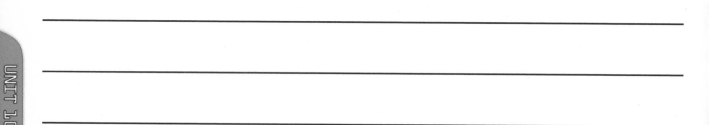

Directions: On the lines below, write an explanation for the distributive property in your own words. Then, write your own example.

_____

_____

_____

_____

_____

Name:_____

Library Words

Directions: Use the words in the Word Bank to complete the crossword puzzle about the library.

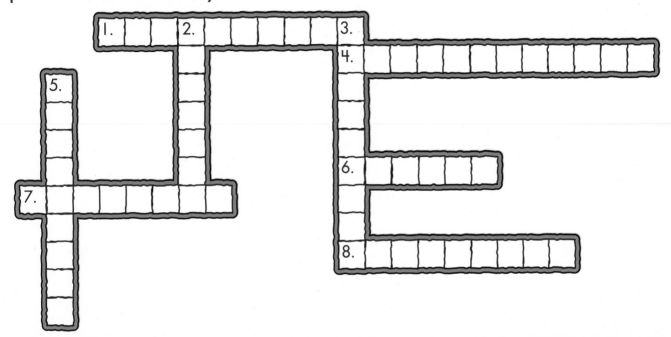

Word Bank

reference	nonfiction	newspaper	magazine
librarian	encyclopedia	fiction	adult's

Across:

1. A book based on facts is _____.
4. You can research Abraham Lincoln's life in this book.
6. If you are not in the children's section, then you may be in the _____ section.
7. This is a kind of periodical.
8. Dictionaries and encyclopedias are included in this section.

Down:

2. A story that someone has made up is _____.
3. This can be delivered to your home every day.
5. If you cannot find what you are looking for, ask this person for help.

UNIT 10

Name:_____

Library Words

A **library** is a place filled with books. People can borrow the books and take them home. When they are finished reading them, people return the books to the library. Most libraries have two sections: One is for adult books and one is for children's books. A **librarian** is there to help people find books.

Directions: Read the title of each library book. On each line, write **A** if the book is written for an adult or **C** if it is written for a child.

1. *Sam Squirrel Goes to the City* _____

2. *Barney Beagle Plays Baseball* _____

3. *Sammy's Silly Poems* _____

4. *Understanding Your Child* _____

5. *Learn to Play Guitar* _____

6. *Bake Bread in Five Easy Steps* _____

7. *The Selling of the President* _____

8. *Jenny's First Party* _____

UNIT 10

Name:_____

Library Words

Directions: Paul and Maria want to learn about the moon. Answer the questions to help them find the information they are looking for.

1. Should they look in the children's section or in the adult's section?

_____

2. Should they look for a fiction book or a nonfiction book?

_____

3. Who at the library can help them?

_____

4. What reference books should they look at?

_____

5. Where can they find information that might have been in the news?

_____

6. What word would they look up in the encyclopedia to get the information they need?

_____

UNIT 10

Transportation Words

Directions: Read about the first cars. Then, use the bold words to complete the puzzle.

   Can you guess how many cars there were in the United States about 100 years ago? Only four! Today, nearly every family has a car. Most families have two cars. **Henry** Ford started the Ford **Motor** Company in 1903. His first car was called the **Model T**. People thought cars would never be used in place of **horses**. Ford had to sell his cars through department **stores**! Soon, cars became popular. By 1920, there were 200 different U.S. companies making **cars**!

Across
2. _____ Ford began making cars in 1903.
4. At first, cars were sold in department _____.
5. By 1920, there were 200 different companies making these.

Down
1. Henry Ford's first car was called a _____.
2. At first, people thought cars would never replace _____.
3. Ford's company was called the Ford _____ Company.

UNIT 10

Name:_____

Words About Simple Machines

Directions: Use the words in the Word Bank to complete the sentences. Then, label the picture with these words: **load**, **force**, and **fulcrum**.

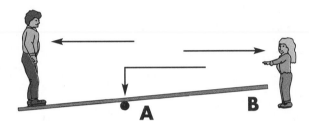

A   B

Mandy wants to try to lift her dad off the ground. Where should Mandy stand on the board? By standing on point B, Mandy can lift her dad.

The board resting on the log is an example of a _____ machine called a lever. A **lever** has three parts—the **force**, the **fulcrum**, and the **load**. Mandy is the force. The point on which the lever turns is called the _____. And Mandy's dad, the object to be lifted, is called the _____. The greater the _____ between the _____ and the fulcrum, the _____ it is to lift the load. The closer the distance between the **force** and the **fulcrum**, the harder it is to lift the load.

Directions: Label the **force**, **fulcrum**, and **load** on the levers.

_____   _____

_____   _____

_____   _____

251

UNIT 10

Name:_____

Words About Simple Machines

Directions: Read the story. Then, answer the questions.

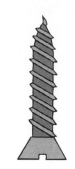

"Poof!" Leroy just shrank himself again in his "Super Electro Shrinking Machine." He is trying to decide which would be easier—climbing around and around the threads of a screw to get to the top or just climbing straight up the side of the screw. He found that the distance up the winding ramp is a lot farther, but the traveling is much easier than going straight up the side. The winding ramp of the screw is like a spiral stairway.

1. Would you travel a farther distance climbing a spiral stairway up three floors or climbing a ladder straight up three floors?

    _____

2. Which would take more force to climb—the stairway or the ladder?_____

3. When you climb a spiral stairway, you travel a greater _____, but you use less _____.

Directions: Read about special inclined planes. Then, label each picture with the word **wedge** or **screw**.

A **screw** is a special kind of inclined plane. A spiral stairway is also an inclined plane. Two or more inclined planes that are joined together to make a sharp edge or point form a wedge. A **wedge** is a special kind of inclined plane. It is used to pierce or split things. A knife is an example of a wedge.

_____   _____   _____   _____

Name:_____

Words About Simple Machines

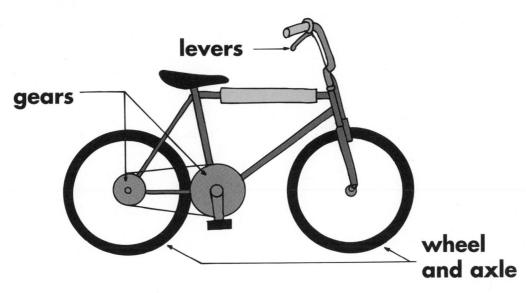

levers

gears

wheel
and axle

Many of the machines that you use each day are made up of two or more simple machines. Look at the simple machines labeled on the bicycle. Machines that are made out of two or more simple machines are called **compound machines**.

Directions: Look at the compound machines. Find the simple machines that make up each compound machine. Label the simple machines you find.

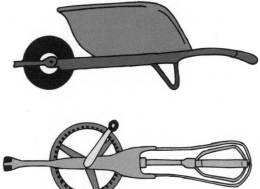

Word Bank			
lever	pulley	wheel and axle	screw

UNIT 10

Name:_____

Unit 10 Review

Directions: Pretend that you are an inventor. Think of a machine that you could invent that would make your life or someone else's life easier. Do research at the library to get ideas. Write about your invention and what it can do. Use vivid and specific words to describe your machine. Then, draw a picture of your invention. Label the simple machines that you used.

_____

_____

_____

_____

_____

_____

UNIT 10

Name:_____

Poetry Words

Poetry tells about feelings, ideas, or events, often with fewer words than regular writing. Some poems rhyme and some poems do not. A poem can be whatever the writer wants it to be. Poems do not need to have complete sentences.

A **couplet** is a pair of rhyming lines. Poems can be made by combining couplets. Line **a** rhymes with another line **a**, and line **b** rhymes with another line **b**.

Sometimes the rhymes are together, like this:

a Carrots, beans, or peas?

a Who wants to eat these?

b I won't tell a lie.

b We'd like cake and pie.

Sometimes the rhymes are apart, like this:

a A timeless tree stood

b on the edge of a dream,

a and thought that he could

b run like the stream.

Directions: Choose the correct word to complete each couplet. Then, write it on the line.

1. a City noises, dirty air, crowded street.
   a Country sun, soaring birds, rows of_____.
      i. corn   ii. wheat   iii. streets

2. a In an alley paved with trash, a flower grows.
   b It stands alone, an upturned bell.
   a How did it get there? The cruel wind knows,
   b A secret the wind will never_____.
      i. knows   ii. stirs   iii. tell

3. a A shower of tears rains down on the stone.
   a This mountain and I are both soaked to the_____.
      i. clothes   ii. bone   iii. skin.

UNIT 11

Name:_____

Poetry Words

A **cinquain** is a special five-line poem. It does not have to rhyme, but the lines follow a specific format.

Line 1: Noun (topic of poem)
Line 2: Two adjectives (describe the topic)
Line 3: Three verbs (actions that relate to the topic)
Line 4: Two more adjectives
Line 5: Noun (another word for the topic)

Directions: Read the cinquain. Then, write your own. Draw a picture to go along with your poem.

Example:

Spring
Bright, cheerful
Raining, blooming, dancing
Fresh, new
Beginning

_____
noun

_____, _____
adjective   adjective

_____, _____, _____
verb   verb   verb

_____, _____
adjective   adjective

_____
noun

UNIT 11

Name:_____

Poetry Words

Directions: A **cinquain** follows the format described below. Write your own cinquain about the sun, moon, or stars.

Star Maiden
Beautiful, bright
Shining, glittering, sparkling
Came to live on earth
Water Lily

Line 1: a noun (topic of poem)
Line 2: two adjectives that describe the noun
Line 3: three verbs with **ing** endings that tell what the noun does
Line 4: a phrase or sentence that tells something special about the noun
Line 5: a synonym for the noun. Repeat the noun if there is no synonym.

_____

_____

_____

_____

_____

Name:_____

Job Words

Directions: Follow the instructions below.

1. In each sentence, circle the word that means the same as **teacher**.

   My educator is a tall man.
   I will ask the professor for help.
   We played basketball outside with the instructor.

2. Look at the word **teacher**. Within this word, underline the smaller word that tells what a teacher does. Then, study the list of verbs in the box. Circle the verbs that mean almost the same as the word you underlined.

educate	sing	inform	dance
instruct	train	stand	read

3. Write one or two complete sentences that tell about your favorite **teacher**. Why do you like him or her? What does he or she teach? Draw a picture of your special **teacher**.

   _____

   _____

   _____

   _____

   _____

   _____

Name:_____

Electricity Words

Have you ever scuffed your feet as you walked across the carpet and then brought your finger close to someone's nose? Zap! Did the person jump? The spark you made was **static electricity**.

Static electricity is made when objects gain or lose tiny bits of electricity called **electrical charges**. The charges are either positive or negative.

Objects that have electrical charges act like magnets, attracting or repelling each other. If two objects have **like charges** (the same kind of charges), they will repel each other. If the two objects have **unlike charges** (different charges), the objects will attract each other.

Directions: Find out more about static electricity. Unscramble the word(s) in each sentence. Then, write the words on the lines.

1. Flashes of (ghtlining) _____ in the sky are caused by static electricity in the clouds.

2. Electrical charges are either (ospivite) _____ or (givnatee) _____.

3. Small units of electricity are called (srgache) _____.

4. Two objects with unlike charges will (arcttat) _____ each other.

5. Sometimes electric charges jump between objects with (unkile) _____ charges. This is what happens when lightning flashes across the sky.

Name:_____

Electricity Words

A **circuit** is a path along which electricity travels. It travels in a loop around the circuit. In the circuit pictured below, the electricity travels through the wire, battery, switch, and bulb. The electricity must have a source. What is the source in this circuit? You're right if you said the battery.

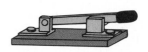

If the wire in the circuit was cut, there would be a **gap**. The electricity wouldn't be able to flow across the gap. Then, the bulb would not light. This is an example of an **open circuit**. If there were no gaps, the bulb would light. This is an example of a **closed circuit**.

Directions: Follow the instructions below.

1. Draw in the wire to the battery, switch, and bulb to make a closed circuit.

   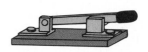

2. Draw in the wire to the battery, switch, and bulb to make an open circuit.

   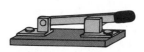

Directions: Unscramble the word at the end of each sentence. Then, write the word on the line.

1. Even the tiniest _____ can stop the electricity from flowing. (apg)

2. A _____ is a path along which electricity flows. (ricituc)

3. If there are no gaps, or openings, a _____ circuit is formed. (sodelc)

UNIT 11

Name:_____

Electricity Words

The bulb won't light in the circuit above. What's wrong with the circuit? It has a gap. How could you fill the gap to make a closed circuit? The easiest way would be to connect the two wires, but with what?

What would happen if you placed a paper clip across the gap? How about a nail? The bulb would light up. The nail or paper clip would form a bridge across the gap. The nail and paper clip carry, or **conduct**, electricity. They are both **conductors**.

Some materials will not carry the electricity well enough to make the bulb light. Try a rubber band. The bulb won't light. Rubber is a poor conductor of electricity. It is called an **insulator**.

```
C O T T O N P
O K G T S O R
P A P E R X K
P L A S T I C
E U D T O R D
R M K E L O S
T I X E R N N
N N G L A S S
R U B B E R Z
K M G R X Z P
```

Directions: Find the different materials hidden in the word search. The materials listed up and down are conductors. Those written across are insulators. Write these materials in the correct group.

Conductor   **Insulator**

_____   _____

_____   _____

_____   _____

_____   _____

                         _____

Directions: Now that you know which materials make good conductors and which make good insulators, write **C** under each object that is a conductor and **I** under each object that is an insulator.

_____   _____   _____   _____

Name:_____

Calendar Words

Directions: Use the calendar to answer the questions. Circle the correct answer.

April

S	M	T	W	T	F	S
				1	2	3
4	5	6	7	8	9	10
11	12	13	14	15	16	17
18	19	20	21	22	23	24
25	26	27	28	29	30	

1. If today is Friday, what day will tomorrow be?
   (A) Tuesday
   (B) Monday
   (C) Sunday
   (D) Saturday

2. If today is Friday, what day will the day after tomorrow be?
   (A) Tuesday
   (B) Monday
   (C) Sunday
   (D) Saturday

3. A carpenter who is building a deck will not work on May 2. What day is that?
   (A) Sunday
   (B) Monday
   (C) Tuesday
   (D) Saturday

4. Imagine that today is Thursday, April 8. What will the date be 3 weeks from now?
   (A) April 22
   (B) April 15
   (C) May 6
   (D) April 29

UNIT 11

Name:_____

Poetry Words

A **diamante** is a special poem that is shaped like a diamond. You can write a diamante poem about any subject.

The diamante has a special format:

Line 1: Noun or pronoun   Monkey
Line 2: Two adjectives   Furry, small
Line 3: Three verbs   Swinging, walking, gathering
Line 4: Four-word phrase   Chewing leaves and twigs
Line 5: Three more verbs   Communicating, caring, moving
Line 6: Two more adjectives   Wild, climber
Line 7: Noun or pronoun   Primate

Directions: Write a diamante about yourself, a feeling, or even a science project!

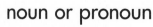

_____
noun or pronoun

_____, _____
adjective   adjective

_____, _____, _____
verb   verb   verb

_____
four-word phrase

_____, _____, _____
verb   verb   verb

_____, _____
adjective   adjective

_____
noun or pronoun

UNIT 11

Name:_____

Poetry Words

An **acrostic poem** has a special format. First, write a word vertically down the page. Then, choose describing words or phrases that begin with each letter of the word.

Example:

Light and breezy
Ever flowing in the wind
Autumn dawns
Fall to the ground

Directions: Write your own acrostic poem. Draw a border around your poem to show what it is about.

_____

_____

_____

_____

_____

_____

_____

UNIT 11

Poetry Words

A **free-verse poem** does not have a special format. It can be in whatever form you like.

Directions: Complete the phrases below to help you write a free-verse poem about you! Then write your final poem in the box. Your poem doesn't have to rhyme!

I am _____.

I hear _____.

I see _____.

I wish _____.

I feel happy when _____.

I feel frustrated when _____.

I get angry when _____.

I am puzzled by _____.

I dream about _____.

I wonder _____.

I plan to _____.

I hope _____.

I know _____.

I understand _____.

I learn _____.

I value _____.

I love _____.

I am afraid of _____.

UNIT 11

Name:_____

Job Words

Directions: It takes many people to build a shopping center. Write a sentence that explains how each person helps to build the shopping center.

1. architect

_____

2. carpenter

_____

3. painter

_____

4. plumber

_____

5. gardener

_____

6. roofer

_____

7. electrician

_____

UNIT 11

Name: _____

Electricity Words

A **light bulb** changes electricity into light. Electricity passes through the very thin wire, called a **filament**, inside the bulb. As electricity flows through the filament, the wire gets hot and gives off light.

Look very closely at the filament in a light bulb. It is made of tiny coils of wire. By using coils, more wire can fit inside the bulb, and the bulb can produce more light.

Directions: Use the words in the Word Bank to label the parts of the light bulb.

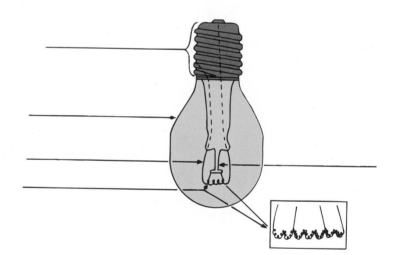

Word Bank

coil filament

glass bulb

wire support

glass support

base

For further investigation:
The first light bulb ever made had a filament made out of cotton! It burned brightly but didn't last long. Find out who invented the first light bulb and when it was invented.

Name:_____

Electricity Words

Directions: Read about electricity. Then, answer the questions.

"Jane, did you remember to turn off the TV?" Jane's parents want Jane to remember to conserve electricity. It takes a lot of fuel to make electricity. We have to be careful not to waste electricity.

Your house has an **electric meter** that measures the amount of electricity your family uses. The meter measures the electricity in **kilowatt hours**. It would take one kilowatt hour to light ten light bulbs (100 watts each) for one hour.

1. Would a 75-watt light bulb use more or less power than the 100-watt light bulb? _____

2. Look at Jane's home. How could Jane conserve electricity?

1._____
2._____
3._____
4._____
5._____
6._____

3. The electric meter on Jane's house is shown in Picture **A**. It reads 2,563 kilowatts. Picture **B** shows Jane's electric meter after one month. Write the number of kilowatts shown on the meter. Then, figure out the number of kilowatt hours Jane's family used in one month.

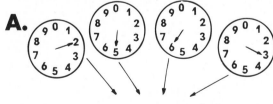

A.

2 5 6 3 kilowatts

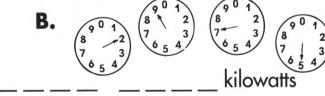

B.

_ _ _ _ _ _ _ _ kilowatts

-2 5 6 3

_ _ _ _ kilowatt hours

Name:_____

Electricity Words

Directions: Read about the telegraph. Then, complete the activities.

In 1877, Samuel Morse used electricity to make the first telegraph. This invention allowed people to communicate directly with one another over long distances.

1. Study the picture of the simple telegraph. Notice how the switch, light bulb, battery, and wire form a circuit. Use the symbols in the key to draw a diagram of the telegraph.

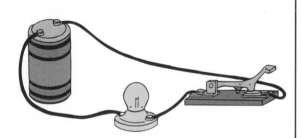

Simple Telegraph Diagram	**Key**
	⊣⊢ wire
	─o─o─ battery
	⊸⊸ switch
	○ light bulb

Directions: Study the Morse Code. Then, decode the message below it.

Morse Code

A	•—	**F**	••—•	**K**	—•—	**P**	•——•	**U** ••—
B	—•••	**G**	——•	**L**	•—••	**Q**	——•—	**V** •••—
C	—•—•	**H**	••••	**M**	——	**R**	•—•	**W** •——
D	—••	**I**	••	**N**	—•	**S**	•••	**X** —••—
E	•	**J**	•———	**O**	———	**T**	—	**Y** —•——
								Z ——••

•—— •—• •• — •   •—   ••• • —•—• •—• • —

—•• •—• ••• ••• •—• ——• •   — ———   •—

••—• •—• •• • —• —••

Name:_____

Calendar Words

Directions: Use the calendar section to answer the questions.

Sun.	Mon.	Tues.	Wed.	Thurs.	Fri.	Sat.
		1	2	3	4	5
6	7	8				

1. Will there be a Friday the thirteenth this month?

_____

2. What date is the third Monday of the month?

_____

3. If today is Wednesday, how many days are there until Monday?

_____

4. What day of the week is the sixteenth?

_____

5. Will the fourteenth fall on a Sunday or a Monday?

_____

6. If today is Thursday, the day before yesterday was

_____ .

7. If today is Tuesday, the day after tomorrow will be

_____ .

8. If yesterday was Monday, tomorrow will be

_____ .

9. If tomorrow will be Thursday, yesterday was

_____ .

10. If the day after tomorrow will be Saturday, what was the day before yesterday?

_____

© 2007 School Specialty Publishing

UNIT 11

Name:_____

Poetry Words

Shape poems are words that form the shape of the thing being written about.

Example:

Directions: Create your own shape poem.

Name:_____

Poetry Words

Haiku is a form of Japanese poetry that is often about nature. There are 3 lines. The first line has 5 syllables. The second line has 7 syllables. The third line has 5 syllables.

Example:

The rain falls softly,	5
Touching the leaves on the trees,	7
Bathing tenderly.	5

Directions: Choose a topic in nature that would make a good haiku. Think of words to describe your topic. Then, write and illustrate your haiku.

_____

_____

_____

Name:_____

Poetry Words

A **limerick** is a fun type of rhyming poem. It has five lines in a special format. Limericks are usually funny or silly! Look at the format below.

	Number of Syllables	Rhyme Scheme
Line 1:	9	a
Line 2:	9	a
Line 3:	5	b
Line 4:	5	b
Line 5:	9	a

Example:
There once was a girl who was silly.
She lived in a place that was hilly.
She sneaked out at night
To fly her new kite.
It tossed her about willy-nilly.

Directions: Write your own limerick.

_____

_____

_____

_____

_____

Name:_____

Job Words

Directions: This is a **Venn diagram**. It shows how things are the same or different. Write the ideas from the Word Bank where they belong in the Venn diagram. Three are done for you.

Word Bank			
help people	fight fires	ride cars	ride fire engines
fight crime	are brave	use sirens	give traffic tickets

police officers — **police officers and firefighters** — **firefighters**

ride cars — are brave — ride fire engines

Directions: Use the information in the Venn diagram to complete this compare-and-contrast paragraph.

Police officers and firefighters are brave. They both _____ to alert people on the road, but police officers _____ , while firefighters _____ . They both help people, but in different ways. Police officers _____ and firefighters _____ . My dad only wishes that police officers didn't also _____ !

Name:_____

Electricity Words

Steve and Lenny really enjoyed listening to the radio while they fished. Radios need electricity to work. Where did Steve's radio get its power? From a **dry cell battery**, of course. Dry cells are sources of portable power.

Most portable radios use dry cells. A dry cell makes electricity by changing chemical energy into electrical energy. Chemicals in the dry cell act on each other and make **electrons** flow. The flow of electrons is called **electricity**.

Directions: Use the words in the Word Bank to label the parts of the dry cell. You can use a science book for help, but first try to figure out each part by yourself.

Word Bank

chemical paste

carbon rod

zinc case

terminal

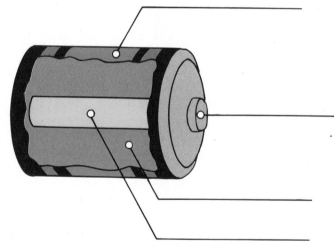

Directions: Write the names of the appliances, tools, or toys in your house that are powered with dry cells.

_____   _____

_____   _____

_____   _____

_____   _____

_____   _____

UNIT 11

Name: _____

Electricity Words

Directions: Someone is responsible for inventing each of these appliances. Try to think of your own invention. Describe it below.

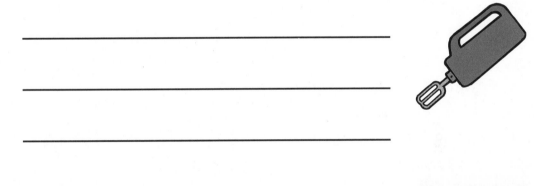

_____

_____

_____

_____

_____

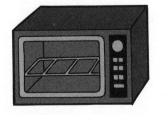

Electricity Words

Directions: Make your own battery with the help of an adult.

You will need:
a lemon
two different pieces of metal (for example, a brass thumbtack and a
                                    steel paperclip)
copper wire
a flashlight bulb

Directions:
Push the two pieces of metal into the lemon. Make sure that the two metals
do not touch one another!
Wrap copper wire around the ends of the metals and connect the other
ends of the wire to a flashlight bulb.
The light bulb should light up.

The acid in the lemon acts as the electrolyte that allows particles to move to
the electrodes (the thumbtack and the paperclip). The electricity then flows
through the light bulb until the electrolyte (acid) around the metal pieces is
no longer able to react.

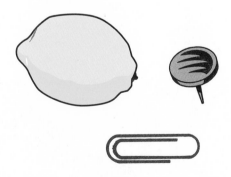

UNIT 11

Name:_____

Unit 11 Review

Directions: Draw a line to match each word to its description.

1. teacher   a rhyming pair of lines

2. month   the thin wire inside a light bulb

3. circuit   types of electrical charges

4. terminal   a protector

5. Haiku   the number of days in a week

6. couplet   a material that carries electricity

7. cotton   a special five-line poem

8. filament   a poem that has no special format

9. positive and negative   a type of insulator

10. free verse   a form of Japanese poetry

11. conductor   someone who educates

12. seven   12 of these make up a year

13. cinquain   the path along which electricity travels

14. police officer   part of a battery

UNIT 11

UNIT 12

Name:_____

Words in an Expository Paragraph

An **expository paragraph** gives detailed information about a topic. It tells facts, opinions, or both.

Example: My favorite sport is swimming. It is not only fun and refreshing on a hot day, but it is also a great way to exercise. I go swimming almost every day in the summer.

Directions: Write an expository paragraph to tell about each subject.

1. My favorite pastime is

_____

_____

_____

2. Summer is important to me because

_____

_____

_____

3. My ambition in life is to be a

_____

_____

_____

4. If I could be anywhere in the world,

_____

_____

_____

UNIT 12

Name:_____

Words in a Compare-and-Contrast Paragraph

To **compare** is to notice the similarities and differences between two things. Another way to say this is **compare and contrast**.

Directions: Compare books and movies. Write a list of the ways they are the same and a list of the ways they are different.

Ways they are the same:

_____

_____

Ways they are different:

_____

_____

Directions: Use your ideas to write a paragraph about the similarities between books and movies and a paragraph about their differences. Begin both paragraphs with topic sentences.

_____

_____

_____

_____

_____

_____

_____

_____

UNIT 12

Name:_____

Words in a Persuasive Paragraph

A **persuasive paragraph** is a way to express strong opinions and to try to make others feel the same way.

To write a persuasive paragraph:

- Choose a topic.

- Write a topic sentence that states your strong opinion and why you feel this way.

- Write several supporting sentences that give your reasons. Try to include several facts as well as feelings.

- End with a concluding sentence that summarizes your strong opinion.

Directions: Follow the steps to plan a persuasive paragraph.

1. Topic (state your opinion)

    _____

2. Topic Sentence _____

    _____

3. Supporting Sentences _____

    _____

    _____

    _____

4. Concluding Sentence _____

    _____

    _____

Name:_____

Words About Famous People

Directions: Read the paragraph about Neil Armstrong. Then, answer the questions.

Neil Armstrong was born on August 5, 1930. From an early age, Armstrong took a great interest in planes and began flying lessons as soon as he was old enough. In college, he studied aerospace engineering. After college, Armstrong worked in a number of different fields of flight, finally joining the National Aeronautics and Space Administration (NASA) in 1962. It wasn't until 1969 that Armstrong participated in the legendary flight of Apollo 11 to the moon, serving as the first human being to ever set foot on its surface. When Armstrong took his first step, he made the famous statement, "That's one small step for [a] man, one giant leap for mankind."

1. What does "aerospace" mean?

   _____

   _____

2. Summarize Armstrong's life leading up to his flight on Apollo 11.

   _____

   _____

   _____

3. Imagine you were Armstrong, taking your first step on the moon. Describe your experience.

   _____

   _____

   _____

Name:_____

Words About Earth

Thousands of years ago, people made up stories to explain things that happened in their world. Those stories are called **myths**.

Directions: Read the myths about Earth. Then, complete the activity at the bottom of the page.

1. Some ancient cultures believed that Earth was held by huge figures. For example, the Greeks believed that Atlas carried the sky on his shoulders. When he shrugged his shoulders, an earthquake took place.

2. Another Greek legend says that when Poseidon, the sea god, was angry, he banged the sea floor with his trident (or spear), causing storms at sea.

3. Aerial views of craters look like giant eyes. Mount Vesuvius's crater may have inspired the Greek myth of the Cyclops, a tribe of one-eyed giants.

4. It is said that the powerful goddess, Pele, lives in the crater Halemaumau at the summit of Kilauea on Hawaii and makes mountains, melts rocks, destroys forests and builds new islands.

Extension activity:
Look up natural disasters in almanacs and/or encyclopedias. On a separate sheet of paper, write a myth to explain its event. Give the main characters (quakes, volcanoes, gods, animals, etc.) human characteristics and motions. The name of your story should be the name of the natural disaster.

Myths

UNIT 12

Name:_____

Words About Earth

Directions: Follow the recipe to learn more about Earth's layers.

You will need:

an adult, 2 large bowls (one that can go in the freezer), a rolling pin, a wooden spoon, a large wooden cutting board, a saucepan, measuring spoons, a long sharp knife, paper plates, plastic forks, the ingredients listed below

Cover the inside of the bowl that will go in the freezer with a nonstick spray.

INGREDIENTS:

Crust   4 tablespoons powdered sugar
               1/2 cup butter
               2 cups graham crackers

Mantle   1/2 cup crushed, unsalted peanuts
               chocolate ice cream

Outer Core   orange, red, and yellow sorbet
               M&M's™

Inner Core   vanilla ice cream
               red and green food coloring

— **crust**
— **mantle**
— **outer core**
— **inner core**

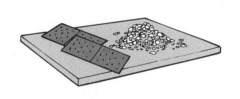

CRUST: Crush graham crackers on the cutting board. Mix powdered sugar with melted butter in a bowl. Line all sides of sprayed bowl with the mixture. Pat it inside the bowl to about 1/4 - 1/2 " thickness. Put it in the freezer until frozen.

Make layers in the order shown above, one layer at a time. Freeze each layer in the bowl before you go on to the next step. (Before mixing and adding each layer, let the ice cream soften, without completely melting.)

When Earth's cross section is frozen, take it out of the freezer. Cut it in half and then in fourths. Remove one quarter at a time. Slice it like a cake so that each serving has a little of each of Earth's layers. Put it on plates and serve.

Name:_____

Words About Earth

Erosion is the wearing away of Earth's surface by wind or water. Complete the following activity to learn about the effects of erosion on Earth.

You will need:
dirt, five 12" square pieces of thick cardboard, 5 roasting-type pans (you may wish to purchase disposable ones), grass seed, small rocks, leaves, twigs, paper towels, a small watering can, water, a quart-size jar

Directions: Cover the 5 pieces of cardboard with at least an inch or two of moist dirt. Then, do one of the following with each piece of cardboard:

1. Leave one piece of cardboard as is.
2. Set the leaves into the dirt in one.
3. Set the twigs into the dirt in one.
4. Set the rocks into the dirt in one.

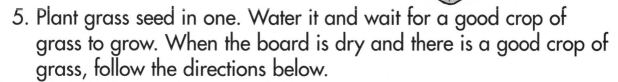

5. Plant grass seed in one. Water it and wait for a good crop of grass to grow. When the board is dry and there is a good crop of grass, follow the directions below.

Lean the cardboard against the inside of a pan. Fill a quart jar with water and pour it into a watering can. Holding the spout about 2" above the cardboard, sprinkle water over it and observe the water flowing over the dirt into the pan.

To compare the amount of dirt that has been eroded, fold a paper towel into a cone shape. Place it in the mouth of the jar and pour the muddy water from the pan into it. Compare what each piece of cardboard looks like and the amount of dirt on the paper towels. Why do you think there are differences?

Earth Science

287

Name:_____

Words About Place Value

The **place value** of a digit or numeral is shown by where it is in the number. For example, in the number **23**, **2** has the place value of **tens** and **3** is **ones**.

Directions: Add the tens and ones. Then, write your answers on the lines

Example:

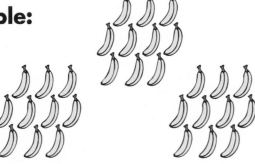

+   =   33

3 tens   +   3 ones   =   33

1. 7 tens + 5 ones   = _____   4. 4 tens + 0 ones   = _____

2. 2 tens + 3 ones   = _____   5. 8 tens + 1 one   = _____

3. 5 tens + 2 ones   = _____   6. 1 ten + 1 one   = _____

Directions: Draw lines to match the numbers. The first one is done for you.

2 tens + 5 ones   38

3 tens + 8 ones   25

1 ten + 0 ones   6

0 tens + 6 ones   10

Name:_____

Words in a How-To Paragraph

A **how-to** paragraph gives instructions to the reader about how to do something. The paragraph should give step-by-step instructions.

Directions: Number the sentences in order from 1 to 7 as they should appear in a how-to-paragraph.

How to Use a Hula Hoop

_____ Let go of the hoop.

_____ Bring the hoop up around your waist.

_____ Twist the hoop.

_____ Keep swiveling your hips.

_____ Hold the hoop in both hands.

_____ Swivel your hips.

_____ Step into the hula hoop.

Directions: Write a paragraph that explains how to use a hula hoop using the steps above. Add your own topic sentence and concluding sentence. Add details to make your instructions more interesting.

_____

_____

_____

_____

_____

_____

_____

Paragraphs

289

UNIT 12

Name:_____

Words in an Informative Paragraph

An expository paragraph gives information or explains something. One type of expository writing is an **informative paragraph**. It gives information.

Directions: Only five of these sentences belong in a paragraph together. Draw a line through the sentences that do not belong. Then, rewrite the paragraph.

There are many kinds of snakes. Kenny has two snakes. Some pythons are as long as a bus. Water snakes live in rivers or lakes. The snake at the zoo is named Monty. Garter snakes are very small. I like snakes. All snakes are reptiles.

_____

_____

_____

_____

_____

_____

_____

_____

_____

UNIT 12

Name:_____

Words in a Descriptive Paragraph

A **descriptive paragraph** tells about something that can be observed or experienced. Notice how the paragraph below begins with a topic sentence. It is followed with support sentences that give descriptive details.

Example:

The banana split was an ice-cream lover's dream come true. A large blue oval dish was lined with long slices of bananas. On the bananas were three huge scoops of ice cream: chocolate fudge, vanilla, and strawberry. Drizzled over the vanilla scoop was loads of hot fudge sauce. Butterscotch sauce was dripping down the other two scoops. Lastly, chopped nuts were sprinkled over the sauce with a puff of whipped cream and a cherry to top it off!

Directions: Choose a topic from the list in the box. Then, write a list of details that could describe it.

My Classroom	My Favorite Outfit	Sledding
In-Line Skating	Around the Campfire	My Pet
Thanksgiving Dinner	Riding a Roller Coaster	

Topic: _____

Details: _____   _____

_____   _____

_____   _____

_____   _____

_____   _____

Name:_____

Words About Famous People

Directions: Read about Christopher Columbus. Then, answer the questions.

What do you know about Christopher Columbus? He was a famous sailor and explorer. Columbus was 41 years old when he sailed from southern Spain on August 3, 1492 with three ships and 90 men. Thirty-three days later, they landed on Watling Island in the Bahamas. The Bahamas are islands located in the West Indies. The West Indies are a large group of islands between North America and South America.

1. How old was Columbus when he set sail from southern Spain?

   _____

2. How many ships did he take?

   _____

3. How many men were with him?

   _____

4. How long did it take him to reach land?

   _____

5. Where did Columbus land?

   _____

6. What are the West Indies?

   _____

Words About Earth

Directions: Earth is made of **rocks** and **minerals**. A rock is a solid mass made up of minerals. Minerals are substances that are not made of animals or plants. Gold, silver, iron, and salt are minerals. Here is how you can make your own crystal rock candy.

You will need:

an adult, 4 cups of sugar, water, string, pencils, glasses that will not break when hot water is added, saucepans, spoons, measuring cups, a magnifying glass, food coloring, a stove, a pen, scissors, a stainless steel spoon, 9" x 12" sheets of drawing paper cut into four equal pieces

Directions:

Pour one cup of water into a saucepan. Add two cups of sugar. Stir over heat until sugar is dissolved. Add two more cups of sugar and continue heating and stirring until clear. Pour sugar water into glasses. (As a precaution against breakage, put a stainless spoon in each glass while pouring.)

Tie a piece of string to the center of each pencil—one per glass. The string should be long enough so that the string will hang in the solution, just above the bottom of the glass. Measure off and tie two more pieces of string to the same pencil. Cut them off and let them hang in the solution, too. Add food coloring if you want the crystals to have color.

In a few hours, examine the string in the glass. Some crystals should have formed. Look at them with a magnifying glass and draw a picture of them. Taste one. If you like it, you can eat it.

Name:_____

Words About Earth

Directions: The Seven Summits are the highest mountains of each of the seven continents. Use the Word Bank to write the name of each mountain on the correct continent. Then, color the continents.

Word Bank			
Everest	Aconcagua	Mount McKinley	
Kilimanjaro	Elbrus	Vinson Massif	Kosciuszkor

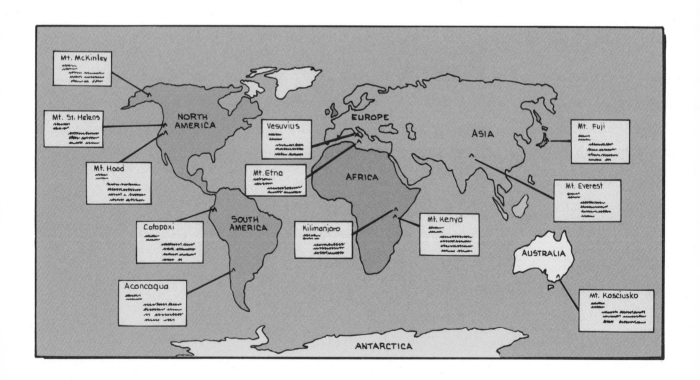

Name:_____

Words About Earth

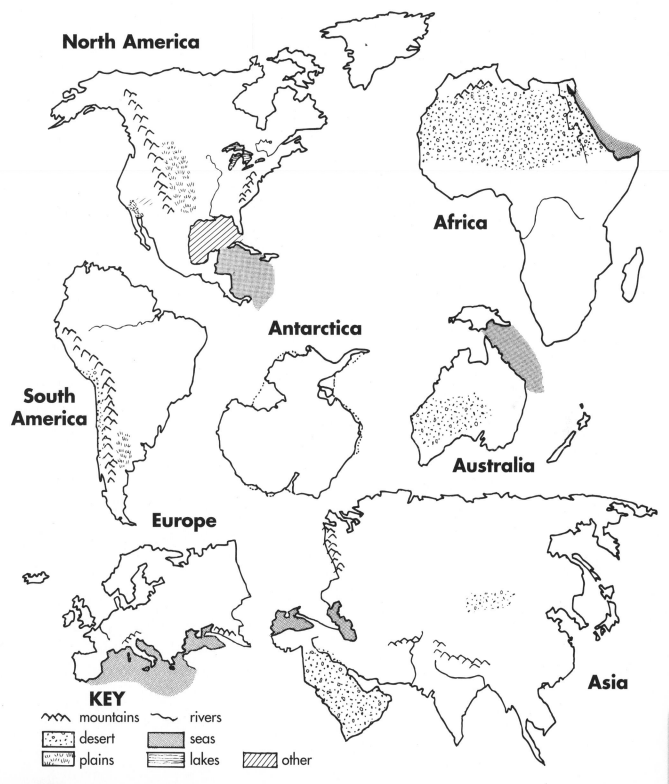

North America

Africa

Antarctica

South
America

Australia

Europe

Asia

KEY

ᗰᗰᗰ mountains   ⌒ rivers

▨ desert   ▨ seas

▨ plains   ▨ lakes   ▨ other

UNIT 12

Name:_____

Words About Place Value

The **place value** of a digit, or numeral, is shown by where it is in the number. For example, in the number 1,234, 1 has the place value of **thousands**, 2 is **hundreds**, 3 is **tens**, and 4 is **ones**.

Hundred Thousands	Ten Thousands	Thousands	Hundreds	Tens	Ones
9	4	3	8	5	2

Directions: Draw lines to match the numbers in Column A with the place values listed in Column B. The first one is done for you.

A	B
62,453	two hundred thousand
7,641	three thousand
486,113	four hundred thousand
11,277	eight hundreds
813,463	seven tens
594,483	five ones
254,089	six hundreds
79,841	nine ten thousands
27,115	five tens

Words in a Cause-and-Effect Paragraph

Expository writing gives information or explains something. A **cause-and-effect paragraph** is expository writing that explains why something happened.

Directions: Draw a line to match each cause to its effect. Notice that the cause happens before the effect.

Cause	**Effect**
Don't pet the snake from tail to head.	The wrong food will make a snake sick.
Snakes should not be kept in a cold place.	Doing this could hurt its scales.
Never feed a snake something it should not eat.	A snake cannot make itself warm, and it could get sick.

Directions: Read the cause-and-effect paragraph. Underline the causes. Circle the effects. (Hint: There are three of each.)

I have to watch my snake, Jake, more closely. Yesterday, I took him out of his cage to clean it. He got away when I was not looking. He slithered as fast as lightning into the kitchen. My mom screamed loudly and jumped on a chair. Jake hid under the stove. I looked for a long time before I found him. Now, he is back in his cage. Next time, I plan to put him in a box while I clean his cage.

Name:_____

Words in an Expository Paragraph

Compare-and-Contrast Paragraph	Persuasive Paragraph	How-To Paragraph

topic sentence
first comparison or contrast
second comparison
  or contrast
third comparison
  or contrast
concluding sentence
	state opinion
	first reason for
	second reason for
	third reason for
	concluding sentence
		topic sentence
		materials
		first step
		second step
		third step
		concluding sentence

Directions: Read each paragraph. Decide what type of paragraph it is. Write its name on the line.

1. _____

Mom and Dad, I think I should be able to have a birthday party for three reasons. First, I think it would be fun to spend time with my friends. We also have not had cake and ice cream lately. My sister and brothers would enjoy the party, too. Surely, it is a good idea to have a party.

2. _____

This is how I can invite all my friends to my birthday party. My dad and I will buy invitations at the store. The first thing I will do is write the day and time inside each invitation. Next, I will write each friend's name on the outside of each envelope. Last, I will give them to my friends. I cannot wait for the party!

3. _____

I wonder if I should ask for a puppy or a video game. Both would be fun to have, but a dog would take a lot of care. A video game cannot snuggle at night, but it takes very little care. A dog has many other costs, such as food, vets, and grooming. I think the video game would be best for me.

UNIT 12

Words in an Expository Paragraph

Informative Paragraph	Descriptive Paragraph	Cause-and-Effect Paragraph
topic sentence	topic sentence	topic sentence
first fact	descriptive sentence	cause or effect
second fact	descriptive sentence	cause or effect
third fact	descriptive sentence	cause or effect
concluding sentence	concluding sentence	concluding sentence

Directions: Read each paragraph. Decide what type of paragraph it is. Write its name on the line.

1. _____

What a beautiful birthday cake I have! Mom made it look just like a puppy. It has floppy ears with a shiny, black gumdrop nose. The dog cake even has a blue frosting collar that says, "Snoopy." When I saw the cake, I was sure I was getting a video game. I think Mom and Dad are hinting that my cake is the only dog I'm going to get.

2. _____

My birthday cake was nearly ruined. First, Felix tried to pin the tail on the cat. The poor cat ran through the kitchen and jumped up on the table. Mom grabbed the cake just before the cat ran into it. We almost had a cat in our dog cake!

3. _____

I had my birthday party on Saturday. Four boys and three girls came to the party. Everyone had a piece of my dog birthday cake with a scoop of vanilla ice cream. My parents gave me a white beagle puppy named "Snoopy." Everyone who came to the party said that it was really fun, and they all loved my new dog!

Name:_____

Words About Famous People

Directions: Read about Babe Ruth. Then, answer the questions.

The great baseball champion **Babe Ruth** was born in Baltimore, Maryland on February 6, 1895. He could hit a ball father than most major-league players when he was only 13 years old. He did not have a very good home life, so he spent most of his early years living in a school for boys. He played baseball whenever he could, so he became very good.

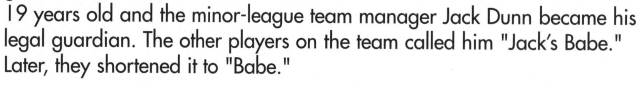

His real name was George Ruth. People gave him the nickname "Babe" when he was 19 years old and the minor-league team manager Jack Dunn became his legal guardian. The other players on the team called him "Jack's Babe." Later, they shortened it to "Babe."

1. When was Babe Ruth born?

_____

2. Where was he born?

_____

3. What did the players originally call Babe Ruth?

_____

4. How old was Babe when he got his nickname?

_____

Name:_____

Words About Earth

Directions: Write a descriptive shape poem about a type of natural disaster. List different kinds of natural disasters, such as tornadoes, floods, monsoons, volcanic eruptions, earthquakes, typhoons, and hurricanes. Under each one, list words associated with that disaster.

Choose one of the natural disasters to be the theme of your **shape poem**. A shape poem takes the shape of the subject it describes. Use the words you have listed to create the picture of the disaster.

UNIT 12

Name:_____

Words About Earth

Earth is made of several layers. This is what they are called and their composition (what they are made of), from the inside out:

Inner core: solid iron and nickel
Outer core: melted iron and nickel
Mantle: thick layer of solid rock
Crust: upper layer that is brittle and can break

Directions: Complete the activity to understand Earth's composition.

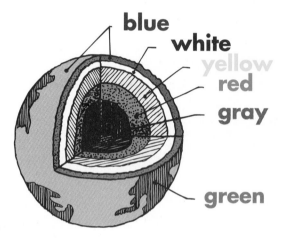

blue
white
yellow
red
gray
green

You will need:

green, blue, red, gray, white, and yellow plasticine clay; knives; a lemon, a small apple, an orange, a small grapefruit (or their equivalent sizes); paper; pen or chalk

Directions: Put the fruit on display. Make Earth's inner core using gray plasticine. Roll it into a ball about the size of a lemon. Then, add red plasticine around it to make the outer core. The total size should now be equal to that of an apple. Next, add yellow clay to make the mantle. When this is added, the clay should be about the size of an orange. The last layer of Earth is the crust. Put a 1/4" white layer of clay around the mantle. Next, put on what is visible—a thin layer of blue (water) and green (continents). Cut out a wedge to show the cross section of Earth's different layers.

Name:_____

Words About Earth

A **volcano** is an opening in Earth's crust through which melted rock, ash, and gases are forced out.

Directions: Complete the activity to make a volcano erupt!

You will need:

vinegar, red food coloring, a large cardboard box, baking soda, a narrow plastic beaker, sand, a paper towel tube, scissors, clay, a flat box (3-4" high), a knife, masking tape

Cut and tape a flat box together so that it is about 10" square. Color the vinegar with red food coloring. Wear old clothes for the eruption.

Directions:

1. Fill half of a beaker with baking soda.

2. Cut two or three holes in the paper towel tube. Put it over the beaker.

3. Mold clay around the tube. Leave the top and the holes you poked open.

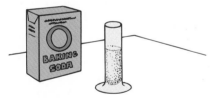

4. Make tunnels out of clay that lead down to the holes.

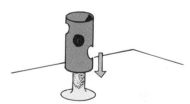

5. Put the beaker with the tube molded with clay in the large box. Pile damp sand around the clay volcano. Pat it to make it into a volcano shape. Leave the top and tunnels exposed.

6. When it is time to make it erupt, take it outside. Pour red vinegar into the beaker. Stand back. **VOOM!**

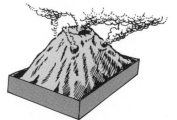

Earth Science

© 2007 School Specialty Publishing

UNIT 12

Unit 12 Review

Directions: Use a word in the Word Bank to complete each sentence.

Word Bank				
concluding	baseball	Atlas	ones	wind
minerals	similarities	natural	Spain	how
crust	inner	opinion	aerospace	

1. Christopher Columbus set sail from _____ to discover the new world.
2. _____ is the mythical man who carried the sky on his shoulders.
3. In a compare-and-contrast paragraph, you write about the _____ and differences between two things.
4. Hundreds, tens, and _____ are words used to describe place value.
5. The wearing away of the earth's surface is caused by _____ and water.
6. _____ are substances formed in the earth that are not made of animals or plants.
7. Neil Armstrong studied _____ engineering to prepare himself to become an astronaut.
8. Floods, earthquakes, and hurricanes are kinds of _____ disasters.
9. Each paragraph should end with a _____ sentence.
10. The _____ is the layer of the earth's surface that is brittle and can break.
11. A _____–to paragraph gives step-by-step instructions.
12. If you wanted to express your _____ on a topic, you would write a persuasive paragraph.
13. Babe Ruth was a famous _____ player.
14. The layer closest to the center of the earth is called the _____ core.

UNIT 12

Words That Are Nouns

A **noun** names a person, place, or thing.

person	• chef • postman • florist
place	• meadow • beach • island
thing	• bowl • doorknob • jacket

Directions: Read the story. Then, circle all the nouns.

There is a magical (chef) who lives on a small, windy (island) off the (coast) of (Ireland). His (name) is (Happy O'Reilly) and (people) travel from all over the (world) to see (Happy). He has jolly red (cheeks) twinkling blue (eyes) and a (smile) for (everybody). He lives by himself in a small, stone (cottage) that has a giant stone (fireplace) right in the middle. In that magical (fireplace), he makes his potato (bread) and vegetable beef (stew) that will cure any (sickness). In the summertime, he makes his apple cobbler (dessert) which will keep a (smile) on your (face) for an entire (year). Go visit (Happy O'Reilly)—if you can find him!

6

Words That Are Nouns

Nouns can also name **ideas**. Ideas are things we cannot see or touch, such as **bravery**, **beauty**, and **honesty**.

Directions: Read the sentences. Then, underline each idea noun. Some sentences may contain more than one.

1. <u>Respect</u> is something that you must earn.
2. We value highly <u>truth</u> and <u>justice</u>.
3. The <u>beauty</u> of the flower garden was breathtaking.
4. You must learn new <u>skills</u> in order to master new <u>things</u>.
5. His <u>courage</u> impressed everyone.
6. She finds <u>peace</u> out in the woods.
7. Their <u>friendship</u> was amazing.
8. The man's <u>honesty</u> in the face of such <u>hardship</u> was refreshing.
9. The dog showed its <u>loyalty</u> toward its owner.
10. <u>Trouble</u> is brewing.
11. The policeman's <u>kindness</u> calmed the scared child.
12. The boy had a <u>fear</u> of the dark.

7

Words That Are Verbs

The word that tells what is happening in a sentence is called a **verb**. Verbs are action words.

Directions: Write a verb from the Word Bank on each line to complete the sentences.

| Word Bank | | | | |
| discovers | dances | eats | drives | shoots |

1. Duffy __drives__ his new, red car.
2. The lady __dances__ on the stage.
3. Coby __shoots__ the arrow at the target.
4. Judy __eats__ pumpkin pie.
5. The archaeologist __discovers__ the hidden doorway.

Directions: Write two sentences using verbs from the Word Bank.

| Word Bank | | | | |
| creates | hammers | builds | mows | scrubs |

1. _Sentences will vary._
2. _____

8

Words About Family

Directions: The puzzle below has two of the words from the Word Bank in it. Find and circle the words. Look across and down.

| Word Bank | | | | | |
| brother | cousin | aunt | mom | sister | dad |

l	m	e	r	x	f	y	h
c	o	u	s	i	n	s	t
y	m	a	a	r	n	m	z
g	w	i	t	b	i	v	s

Now, make your own puzzle. Write the words from the Word Bank in the blank puzzle below. Write some words across and others from top to bottom. Make some words cross each other. Fill the extra squares with other letters. See if someone else can find the words in your puzzle!

Puzzles will vary.

9

Words About Animals

Directions: Read about animals that hibernate. Answer the questions. Then, color the animals that hibernate.

Have you ever wondered why some animals hibernate? Some animals sleep all winter. This sleep is called **hibernation**.

Animals get their warmth and energy from food. Some animals cannot find enough food in the winter. They must eat large amounts of food in the autumn. Their bodies store this food as fat. Then, in winter, they hibernate. Their bodies live on the stored fat. Since their bodies need much less food during hibernation, they can stay alive without eating anymore food during the winter.

Some animals that hibernate are **bats**, **chipmunks**, **bears**, **snakes** and **turtles**.

1. What is hibernation? _a long sleep_
2. When do animals hibernate? _in the winter_
3. Where do animals get their warmth and energy? _from food_
4. Do animals need more or less food when they are hibernating? _less_
5. What are two animals that hibernate? _bats, chipmunks, bears, snakes, or turtles._ Answers should include:

10

Words About Animals

A **food chain** is a series of living things in which each living thing serves as food for the next. For example, bats eat insects and are therefore above them in the food chain.

Directions:
1. Color the pictures.
2. Cut out the pictures and glue them on cardboard.
3. Create a mobile with string and a hanger. Arrange the animals in the order of the food chain from last to first.

Mobile should be arranged in this order:
bear
large fish
small fish
owl
snake
mouse
insect
flower

Color the pictures.

11

Words About Addition and Subtraction

Directions: Write **add** or **subtract** on the line to tell how to solve each problem. **In all** is a clue to add. **Left** is a clue to subtract. The first one is done for you.

1. There are 6 red birds and 7 blue birds. How many birds in all? _____add_____

2. The pet store had 25 goldfish, but 10 were sold. How many goldfish are left? _subtract_

3. There are 8 black cats and 3 brown cats. How many cats in all? _____add_____

4. The store had 18 puppies this morning. It sold 7 puppies today. How many puppies are left? _subtract_

5. There were 11 cats this morning. Someone bought 2 black cats. How many cats are left? _subtract_

13

Words That Are Verbs

Sometimes an action verb needs help from another verb called a **helping verb**.

Common Helping Verbs

am	can	does	is	shall	will
are	could	had	may	should	would
be	did	has	might	was	
been	do	have	must	were	

Directions: Underline the action verb in each sentence. Then, choose the best helping verb to complete each sentence. Write it on the line.

1. Jasmine's family ___is___ planning a recycling project.
   (is had are)

2. They ___are___ talking to their neighbors.
   (is may are)

3. Mr. Chavez ___will___ look for old newspapers and magazines.
   (will do were)

4. The Ong children ___are___ gathering bags to collect plastic bottles.
   (should are did)

5. Jasmine ___might___ open a lemonade stand to make some money.
   (have was might)

6. Mrs. Zanuto said she ___would___ drive us to the recycling center.
   (would be are)

14

Words That Are Verbs

The words **is**, **are**, and **am** are special verbs.

Use **is** with one person, place, or thing.
Example: Mr. Wu **is** my teacher.

Use **are** with more than one person, place, or thing, or with the word you.
Examples: We **are** studying mummies.
You **are** happy.

Use **am** with the word **I**.
Example: I **am** happy today.

Directions: Write **is**, **are**, or **am** to complete each sentence correctly.

1. My house ___is___ brown.
2. My favorite color ___is___ blue.
3. We ___are___ baking cookies today.
4. I ___am___ going to the movies on Saturday.
5. My friends ___are___ going with me.
6. What ___is___ your phone number?
7. You ___are___ standing on my foot.
8. I ___am___ four feet tall.
9. Charles and I ___are___ playing football.
10. Denver ___is___ east of Los Angeles.

15

Words That Are Nouns and Verbs

A **noun** names a person, place, or thing. A **verb** tells what something does or what something is. Some words can be used as both nouns and verbs.

Directions: Write a word from the Word Bank to complete each pair of sentences.

Word Bank

mix	kiss	brush	crash

1. Did your dog ever give you a ___kiss___?
   (noun)

   I have a cold, so I can't ___kiss___ you today.
   (verb)

2. I brought my comb and my ___brush___.
   (noun)

   I will ___brush___ the leaves off your coat.
   (verb)

3. Was anyone hurt in the ___crash___?
   (noun)

   If you aren't careful, you will ___crash___ into me.
   (verb)

4. We bought a cake ___mix___ at the store.
   (noun)

   I will ___mix___ the eggs together.
   (verb)

16

Words About Family

Directions: Use the words in the Word Bank to complete the puzzle about family.

Word Bank

cousin	son	sister	grandma	grandpa	uncle	aunt

Across
1. The child of your aunt and uncle
5. Your mother's mother
7. Your father's father

Down
2. Your mother's child, a boy
3. Your girl sibling
4. Your father's brother
6. Your mother's sister

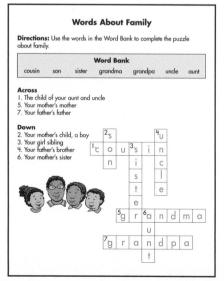

17

Words About Birds

Directions: Looking at a bird's feet can tell you a lot about how they are used. Look at the pictures. Unscramble each bird's name. Then, draw a line to match the bird's name to the sentence that best describes it.

kawh
hawk

ckud
duck

noreh
heron

reckwoodep
woodpecker

"My webbed feet are great for swimming."

"My feet are great for walking up trees."

"I use my feet with long toes to wade in the water and mud."

"I use my strong, powerful feet to catch small animals."

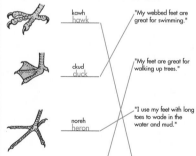

18

Words About Birds

Directions: The shape of a bird's bill can tell you about what it eats. Look at the pictures. Unscramble each bird's name. Then, draw a line to match the bird's name to the sentence that best describes it.

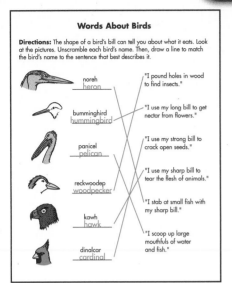

noreh — heron

bumminghird — hummingbird

panicel — pelican

reckwoodep — woodpecker

kawh — hawk

dinalcar — cardinal

"I pound holes in wood to find insects."

"I use my long bill to get nectar from flowers."

"I use my strong bill to crack open seeds."

"I use my sharp bill to tear the flesh of animals."

"I stab at small fish with my sharp bill."

"I scoop up large mouthfuls of water and fish."

19

Words About Birds

Directions: Use the Word Bank to write the word that best describes each kind of bird's bill.

Word Bank		
preying	straining	seed-eating
probing	fish-eating	insect-eating

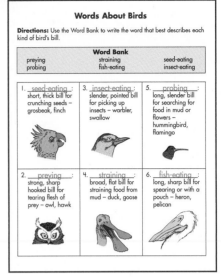

1. __seed-eating__ : short, thick bill for crunching seeds – grosbeak, finch

2. __preying__ : strong, sharp hooked bill for tearing flesh of prey – owl, hawk

3. __insect-eating__ : slender, pointed bill for picking up insects – warbler, swallow

4. __straining__ : broad, flat bill for straining food from mud – duck, goose

5. __probing__ : long, slender bill for searching for food in mud or flowers – hummingbird, flamingo

6. __fish-eating__ : long, sharp bill for spearing or with a pouch – heron, pelican

20

Words About Addition, Subtraction, and Multiplication

Directions: Write **add**, **subtract**, or **multiply** on the line to tell how to solve each problem. Then, solve the problem. The first one is done for you.

1. There were 12 frogs sitting on a log by a pond, but 3 frogs hopped away. How many frogs are left?

   __subtract__ __9__ frogs

2. There are 9 flowers growing by the pond. Each flower has 2 leaves. How many leaves are there?

   __multiply__ __18__ leaves

3. A tree had 7 squirrels playing in it. Then 8 more came along. How many squirrels are there in all?

   __add__ __15__ squirrels

4. There were 27 birds living in the trees around the pond, but 9 flew away. How many birds are left?

   __subtract__ __18__ birds

21

Words That Are Adjectives

Adjectives are describing words that give more information about something. They make writing more interesting.

Examples:			
What Kind:	**white** egg	**small** car	**messy** room
How Many:	**five** flags	**lots** of books	**a half-dozen** donuts
Which One:	**those** ducklings	**that** lamp	**this** bowl

Directions: Look at each picture. Then, write a word that describes it.

Suggested answers:

1. __hot cereal__   4. __sticky shoe__

2. __hungry cat__   5. __happy student__

3. __surprised boy__   6. __two dogs__

22

Words That Are Adverbs

Adverbs are describing words. They describe verbs. Adverbs tell **how**, **when**, or **where** the action takes place.

Examples:	**How**	**When**	**Where**
	slowly	yesterday	here
	gracefully	today	there
	swiftly	tomorrow	everywhere
	quickly	soon	

Directions: Underline the adverb in each sentence. Then, write on the line whether the adverb tells **how**, **when**, or **where**. The first one is done for you.

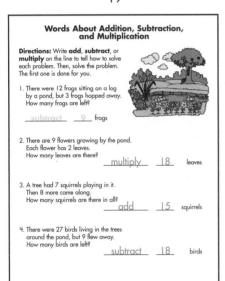

How? When? Where?

1. The children ran quickly home from school. __how__
2. They will have a spelling test tomorrow. __when__
3. Slowly, the children filed to their seats. __how__
4. The teacher sat here at her desk. __where__
5. She will pass the tests back later. __when__
6. The students received their grades happily. __how__

Directions: Write three sentences of your own using any of the adverbs above.

1. __Sentences will vary.__
2. _____
3. _____

23

Words That Are Adjectives and Adverbs

Directions: Write **ADJ** on the line if the bold word is an adjective. Write **ADV** if the bold word is an adverb. The first one is done for you.

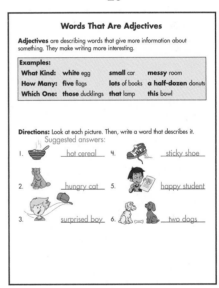

1. __ADV__ That road leads **nowhere**.
2. __ADV__ The squirrel was **nearby**.
3. __ADJ__ Her **delicious** cookies were all eaten.
4. __ADV__ Everyone rushed **indoors**.
5. __ADV__ He **quickly** zipped his jacket.
6. __ADJ__ She hummed a **popular** tune.
7. __ADJ__ Her **sunny** smile warmed my heart.
8. __ADV__ I hung your coat **there**.
9. __ADV__ Bring that **here** this minute!
10. __ADV__ We all walked **back** to school.
11. __ADJ__ The **skinniest** boy ate the most food!
12. __ADJ__ She acts like a **famous** person.
13. __ADJ__ The **silliest** jokes always make me laugh.
14. __ADV__ She must have parked her car **somewhere**!
15. __ADV__ Did you take the test **today**?

24

Words About Family

Directions: Use the words in the Word Bank to write five sentences about the picture. Then, color the picture.

Word Bank				
brother	sister	mom	grandpa	cousin

Color the picture.

1. Sentences will vary.
2. _____
3. _____
4. _____
5. _____

25

Words About Insects

Directions: Read about insects. Then, color the body parts of the insect. Color the head red, the thorax yellow, and the abdomen blue.

yellow red

blue

The largest group of animals belongs to the group called invertebrates—or animals without backbones. This large group is the **insect** group. Insects are easy to tell apart from other animals. Adult insects have three body parts and six legs. The first body part is the **head**. On the head are the mouth, eyes and antennae. The second body part is the **thorax**. On it are the legs and wings. The third part is the **abdomen**. On it are small openings for breathing.

Directions: Draw an insect. Be sure it has the correct number of body parts, legs, wings, and antennae. Fill in the information on the lines.

Pictures will vary.

Insect's name Answers will vary.
Length _____
Where found _____
Food _____

26

Words About Insects

Directions: Use the hints and the Word Bank to write the correct insect name to answer each riddle.

1. I have stout, spiny forelegs.
   I eat insects, including some of my own kind.
   I camouflage well in my surroundings.
   My forelegs make me appear to be praying.
   What am I? praying mantis
2. I have clear wings.
   My body is quite round.
   The males of my species make long, shrill sounds in summer.
   Some of us take 17 years to develop.
   What am I? cicada
3. I have two pairs of long, thin wings.
   I eat mosquitoes and other small insects.
   I live near lakes, ponds, streams and rivers.
   My abdomen is very long . . . as long as a darning needle.
   What am I? dragonfly
4. I am a type of beetle.
   My young are often called glowworms.
   My abdomen produces light.
   What am I? lightning bug
5. I like warm, damp, and dark places and come out at night.
   Humans hate me.
   I am a destructive household pest.
   I am closely related to grasshoppers and crickets.
   What am I? termite

Word Bank		
lightning bug		termite
cicada	dragonfly	praying mantis

27

Words About Insects

Directions: Read about butterflies and moths. Then, answer the questions.

Butterflies and moths belong to the same group of insects. They both have two pairs of wings. Their wings are covered with tiny scales. Both butterflies and moths undergo metamorphosis, or a change, in their lives. They begin their lives as caterpillars. Butterflies and moths are different in some ways. Butterflies usually fly during the day, but moths generally fly at night. Most butterflies have slender, hairless bodies; most moths have plump, furry bodies. When butterflies land, they hold their wings together straight over their bodies. When moths land, they spread their wings out flat.

1. What are three ways that butterflies and moths are alike? Suggested answers:
   a. They both have two pairs of wings.

   b. Their wings are covered with tiny scales.

   c. They both undergo metamorphosis in their lives.

2. What are three ways that butterflies and moths are different?
   a. Butterflies fly during the day. Moths fly at night.

   b. Butterflies have slender, hairless bodies. Moths have plump, furry bodies.

   c. Butterflies hold their wings straight over their bodies when they land. Moths spread their wings out flat.

28

Unit 1 Review

Directions: Use a word from the Word Bank to complete each sentence. Then, on the line beside each sentence, write whether the word you wrote is a noun, verb, adjective, or adverb.

Word Bank			
slowly	strong	bake	plan
toast	beauty	soon	new

1. My dad made __toast__ for breakfast. noun
2. My brother wants a __new__ mountain bike for his birthday. adjective
3. My aunt will __plan__ where to go on her trip. verb
4. The animals will find a place to hibernate __soon__. adverb
5. The __beauty__ of my mother's garden amazed the neighbors. noun
6. I ride my bike __slowly__ beside the busy street. adverb
7. I asked my grandma to __bake__ some cookies for me. verb
8. A hawk uses its __strong__ feet to catch small animals. adjective

Directions: Write **add**, **subtract**, or **multiply** on the line to tell how to solve each problem. Then, solve the problem. Write the answer on the line.

1. There are 3 bats in a cave. Then, 5 more fly in. How many bats in all?
   add 8

2. Three children are outside catching lightning bugs. Each child catches 4 bugs and puts them in a jar. How many lightning bugs are there in all?
   multiply 12

3. There are 15 fish in the pond. A bear catches 9 of them for its dinner. How many fish are left?
   subtract 6

4. Five moths are flying around a lamppost. Five more moths fly over to join them. How many wings do they have in all?
   multiply 20

29

Words That Are Pronouns

A **pronoun** is a word that can take the place of a noun. **He, she, it, they, him, her,** and **them** are all pronouns.

Directions: Read each sentence. Write the pronoun on the line that takes the place of each bold noun.

Example: The **monkey** dropped the banana. It

1. **Dad** washed the car last night. He
2. **Mary and David** took a walk in the park. They
3. **Peggy** spent the night at her grandmother's house. She
4. The baseball **players** lost their game. They
5. **Mike Van Meter** is a great soccer player. He
6. The **parrot** can say five different words. It
7. **Megan** wrote a story in class today. She
8. They gave a party for **Teresa**. her
9. Everyone in the class was happy for **Ted**. him
10. The children petted the **giraffe**. it
11. Linda put the **kittens** near the warm stove. them
12. **Gina** made a chocolate cake for my birthday. She
13. **Pete and Matt** played baseball on the same team. They
14. Give the books to **Herbie**. him

31

Words That Are Pronouns

A **pronoun** is a word that can take the place of a noun.

Directions: Read each underlined noun. Then, in the box above it, write a pronoun from the Word Bank that could replace it. Some pronouns may be used more than once.

Word Bank									
she	it	we	he	his	I	him	they	your	

1. [he] Uncle Nick petted the cat as <u>Uncle Nick</u> walked to the kitchen.
2. [They] <u>The children</u> crowded up to the kitchen door.
3. Granny Little said, "[I] <u>Granny Little</u> wouldn't believe it if [I] <u>Granny Little</u> didn't see it with these old eyes."
4. Lucy said, "[It] <u>The cat</u> is very cute."
5. [We] <u>Will and I</u> left to get some leftovers for the cat.
6. [He] <u>Uncle Nick</u> went upstairs to write [his] <u>Uncle Nick's</u> life story.
7. Granny Little whispered, "Don't bother [She→him] <u>Uncle Nick</u>."
8. I told Uncle Nick, "[They] <u>Lucy and Will</u> want to read [your] <u>Uncle Nick's</u> book."

32

Words That Are Pronouns

Use the pronouns **I** and **we** when you or a group that you are in is doing the action.

Example: I can play ball. **We** can play ball.

Use **me** and **us** when talking about something that is happening to you or a group that you are in.

Example: They gave **me** the ball. They gave **us** the ball.

Directions: Circle the correct pronoun that completes each sentence. Then, write it on the line.

Example: ___We___ are going to the zoo today.   **We, Us**

1. ___I___ wish we did not have to go so soon.   (I) Me
2. Eric threw the ball to ___me___ .   (me) I
3. They made dinner for ___us___ last night.   we,(us)
4. ___I___ am your new teacher.   (I) Me
5. Mom told ___me___ to go to bed.   (me) I
6. ___We___ got our test scores yesterday.   Us,(We)
7. They let ___us___ borrow their car.   (us) we
8. That book belongs to ___me___ .   (me) I
9. She is taking ___me___ with her to the store.   I,(me)
10. Meredith and ___I___ play after school.   (I) me

33

People Words

Directions: Use the words in the Word Bank to write about the people in the picture. Then, color the picture.

Word Bank				
girl	teenagers	mother	man	people

Color the picture.

1. Sentences will vary.
2. _____
3. _____
4. _____
5. _____

34

Words About Dinosaurs

Directions:
Color the dinosaurs.
Cut out the dinosaurs and glue them onto cardboard.
Match the dinosaurs with the descriptions. Write each dinosaur's name on the back of its picture.
Assemble the dinosaurs with string and a hanger to make a mobile.

Color the pictures.

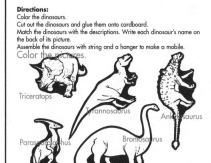

Triceratops
Tyrannosaurus
Ankylosaurus
Parasaurolophus
Brontosaurus

Triceratops: large dinosaur; three horns, one over each eye and one over its nose; large shield of bone protected its neck

Parasaurolophus: large dinosaur; big crest curved backward from its head to beyond its shoulders

Tyrannosaurus: giant meat-eater; large head; jaws filled with sharp teeth

Brontosaurus: giant dinosaur; weighed almost 40 tons; massive body and tail; front legs shorter than its hind legs

Ankylosaurus: body covered with armored plates; large bony club on the end of its tail

35

Words About Dinosaurs

Directions: Find and circle the hidden words in the puzzle. Look forward, backward, up, down, and diagonally. When you have located the words, write the remaining letters at the bottom of the page to spell out a message.

ALLOSAURUS	BIRD HIP	FOSSIL	PLANT-EATER
APATOSAURUS	COELURUS	JURASSIC	PLATED
ARMORED	DINOSAUR	MEAT-EATER	SAUROPOD
ARCHAEOPTERYX	DIPLODOCUS	PALEONTOLOGIST	STEGOSAURUS

Hidden message:
DURING THIS PERIOD SHALLOW SEAS COVERED MUCH OF NORTH AMERICA AND EUROPE AND RAINS CAME TO THE DESERTS.

37

Words About Time

In telling time, the hours between 12:00 midnight and 12:00 noon are **a.m.** hours. The hours between 12:00 noon and 12:00 midnight are **p.m.** hours.

Directions: Draw a line to match the times that are the same.

Example:
7:30 in the morning — 7:30 a.m.
— half-past seven a.m.
— seven thirty in the morning

9:00 in the evening — 9:00 p.m.
— nine o'clock at night

1. six o'clock in the evening — 8:00 a.m.
2. 3:30 a.m. — six o'clock in the morning
3. 4:15 p.m. — 6:00 p.m.
4. eight o'clock in the morning — eleven o'clock in the evening
5. quarter past five in the evening — three thirty in the morning
6. 11:00 p.m. — four fifteen in the evening
7. 6:00 a.m. — 5:15 p.m.

38

ANSWER key

Words That Are Pronouns

Some pronouns show ownership. **My, our, your, his, her, its,** and **their** are called possessive pronouns.
Example: his hat, **her** shoes, **our** dog

You can use the following pronouns by themselves, without a noun: **mine, yours, ours, his, hers, theirs, its.**
Example: That is **mine.**

Directions: Rewrite each sentence replacing the bold words with a pronoun. The first one is done for you.

1. **My dog's** bowl is brown.
   Its bowl is brown.
2. That is **Lisa's** book.
   That is her book.
3. This is **my pencil**.
   This is mine.
4. This hat is **your hat**.
   This hat is yours.
5. Fifi is **Kevin's** cat.
   FiFi is his cat.
6. That beautiful house is **our home**.
   That beautiful house is ours.
7. **The gerbil's** cage is too small.
   Its cage is too small.

39

Words That Are Conjunctions

Or, and, and **but** are called **conjunctions**. This means that they join words or sentences. Use **or** with a choice. Use **and** with similar ideas. Use **but** with **opposite** ideas.

Examples: Is that a skunk **or** a cat? It has black fur **and** a white stripe. It is pretty, **but** it smells bad.

Directions: Rewrite the sentences using **or, and,** or **but** to join each pair of sentences.

1. The skunk has a small head. The skunk has small ears.
   The skunk has a small head and small ears.
2. The skunk has short legs. Skunks can move quickly.
   The skunk has short legs, but it can move quickly.
3. Skunks sleep in hollow trees. Skunks sleep underground.
   Skunks sleep in hollow trees or underground.
4. Skunks are chased by animals. Skunks do not run away.
   Skunks are chased by animals, but they do not run away.
5. Skunks sleep during the day. Skunks hunt at night.
   Skunks sleep during the day but hunt at night.

40

Words That Are Conjunctions

And, but, and **or** are conjunctions. They join two sentences into one longer one.

Use **and** when the sentences are about the same noun or verb.
Example: Tom is in my class, **and** he lives near me.

Use **but** if the second sentence says something different from the first.
Example: Julie walks to school with me, **but** today she is sick.

Use **or** if each sentence names a different thing you could do.
Example: We could go to my house, **or** we could go to yours.

Directions: Rewrite the sentences using **and, but,** or **or** to join the two sentences.

1. Those socks usually cost a lot. This pack of ten socks is cheaper.
   Those socks usually cost a lot, but this pack of ten socks is cheaper.
2. The kangaroo has a pouch. It lives in Australia.
   The kangaroo has a pouch, and it lives in Australia.
3. The zookeeper can start work early. She can stay late.
   The zookeeper can start work early, or she can stay late.

41

People Words

Directions: Use the words in the Word Bank to complete the puzzle about people.

Across
3. A server
4. Someone who finishes school
8. A teacher's boss

Down
1. A writer
2. A rider
5. A king or queen
6. Nephew and _____
7. A store worker

Word Bank
author
clerk
graduate
niece
passenger
principal
ruler
waiter

Crossword solution:
- 1 A / 2 P / 3 WAITER (across)
- 4 GRADUATE (across) with 5 RULER (down)
- 8 PRINCIPAL (across)
- AUTHOR (down), PASSENGER (down), NIECE, CLERK

42

Words About Dinosaurs

Directions: Read about dinosaurs. Then, answer the questions.

Dinosaurs are a group of animals that lived millions of years ago. Some were the largest animals that have ever lived on land. There are none alive today. They became **extinct**, or died off, millions of years ago. This was before people lived on Earth. Many scientists have ideas, but no one can know for sure exactly what happened to the dinosaurs.

1. Why is it not possible to know what caused all the dinosaurs to die?
   Suggested answer: Because dinosaurs died millions of years ago before people lived on Earth.
2. Circle the main idea:
   The dinosaurs died when a comet hit Earth and caused a big fire.
   (There are many ideas about what killed the dinosaurs, but no one knows for sure.)
3. What does **extinct** mean?
   Suggested answer: Extinct means died off; no longer living.
4. Who are the people with ideas about what happened to dinosaurs?
   Scientists have ideas about what happened to dinosaurs.

43

Words About Dinosaurs

Directions: Read about dinosaurs. Then, answer the questions.

Like snakes, dinosaurs may have been cold-blooded. Cold-blooded animals cannot keep themselves warm. Because of this, dinosaurs were likely not very active when it was cold. When the sun grew warm, the dinosaurs likely became active. The sun warmed the dinosaurs and gave them the energy they needed to move about.

Suggested answers:
1. Why would dinosaurs have been inactive when it was cold?
   Dinosaurs would not have been able to keep themselves warm when it was cold.
2. What time of day would dinosaurs have been most active?
   Dinosaurs would have been most active during the day when the sun was out.
3. What time of day would dinosaurs have been least active?
   Dinosaurs would have been least active at night when the sun was down.
4. Why did dinosaurs need the sun?
   Dinosaurs needed the sun to warm themselves to give them the energy to move about.

44

Words About Reptiles

Directions: Read the statements about snakes. Write **fact** if the statement can be proven. Write **opinion** if the statement expresses a belief that cannot be proven.

1. ___opinion___ It is easy to take care of snakes.
2. ___fact___ Snakes do not shed fur all over the house.
3. ___opinion___ Mom does not want to feed a snake.
4. ___fact___ My sister is afraid of snakes.
5. ___fact___ Snakes do not need to go for walks.
6. ___fact___ Snakes are cold-blooded.
7. ___fact___ Snakes need a heat lamp at all times.
8. ___fact___ Snake

Directions: Write your opinion about snakes.

Answers will vary.

45

Words About Time

Directions: Read each sentence. Then, choose the best word or phrase to replace the underlined word. Circle the letter next to the correct answer.

1. Tim was born near the end of the 1900s, the <u>century</u> before this one.
   (a.) 100-year period
   b. 10-year period
   c. weekend
   d. 1,000-year period

2. The paint needs to dry for a <u>day</u>.
   a. 2-hour period
   (b.) 24-hour period
   c. weekend
   d. 1-hour period

3. Clothing styles change about every <u>decade</u>.
   a. 100-year period
   b. year
   (c.) 10-year period
   d. minute

4. I will see you one <u>week</u> from now.
   a. 2-day period
   (b.) 7-day period
   c. 10-minute period
   d. 10-day period

46

Words That Are Conjunctions

Words that combine sentences or ideas, such as **and**, **but**, **or**, **because**, **when**, **after**, and **so**, are called **conjunctions**.

Examples: I played the drums, **and** Sue played the clarinet.
She likes bananas, **but** I do not.
We could play music **or** just enjoy the silence.
I needed the book, **because** I had to write a report.
He gave me the book **when** I asked for it.
I asked her to eat lunch **after** she finished the test.
You wanted my bike **so** you could ride it.

Using different conjunctions can affect the meaning of a sentence.
Example: He gave me the book **when** I asked for it.
He gave me the book **after** I asked for it.

Directions: Choose the best conjunction to combine each pair of sentences. Write the new sentence on the line. The first one is done for you.

1. I like my hair curly. Mom likes my hair straight.
   I like my hair curly, but Mom likes it straight.
2. I can remember what she looks like. I can't remember her name.
   I can remember what she looks like, but I can't remember her name.
3. We will have to wash the dishes. We won't have clean plates for dinner.
   We will have to wash the dishes, because we won't have clean plates for dinner.
4. The yellow flowers are blooming. The red flowers are not.
   The yellow flowers are blooming, but the red flowers are not.
5. I like banana cream pie. I like chocolate donuts.
   I like banana cream pie and chocolate donuts.

47

Words That Are Conjunctions

If and **when** can be conjunctions, too.

Directions: Rewrite the sentences using **if** or **when** to join the two sentences.

Example: The apples will need to be washed.
The apples are dirty.

The apples will need to be washed if they are dirty.

1. The size of the crowd grew. It grew when the game began.
   The size of the crowd grew when the game began.
2. Be careful driving in the fog. The fog is thick.
   Be careful driving in the fog if it is thick. OR:
   Be careful driving in the fog when it is thick.
3. Pack your suitcase. Do it when you wake up in the morning.
   Pack your suitcase when you wake up in the morning.

48

Words That Are Conjunctions

Other words that can join sentences are **when**, **after**, and **because**.

Examples: **When** we got there, the show had already started.
After I finished my homework, I watched TV.
You can't go by yourself, **because** you are too young.

Directions: Use the joining words in the balloons to rewrite the sentences.

1. The keeper opened the door. The bear got out.
   When the keeper opened the door, the bear got out.
2. I didn't buy the tickets. They cost too much.
   I didn't buy the tickets, because they cost too much.
3. The kangaroo ate lunch. It took a nap.
   After the kangaroo ate lunch, it took a nap.
4. The door opened. The crowd rushed in.
   When the door opened, the crowd rushed in.
5. I cut the bread. Everyone had a slice.
   After I cut the bread, everyone had a slice.

49

People Words

Directions: Use the people words from the Word Bank to write about each picture.

Word Bank			
teenagers	toddler	adult	boy

1. Sentences will vary.

2.

3.

4.

50

Words About Reptiles

Snakes are a kind of **reptile**. A reptile is a cold-blooded animal with a skeleton inside its body and dry scales or hard plates on its skin. There are many kinds of snakes, in all sizes and colors. Pythons can be as long as a bus. Corn snakes are red and white, just like a candycane. Milk snakes are gentle and shy. They are usually tri-color, with rings of red, black, and white. Garter snakes have yellow stripes on brown or black. Garter snakes are very common, so they may be in your own backyard!

Directions: Choose a snake mentioned above. Find out more information about it. Then, write three interesting facts about your snake.

1. Answers will vary.
   _____
   _____
   _____

2. _____
   _____
   _____
   _____

3. _____
   _____
   _____
   _____

51

Words About Reptiles

Directions: Read about the rainforest lizard. Then, answer the questions.

The **rainforest lizard** is a reptile. It grows to be as large as a dog! It has scales on its skin. It has a very wide mouth. It has spikes sticking out of the top of its head. It looks scary, but don't be afraid! This lizard eats mostly weeds. Snakes and birds eat these lizards. Some people in the rainforest eat them, too!

1. What is the size of the rainforest lizard?
   The rainforest lizard is as large as a dog.

2. Where do its scales grow?
   Its scales grow on its skin.

3. Which kind of food does the lizard eat?
   The lizard eats mostly weeds.

4. What animals eat these lizards?
   Snakes and birds eat these lizards.

5. Would you like to see this lizard? Why or why not?
   Answers will vary.

52

Words About Reptiles

Directions: The five snakes described are held in the cages below. Use the descriptions and the clues under the cages to write each snake's name on the correct cage.

The King Cobra is the longest poisonous snake in the world. One of these snakes measured almost 19 feet long. It comes from southeast Asia and the Philippines.

The Gaboon Viper, a very poisonous snake, has the longest fangs of all snakes (nearly 2 inches). It comes from tropical Africa.

The Reticulated Python is the longest snake of all. One specimen measured 32 feet 9 1/2 inches. It comes from southeast Asia, Indonesia, and the Philippines. It crushes its prey to death.

The Black Mamba, the fastest-moving land snake, can move at speeds of 10–12 m.p.h. It lives in the eastern part of tropical Africa.

The Anaconda is almost twice as heavy as a reticulated python of the same length. One anaconda that was almost 28 feet long weighed nearly 500 pounds.

| #1 The Anaconda | #2 The King Cobra | #3 The Reticulated Python | #4 The Gaboon Viper | #5 The Black Mamba |

Clues:
- The snake in cage #5 moves the fastest on land.
- The longest snake of all is between the snake that comes from tropical Africa and the longest poisonous snake.
- The very heavy snake is to the left of the longest poisonous snake.

53

Unit 2 Review

Directions: Read each sentence. Write the pronoun on the line that takes the place of each underlined noun or nouns.

1. My friend and I like to play together after school.   We

2. The children's cat chased the lizard.   Their

3. The Brontosaurus was a giant dinosaur that weighed almost 40 tons.   It

4. My mother gets up at six o'clock in the morning to get ready for work.   She

5. The teenagers like to go to the movies on Friday night.   They

6. That brand new bike belongs to Catherine.   her

7. Spot is Steven's dog.   his

8. The paleontologist wrote about her findings in a science journal.   She

9. Julia and William have to go to bed at eight o'clock on school nights.   They

Directions: Complete each sentence.
Sentences will vary.
1. The girl is tall and athletic, but her sister is _____.
2. We should eat fruits and vegetables, because _____.
3. I got in trouble when _____.

54

Transition Words

In some paragraphs, the order or sequence of the sentences is very important. **Transition words**, such as **first**, **next**, **after**, **then**, **finally**, and **last**, offer clues to help show the sequence of the sentences.

Directions: Read the story. Then, circle the transition words.

My family is entering the bake-off contest at the local fair. My dad thinks that we have the best apple pie recipe. Our friends agree.

(First,) dad takes us to the apple orchard to choose the ripest apples. (Next,) we go home to prepare the pie. (After) we wash and slice the apples, we mix in the rest of the ingredients. (Then,) while we make the crust, we wait for the oven to preheat. (Finally,) we add the apples in the crust. We bake the pie until it is cooked to perfection. (Last,) we take our apple pie to the fair and keep our fingers crossed that we win the blue ribbon!

56

Story Words

The **main idea** of a story is what the story is about. Story **details** are the characters and the events that make up the story.

Directions: Read each main idea sentence. Then, read the detail sentences that follow. Draw a ✓ on the line beside each detail that supports the main idea.

Example: Niagara Falls is a favorite vacation spot.
_____ There are so many cars and buses that it is hard to get around.
_____ My little brother gets sick when we go camping.
_____ You can see people there from all over the world.

1. Hummingbirds are interesting birds to watch.
   ✓ They look like tiny helicopters as they move around the flowers.
   ✓ One second they are "drinking" from the flower; the next, they are gone!
   _____ It is important to provide birdseed for the winter for our feathered friends.

2. Boys and girls look forward to Valentine's Day parties at school.
   ✓ For days, children try to choose the perfect valentine for each friend.
   _____ The school program is next Tuesday.
   ✓ Just thinking about frosted, heart-shaped cookies makes me hungry!

57

ANSWER key

Story Words

All short stories have a plot, a setting, a theme, and characters.

The **plot** is what the story is about.
The **characters** are the people or animals in the story.
The **setting** is where and when the story occurs.
The **theme** is the message or idea of the story.

Directions: Use the diagram to plan a story that you would like to write.

Answers will vary.

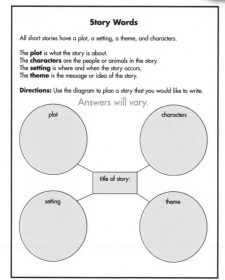

plot

characters

title of story:

setting

theme

58

Words Around the House

Word Bank				
cabinet	curtains	cushion	drawer	mirror
quilt	sofa	sweep	towel	trash

Directions: Write a word from the Word Bank to fit each clue. The letters in the boxes will reveal the name of some of the noisiest things in people's homes.

1. Garbage — t r a s h
2. Thirsty cloth — t o w e l
3. Bed covering — q u i l t
4. Cupboard — c a b i n e t
5. You do it with a broom. — s w e e p
6. Couch pillow — c u s h i o n
7. I can see myself in it. — m i r r o r
8. Window coverings — c u r t a i n s
9. A home for socks — d r a w e r
10. Couch — s o f a

Directions: Imagine that you are a prince or a princess. On a separate sheet of paper, describe a room in your palace. Use the words in the Word Bank.

59

Words About the Human Body

Directions: Read about the human body. Then, use the bold words to finish the sentences below.

What gives you your **shape**? Like a house's frame, your body also has a frame. It is called your **skeleton**. Your skeleton is made of more than two hundred bones.

Your skeleton helps your body move. It does this by giving your **muscles** a place to attach. Your skeleton also **protects** the soft organs inside your body from injury.

Each bone has a hard, outer layer of **calcium**. Inside is a soft, **spongy** layer that looks like a honeycomb. The hollow spaces in the honeycomb are filled with **marrow**. Every minute, millions of **blood** cells die. But you don't need to worry. The bone marrow works like a little factory, making new blood cells for you.

1. Your skeleton p r o t e c t s your soft organs.
2. Bone m a r r o w makes new blood cells.
3. Inside the bone is a soft, s p o n g y layer.
4. Millions of b l o o d cells die every minute.
5. The hard, outer layer of bone is made of c a l c i u m.
6. More than two hundred bones make up your s k e l e t o n.
7. Your skeleton is a place for m u s c l e s to attach.
8. Your skeleton gives your body its s h a p e.

60

Words About the Human Body

Directions: Read about the human body. Then, use the bold words to answer the clues to complete the puzzle.

Your body is like an amazing **machine**. Every minute, your heart pumps six quarts of blood. Your brain sends thousands of **messages** to other parts of your body. The messages travel along the nerves at more than 100 miles an hour! Your **lungs** fill with air. Your **ears** hear **sounds**. Your eyes see **pictures**. And you thought you were just sitting here reading! Your body is always very **busy**, even when you sleep.

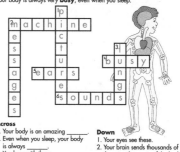

Across
2. Your body is an amazing _____.
4. Even when you sleep, your body is always _____
5. You hear with these.
6. This is what you hear.

Down
1. Your eyes see these.
2. Your brain sends thousands of these to other parts of the body.
3. These fill with air.

61

Words About the Human Body

Directions: Read about your lungs. Then, answer the questions.

Imagine millions of teeny, tiny balloons joined together. That is what your **lungs** are like. When you breathe, the air goes to your two lungs. One lung is located on each side of your chest. The heart is located between the two lungs. The lungs are soft, spongy, and delicate. That is why there are bones around the lungs. These bones are called the **rib cage**. The rib cage protects the lungs so they can do their job. The lungs bring **oxygen** into the body. They also take waste out of the body. This waste is called **carbon dioxide**. We could not live without our lungs!

1. Circle the main idea:

The lungs are spongy and located in the chest. They are like small balloons.

(The lungs bring in oxygen and take out carbon dioxide. We could not live without our lungs.)

2. What is the name of the bones around your lungs? rib cage
3. What is located between the lungs? the heart
4. What goes into your lungs when you breathe? oxygen
5. Why are there bones around your lungs? to protect them because they are soft, spongy, and delicate

62

Money Words

Directions: Circle the letter beside the answer that correctly completes each sentence.

1. One quarter equals
   (a.) twenty-five pennies
   b. fifty cents
   c. five dollars
   d. twenty-five dimes

2. A half dollar equals
   a. five nickels
   (b.) two quarters
   c. five quarters
   d. twenty dimes

3. One ten-dollar bill equals
   a. one hundred dimes
   b. five dollars
   (c.) two five-dollar bills
   d. ten quarters

4. Two dimes are worth less than
   a. two nickels
   (b.) one quarter
   c. fifteen pennies
   d. three nickels

5. George Washington is pictured on a
   a. nickel
   b. five-dollar bill
   (c.) dollar bill
   d. penny

63

313

Story Words

The **main idea** of a story is what the story is about. Story **details** are the characters and the events that make up the story.

Directions: Read the story about spiders. Then, answer the questions about the main idea and story details.

Many people think spiders are insects, but they are not. Spiders are the same size as insects, and they look like insects in some ways. But there are three ways to tell a spider from an insect. Insects have six legs, and spiders have eight legs. Insects have antennae, but spiders do not. An insect's body is divided into three parts; a spider's body is divided into only two parts.

1. The main idea of this story is:

Spiders are like insects.

(Spiders are like insects in some ways, but they are not insects.)

2. What are three ways to tell a spider from an insect?

a) Spiders have eight legs; insects have six.

b) Spiders do not have antennae; insects do.

c) A spider's body is divided into two parts; an insect's is divided into three.

Circle the correct answer.

3. Spiders are the same size as insects. (True)   False

64

Story Words

A good story contains these story elements:

Characters: the people, animals, or objects in the story
Setting: where and when the story takes place
Plot: the sequence of events
Conclusion: what happens in the end

Directions: Read the story. Then, answer the questions.

Ann and Tony are in line to go on the roller coaster. Ann is glad. She has never been on such a big ride before. She bites her lip, because she is nervous. Tony says he does not want to go with her. Ann does not want to go alone. She is not happy, but she steps out of the line with Tony. Then, Tony changes his mind. "I'll go with you," he says. Ann is glad her friend will go, too.

Suggested answers:

1. Who are the characters in the story? Ann and Tony

2. What is the setting? amusement park; line for the roller coaster ride

3. What is the plot? Ann and Tony wait in line to ride a roller coaster; Ann is nervous; Tony doesn't want to go with Ann on the ride.

4. What is the conclusion? Tony changes his mind and agrees to go with Ann on the roller coaster.

65

Story Words

The end of a story should bring all the parts of the story together and provide a satisfying conclusion. The elements of a story ending include:

The climax – the most thrilling part of the story where the problem is either solved or the plot thickens.

The resolution – how the characters solve the story problem.

The conclusion – what happens to the characters in the end.

Directions: Choose your favorite story. Think about its climax, resolution, and conclusion. Write why you think the ending is good, or write another ending for the story.

Answers will vary.

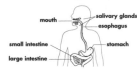

66

Words Around the House

Word Bank			
cabinet	curtains	cushion	drawer
quilt	sofa	sweep	towel

Directions: Write the word from the Word Bank that best completes each group.

1. cupboard, shelves, closet, cabinet

2. pillow, pad, soft, cushion

3. living room, couch, long, sofa

4. broom, clean, brush, sweep

5. bed, blanket, warm, quilt

6. bath, shower, drying, towel

7. window, drapes, cloth, curtains

8. dresser, socks, slide, drawer

Directions: Choose the word that best completes each sentence. Write the correct letter on the line.

1. You use a towel when you are __g__ .   a. pillow

2. To sweep the floor you need a __d__ .   b. shelves

3. In a kitchen drawer we keep __h__ .   c. windows

4. Flowered curtains cover my bedroom __c__ .   d. broom

5. This cabinet has four __b__ .   e. bed

6. A cushion is soft like a __a__ .   f. living room

7. There is a warm quilt on my __e__ .   g. wet

8. We have a comfortable sofa in our __f__ .   h. forks

67

Words About the Human Body

Directions: Use the diagram to number the sentences below in the correct order from 1 to 8 to show what happens when you swallow a bite of food.

mouth — salivary glands — esophagus — small intestine — stomach — large intestine

__2__ While your teeth are breaking the food into tiny pieces, saliva is making the food softer.

__8__ Whatever the body cannot use goes into the large intestine.

__5__ While the food is in your stomach, more juices help to dissolve it.

__3__ When the food in your mouth is soft enough, you swallow it.

__6__ When the food has dissolved in your stomach, it goes to your small intestine.

__4__ As you swallow your food, it moves down the esophagus to your stomach.

__1__ You use your teeth to take a bite out of a sandwich.

__7__ While the food is in your small intestine, the body absorbs whatever it needs.

68

Words About the Human Body

Directions: Read about the functions of blood in the human body. Then, use the bold words to complete the sentences below.

If you could look at a drop of your blood under a microscope, you would see some odd-shaped cells floating around in a liquid called **plasma**. These are the **white blood cells**. White blood cells are "soldiers" that fight germs which cause disease.

You would also see many smaller, saucer-shaped cells called **red blood cells**. Red blood cells give your blood its red color. They also have the important job of carrying **oxygen** to all of the cells in your body.

Blood **platelets** go to work when you have a cut. They form a plug, called a clot, that stops the bleeding.

Blood travels throughout your whole body. It goes to the **lungs** to pick up oxygen and to the intestines to pick up digested food. It carries the oxygen and **food** nutrients to all parts of your **body**. It also takes away carbon dioxide and other waste products.

red blood cell

platelet

white blood cell

1. Red blood cells carry oxygen.

2. The blood gets oxygen from your lungs.

3. Blood carries food nutrients from the intestines.

4. White blood cells fight germs.

5. Blood travels to all parts of your body.

6. The liquid part of the blood is called plasma.

7. Red blood cells give blood its color.

8. Platelets form blood clots.

69

Words About the Human Body

Directions: Read about the circulatory system. Then, complete the activities.

Blood travels through three kinds of tubes. **Arteries** carry oxygen-rich blood from your heart to other parts of your body. Blood vessels called **veins** carry carbon dioxide-rich blood back to your heart. **Capillaries** are tiny vessels that connect arteries and veins. Capillaries take carbon dioxide from the cells and give the cells oxygen. Capillaries are fifty times thinner than a hair. They are so small that the blood cells must line up one at a time to travel through them.

Your heart, blood, arteries, veins, and capillaries work as a team. This team is called your **circulatory system**.

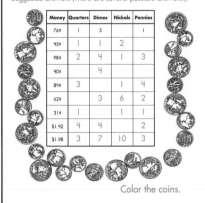

veins
arteries

1. Name three kinds of blood vessels.

a. arteries

b. veins

c. capillaries

2. The picture shows your circulatory system.
• Color the veins **blue**.
• Color the arteries **red**.
• Color the heart **brown**.

70

Money Words

Directions: Figure out which coins you need to make each amount. Then, color the coins.

Suggested answers (There are several possible answers.):

Money	Quarters	Dimes	Nickels	Pennies
76¢	1		5	1
45¢	1	1	2	
98¢	2	4	1	3
40¢		4		
84¢	3		1	4
62¢		3	6	2
31¢	1		1	1
$1.42	4	4		2
$1.98	3	7	10	3

Color the coins.

71

Story Words

Directions: Read the story. Then, answer the questions.

On Saturday, Tracy and her parents were watching television at home. Snow began falling around noon. Wow! It was really coming down. They turned off the television and looked out the window. The snow looked like a white blanket. They decided to put on their coats and go outside. All of the neighbors came out to see the snow. Tracy saw her friend, Jim. They built a snowman together. It was a great day!

1. Who are the characters of the story? Tracy, her parents, Jim

2. Where and when does the story take place? Tracy's house on Saturday afternoon

3. What is the plot? Tracy and her parents were watching television; it started snowing; Tracy and her parents went outside.

4. What is conclusion? Tracy saw her friend, Jim; they built a snowman together; they had a great day.

72

Story Words

A **concluding sentence** ties the story together.

Directions: Read each story. Then, choose the correct concluding sentence for the story. Write the sentence on the line.

1. **Corn on the Cob**

Corn on the cob used to be my favorite food. That is, until I lost my four front teeth. For one whole year, I had to sit and watch everyone else eat my favorite food without me. Mom gave me creamed corn, but it just wasn't the same. When my teeth finally came in, Dad said he had a surprise for me. I thought I was going to get a bike or a new CD player or something. I was just as happy to get what I did.

a. He gave me a new pair of shoes!
b. He gave me all the corn on the cob I could eat!
c. He gave me a new eraser!

(b) He gave me all the corn on the cob I could eat!

2. **A Train Ride**

When our family took its first train ride, my sister brought along a big box. She would not tell anyone what she had in it. In the middle of the trip, we heard a sound coming from the box. "Okay, Jan, now you have to open the box," said Mom. When she opened the box, we were surprised.

a. I would like to take a train ride every year.
b. Trains move faster than I thought they would.
c. She had brought her new gerbil along for the ride.

(c) She had brought her new gerbil along for the ride.

73

Story Words

Word Bank						
plot	events	character	setting	read	sentence	time

Directions: Write a word from the Word Bank to fit each clue. The letters in the boxes will reveal the name of things you read.

1. The time and place a story takes place — s e t t i n g

2. The person or animal the story is about — c h a r a c t e r

3. What the story is about — p l o t

4. What you do with a story — r e a d

5. The setting is the place and _____ . — t i m e

6. The concluding _____ ties the story together. — s e n t e n c e

7. The things that happen in a story — e v e n t s

74

Words Around the House

Directions: Read each sentence. Then, choose the best word or phrase to replace the underlined word. Circle the letter beside the correct answer.

1. We keep plates, cups, and glasses in the <u>cabinet</u> near the sink.
a. dresser   c. refrigerator
(b) cupboard   d. bookcase

2. I opened the window <u>curtains</u> so I could see outside.
a. doors   (c) cloth coverings
b. locks   d. wooden frames

3. I lay on the couch with my head on a soft <u>cushion</u>.
(a) pillow   c. blanket
b. stuffed animal d. warm sweater

4. We keep knives, forks, and spoons in a kitchen <u>drawer</u>.
a. closet for coats and jackets   c. closet for mop and brooms
b. shelf behind a glass door   (d) box that slides in and out

75

Words About the Human Body

Directions: Read about muscles. Then, use the bold words to complete the puzzle.

Muscles are tissues that move parts of the body. Each set of muscles has a **job** to do. The names of muscles have to do with the jobs they perform. The muscles that pull your forearms down are called **triceps**. Tri means "three." The triceps have three parts of muscle working together. The muscles that pull your forearms up are called **biceps**. Bi means "two." The biceps have two parts of muscle working together. Each set of muscles has a certain job to do. Muscles in the front of the foot pull your **toes** up. Muscles on the back of the thighs bend your **knees**.

Crossword answers:
- Across 2 / Down: m u s c l e s
- ²j o b
- ³b i c e p s
- ⁴t r i c e p s
- ⁵k n e e s

Across
2. Each set of muscles has a certain _____ to do.
4. These muscles pull your forearms down.
5. Muscles on the back of the thighs bend these.

Down
1. Without these, you would be a "bag of bones."
3. These muscles pull your forearms up.
4. Muscles on the front of your foot pull these up.

76

Words About the Human Body

Directions: Use the drawing of the tooth to complete the sentences.

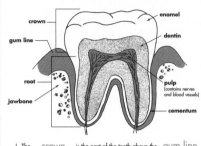

Labels: crown, enamel, dentin, gum line, pulp (contains nerves and blood vessels), root, jawbone, cementum

1. The ___crown___ is the part of the tooth above the ___gum line___.
2. The ___root___ of the tooth grows into the ___jawbone___.
3. The outer covering of the crown is called ___enamel___.
4. The majority of the tooth is made of ___dentin___.
5. Any pain is transmitted to the brain through nerves in the ___pulp___.
6. ___Cementum___ covers the dentin in the root.

77

Words About the Human Body

Directions: Read about your heart. Then, answer the questions.

Make your hand into a fist. Now, look at it. That is about the size of your **heart**, the muscle that pumps blood through your body! Your heart works all the time. Right now it is beating about 90 times a minute. When you run, it beats around 150 times a minute.

Inside, your heart has four spaces. The two spaces on the top are called **atria**. This is where blood is pumped into the heart. The two spaces on the bottom are called **ventricles**. This is where blood is pumped out of the heart. The blood is pumped to every part of your body. How? Open and close your fist. See how it tightens and loosens? The heart muscle tightens and loosens, too. This is how it pumps blood.

1. How often does your heart work? ___all the time___
2. How fast does it beat when you are sitting? ___90 times a minute___
3. How fast does it beat when you are running? ___150 times a minute___
4. How many spaces are inside your heart? ___four___
5. What are the heart's upper spaces called? What are the lower spaces called?
   ___atria___ ___ventricles___

78

Unit 3 Review

Directions: Write the letter of the description on the right that best matches the word(s) on the left.

__h__ 1. details   a. twenty-five cents

__g__ 2. capillaries   b. the human body's frame

__j__ 3. conclusion   c. three

__n__ 4. ears   d. bed covering

__l__ 5. first, next, last   e. the sequence of events in a story

__i__ 6. esophagus   f. the part of the tooth you can see

__m__ 7. oxygen   g. tiny vessels that connect arteries and veins

__c__ 8. tri   h. the characters and events that make up a story

__a__ 9. quarter   i. the tube that connects your mouth to your stomach

__k__ 10. atria   j. the end of a story

__b__ 11. skeleton   k. the heart's upper spaces

__f__ 12. crown   l. transition words

__e__ 13. plot   m. what red blood cells carry

__d__ 14. quilt   n. the body part that allows you to hear sounds

79

Genre Words

A **genre** is a category people use to organize different kinds of books. Everything you read can be classified in a specific genre.

Fiction is a genre. A fiction book is about things that are made up or are not true. Nonfiction is also a genre. A **nonfiction** book is about things that have really happened or are true. Books can be classified into more types within these two categories.

Mystery — a book that has clues that lead to solving a problem or mystery

Biography — a book about a real person's life

Poetry — a book that has a collection of poems, which may or may not rhyme

Fantasy — a book about things that cannot really happen

Sports — a book about different sports or sport figures

Travel — a book about going to other places

Directions: Read the titles. Then, write **biography**, **fantasy**, **mystery**, **poetry**, **sports**, or **travel** next to each title.

1. Marty Frye, Private Eye — ___mystery___
2. Yoga Activities for Kids — ___sports___
3. The Chronicles of Narnia — ___fantasy___
4. A Sightseer's Guide to New York City — ___travel___
5. Silly Verse for Kids — ___poetry___
6. 100 Americans Who Shaped American History — ___biography___

81

Genre Words

Directions: Each genre listed below is nonfiction, which means it is about things that have really happened. Read the description for each genre. Then, draw a line to match each genre to the correct title.

An **autobiography** is the story of a person's life written by that person.

Ben Franklin and His First Kite

A **biography** is the story of a person's life written by another person.

My Story: In My Own Words

An **informational passage** gives information about a subject.

Heavy Rains Blamed for Flooding in the South

82

ANSWER key

Genre Words

Directions: Read each passage. Then, choose the genre that best describes it. Write **autobiography**, **biography**, or **informational passage** on the line.

Americans began playing baseball on informal teams, using local rules, in the early 1800s. By the 1860s, baseball was being described as America's "national pastime." Alexander Cartwright invented the modern baseball field in 1845. He and members of his baseball club came up with the first rules and regulations for the modern game of baseball. The first recorded baseball game occurred in 1846 in New Jersey.

informational passage

Ted Williams was born on August 30, 1918 in San Diego, California. He made his major league debut with the Boston Red Sox at the age of 21. His batting records earned him the nickname, "The Splendid Splinter." He was an All-Star hitter who earned 2 MVP awards. His accomplishments on the field led to his induction in the Baseball Hall of Fame in 1966. Ted Williams died on July 5, 2002, in Inverness, Florida.

biography

Although people consider me a legendary baseball player, I am most proud of the time I served my country as a Marine Corps pilot during World War II and the Korean War. During the Korean War, John Glenn and I served in the same unit. I missed nearly five full seasons of baseball due to my military service. While these absences limited my career baseball totals, I will never regret my time in the Marines.

autobiography

83

Words About the United States

Directions: Read about Delaware and Hawaii. Then, fill in the chart.

Fifty states make up the United States of America. Delaware became the first state on December 7, 1787. Hawaii became the fiftieth state on August 21, 1959.

Delaware is the second smallest state. Its nickname is First State. It is located on the east coast next to the Atlantic Ocean. The capital city of Delaware is Dover. The main industry is manufacturing.

Hawaii, nicknamed the Aloha State, actually consists of over 100 islands in the Pacific Ocean. Only three states are smaller than Hawaii. Honolulu is the capital city, located on the island of Oahu. Tourism is Hawaii's most important industry.

	Delaware	**Hawaii**
Date it became a state	December 7, 1787	August 21, 1959
Nearby ocean	Atlantic	Pacific
Main industry	manufacturing	tourism
Capital city	Dover	Honolulu
Size of state	second smallest state	fourth smallest state
Nickname	First State	Aloha State
Would you like to visit?	Answers will vary.	

84

Words About Nutrition

Vitamins are natural or human-made substances that our bodies need to grow and to stay healthy. We can get all of the vitamins we need by eating a well-balanced diet.

Directions: Using different colors, guide the Vita-Men on the left through the mazes to find out the jobs they do.

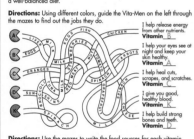

I help release energy from other nutrients.
Vitamin _B_

I help your eyes see at night and keep your skin healthy.
Vitamin _A_

I help heal cuts, scrapes, and scratches.
Vitamin _C_

I give you good, healthy blood.
Vitamin _K_

I help build strong bones and teeth.
Vitamin _D_

Directions: Use the mazes to write the food sources for each vitamin.

Vitamin A	Vitamin B	Vitamin C	Vitamin D	Vitamin K
liver	eggs	oranges	milk	spinach
milk	milk	strawberries	eggs	broccoli
spinach	tuna	tomato	fish	milk
carrots	red meat	grapefruit	cheese	
	nuts	spinach		
	chicken			

85

Words About Nutrition

The food you eat must be digested before your body can use it. Digested food is changed into nutrients that help your body grow and give you energy.

Word Bank
proteins
vitamins
minerals
carbohydrates
water
fats

Directions: Use the Word Bank to unscramble the names of the six nutrient groups.

1. netroips _proteins_
2. ralmenis _minerals_
3. afts _fats_
4. ratew _water_
5. timnivas _vitamins_
6. droracbaytesh _carbohydrates_

Directions: Write each nutrient name from the Word Bank on the line that best describes the job that it does for your body.

Needed: Nutrient to Deliver Food and Waste
fats

Wanted: Muscle Builder and Body Repair Worker
water

Wanted: Nutrient to Store Energy
proteins

Needed: Quick Energy Supplier
carbohydrates

Needed: Growth and Good Health Helper
minerals

Needed: Nutrients for Many Jobs
vitamins

86

Words About Nutrition

Directions: A nutritious diet helps your body fight diseases. Write the foods from the Word Bank in the correct category.

Word Bank
tomatoes, bread, eggs, milk, potatoes
oranges, sugar, fish, cereal, green beans
chicken, margarine, cheese, noodles, rice
apples, red meat, butter

Carbohydrates
bread
cereal
noodles
potatoes
rice

Proteins
chicken, milk
eggs
fish
cheese
red meat

Fats
sugar
margarine
butter

Minerals
tomatoes, green beans
oranges
apples

Directions: Write what you ate yesterday in each group. Did you get enough servings of each?

Dairy Group (2–3 servings a day)

Meat & Protein Group (2–3 servings a day)

Answers will vary.

Grain Group (6–11 servings a day)

Fruit & Vegetable Group (5–9 servings a day)

87

Fraction Words

A **fraction** is a part of a whole.

Directions: Read each fraction problem. Then, solve it. Write your answer as a fraction.

1. Fred played the ring-toss game. He tossed 27 rings. One-third of the rings landed on the ground. What fraction of rings landed on the bottles?

   Answer: _two-thirds_

2. Charlotte worked at the refreshment stand. She served 30 glasses of lemonade, 15 glasses of milk, and 45 glasses of water. What fraction of people ordered water that day?

   Answer: _one-half_

3. A book of tickets for rides contains 24 tickets. Mr. Dell gave one-fourth of the tickets to his son. What fraction of tickets does he have left?

   Answer: _three-fourths_

4. A hot dog and soda costs $3.00. At the end of the day, Mrs. Ross sold the hot dog and soda for $1.50. What fraction of the original cost did people have to pay?

   Answer: _one-half_

5. Lenny had a dozen yellow, red, and green balloons. Half of them were yellow. One-fourth were green. What fraction of the balloons were red?

   Answer: _one-fourth_

88

Genre Words

Fiction writing is a story that has been invented. The story might be about things that could really happen (realistic) or about things that couldn't possibly happen (fantasy). **Nonfiction** writing is based on facts. It usually gives information about people, places, or things. A person can often tell while reading whether a story or book is fiction or nonfiction.

Directions: Read the paragraphs. Decide whether each paragraph is fiction or nonfiction. Circle the letter **F** for fiction or the letter **N** for nonfiction.

1. "Do not be afraid, little flowers," said the oak. "Close your yellow eyes in sleep and trust in me. You have made me glad many a time with your sweetness. Now I will take care that the winter shall do you no harm." **(F) N**

2. The whole team watched as the ball soared over the outfield fence. The game was over! It was hard to walk off the field and face parents, friends, and each other. It had been a long season. Now, they would have to settle for second place. **(F) N**

3. Be careful when you remove the dish from the microwave. It will be very hot, so take care not to get burned by the dish or the hot steam. If time permits, leave the dish in the microwave for 2 or 3 minutes to avoid getting burned. It is a good idea to use a potholder, too. **F (N)**

89

Genre Words

Something that is **real** could actually happen. Something that is **fantasy** is not real. It could not happen.

Examples: Real: Pigs can wallow in mud.
Fantasy: Pigs can fly.

Directions: Read each sentence. Then, write **real** or **fantasy** on the line next to each one.

1. Lightning flashed across the sky during the storm. _____real_____
2. We will fly by your house on our rocket-powered skates. _____fantasy_____
3. My mother uses a wheelbarrow to move dirt to her garden. _____real_____
4. I have to wear boots and a coat when it is cold outside. _____real_____
5. A caterpillar goes through four changes as it becomes a butterfly. _____real_____
6. The mermaid left the water and walked along the beach. _____fantasy_____
7. The alien blasted off in his spaceship. _____fantasy_____
8. Leaves change their colors in autumn. _____real_____
9. The tree spoke to me as I walked past it on my way to school. _____fantasy_____
10. We go to the beach when it is hot. _____real_____

90

Genre Words

Directions: Read about fiction and nonfiction books. Then, look at each different type of book listed. Write **F** if the book is fiction. Write **NF** if the book is nonfiction.

There are many kinds of books. Some books have make-believe stories about princesses and dragons. Some books contain poetry and nursery rhymes, like Mother Goose. These are **fiction**.
Some books contain facts about space and plants. And still other books have stories about famous people in history like Abraham Lincoln. These are **nonfiction**.

NF	1. dictionary entry about horses
NF	2. history of sports
F	3. riddles and jokes
NF	4. true life story of a president
F	5. Aesop's fables
NF	6. an encyclopedia entry about clouds
F	7. story about a talking puppet
F	8. nursery rhyme
F	9. story about a panda that talks to zoo visitors
NF	10. story about the first space flight

91

Words About the United States

In 1803, President Thomas Jefferson sent Meriwether Lewis and William Clark to find a water route to the Pacific and explore the uncharted West. They began their journey along the Missouri river from their St. Louis-area camp. As they traveled, Clark spent most of his time on a boat, charting the course and making maps. Meanwhile, Lewis was often ashore, studying the rock formations, soil, animals, and plants along the way. Lewis and Clark encountered many interesting things: over 300 species unknown to science, nearly 50 Indian tribes, and the Rockies. They journeyed all the way to Fort Clatsop, which sits on the border between Oregon and Washington. After nearly two and half years, Lewis and Clark returned to St. Louis on September 23, 1806.

Directions: Color the states that Lewis and Clark traveled through on their expedition. Then, choose a state and do research to find out what Lewis and Clark discovered there.

92

Words About Nutrition

Carbohydrates are the main source of quick energy. Foods with lots of sugar and starch are rich in carbohydrates. You get carbohydrates from many foods like spaghetti, bread, cake, and candy.

Directions: Write a word from the Word Bank to complete each sentence and learn more about carbohydrates.

1. Carbohydrates are the **first** foods to be digested.
2. **Starches** are changed to sugars.
3. Sugar gives us **energy**.
4. Leftover sugar is stored as **fat**.

Word Bank
fat
first
starches
energy

Directions: Fill in the plate with carbohydrate-rich foods. Find pictures of these foods in magazines. Cut them out and glue them on the plate.

Pictures will vary.

93

Words About Nutrition

Directions: Read about snack foods. Then, take the snacker's survey.

Do you have a bad case of the munchies, crunchies, or nibbles? Some snack foods can be healthy for you, while others are not. Foods that are lower on the food pyramid are usually much better for you because they contain smaller amounts of fat.

Snacker's Survey

Write the food group to which each snack belongs. Then, using a scale of 1–10, with 1 being the lowest, give each snack a taste score and a nutrition score.

Snack	Food group	Taste score	Nutrition score
Apple	Fruits		
Cheese	Dairy	Answers	
Cookie	Fats	will	
Potato Chips	Fats	vary.	
Orange	Fruits		
Carrot	Vegetables		
Cake	Fats		
Candy Bar	Fats		
Bagel	Grains		
Beef Jerky	Meat & Protein		
Popcorn	Grains		
Pretzels	Grains		

94

Words About Nutrition

Fat is a white or yellow oily substance found in some parts of animals or plants. Our bodies need some fat to stay healthy.

Directions: Many of the foods we eat contain fat. Try this fat test on several foods.

Materials Needed
6" x 6" pieces of brown paper bags (one per person)
6 containers each containing 1/4 cup of the following:
    water, oil, peanut butter, soft cheese,
    orange juice, soft margarine
6 toothpicks (one in each container)

Directions:
• Predict which foods contain fat on the chart below.
• Use the toothpick from each container to make a spot on your bag. Be careful to use small amounts of each item so they won't run together.
• Wait several minutes and check the spots. Those with fat will leave a greasy spot. Record your observations.

Name of Food	I Predict . . .		I Observed . . .	
	Fat	No Fat	Fat	No Fat
	Answers will vary.			

1. Which food seemed to have the most fat? Why? _Answers will vary._
2. Which food surprised you? _____
3. Which of the foods do you eat often? _____
4. What could you eat instead of the fatty foods? _____

Fraction Words

Directions: Color the number of items that show each fraction.

1. Color **one-third** of the cookies.
Color four cookies.

2. Color **one-fourth** of the dog treats.
Color six bones.

3. Color **one-fifth** of the pepperoni.
Color five pepperoni.

4. Color **one-half** of the books.
Color nine books.

Genre Words

Directions: Read each sentence about books. The book titles are in italics. Decide what type of book each title is. Then, on the line, write **mystery**, **biography**, **poetry**, **fantasy**, **sports**, or **travel**.

1. I read aloud to my sister from the book *Read-Aloud Rhymes for the Very Young*. — poetry

2. *The Secret of Shadow Ranch* features my favorite detective, Nancy Drew. — mystery

3. I will lend you my copy of *A Wrinkle in Time*. — fantasy

4. Mom bought us *Games You Can Play in the Car* to keep us busy on our road trip. — travel

5. I like baseball, so my dad bought me the book *The Story of Jackie Robinson*. — biography

6. *Kids in Sports* is a great book about child athletes. — sports

7. *Harry Potter and the Sorcerer's Stone* is one of the top-selling books of all time. — fantasy

8. *The Last Flight of Amelia Earhart* is an interesting story about aviation. — biography

9. I borrowed *The Case of the Treasure Hunt* from the library. — mystery

10. My dad bought me *A Complete Handbook to Soccer* to help me with my game. — sports

Genre Words

A **mystery** story usually has lots of suspense and exciting events. At the end, you get to find out "who did it"!

Directions: Follow these directions to make a mystery cube:

1. Cut a 12 x 16 1/2-inch piece of cardboard.
2. Draw the outline of the cube as shown below.
3. Cut out the shape.
4. Measure three 4-inch segments horizontally. Draw a dotted line between each segment.
5. Measure three 4-inch segments and one 4 1/2-inch segment vertically. Draw a dotted line between each segment.
6. Fold along the dotted lines.
7. Carefully tape the edges with clear tape.
8. Tuck the flap into the top of the cube.
9. Write the following on your cube:
   Top: Title
   Right side: Characters
   Left side: Where the story takes place
   Front: What is the mystery?
   Back: Three clues that help solve the mystery
   Bottom: Author's name
   Inside top: Solution to the mystery
10. Place some items inside the cube that symbolize the mystery or how it was solved.
11. Illustrate or decorate the cube.

		Front	
Left Side	Bottom	Right Side	
	Back		
	Top		

Genre Words

An **autobiography** is the story of your life written by you! An outline can help you to organize details about your life.

Directions: Use the outline to write information about your life.

I. My Early Years   Answers will vary.
   A. Birthdate _____ Place _____
   B. Favorite activities _____
   C. Family members _____
   D. Things I learned _____
   E. First school _____
II. My Present
   A. School grade _____
   B. Friends _____
   C. Favorite subjects _____
   D. Sports or hobbies _____
   E. Family fun _____
III. My Future
   A. Middle school/High school _____
   B. College _____
   C. Ambitions _____
   D. Places I would like to see _____
   E. Things I would like to accomplish _____
   _____

Words About the United States

Directions: Study the map of the United States. Then, fill in the circle beside each correct answer.

1. Which state is a peninsula?
   (A) Nevada
   (B) Florida
   (C) Washington
   (D) Georgia

2. Which state is farthest north?
   (A) Texas
   (B) Arizona
   (C) New York
   (D) Kansas

3. Which state is on the West Coast?
   (A) California
   (B) North Carolina
   (C) Utah
   (D) Minnesota

4. Which state is east of Nebraska?
   (A) Oregon
   (B) Mississippi
   (C) Idaho
   (D) New Mexico

Words About Nutrition

Nutritious food is not dull, boring food. Angelo's pizza is very nutritious. It has food from all six food groups.

Directions: Draw a line to match each ingredient with its food group. Then, with an adult's help, follow the recipe to make the pizza.

Angelo's Pizza Supreme
1 loaf frozen bread dough, thawed
Mozzarella cheese (shredded) — Grains
hamburger (cooked)
pepperoni (sliced)
anchovies
sausage (cooked) — Dairy
vegetable oil
pizza sauce (6 oz. can) — Meat and Protein
tomatoes (chopped)
onion (chopped)
green pepper (chopped) — Fats
mushrooms (sliced)
olives (sliced) — Fruits and Vegetables

Press thawed bread dough onto a greased pizza tin. Prick with a fork and brush with oil. Bake at 400° until light brown (about 10 minutes). Cover crust with tomato sauce, cheese, and other ingredients. Bake at 400° until cheese is melted.

101

Words About Nutrition

Directions: Write the letter of each of the fruits and vegetables under the correct plant part.

Leon's Fresh Produce

A. celery B. spinach C. peanuts D. asparagus E. onion
F. carrots G. broccoli H. orange I. radish J. garlic
K. cabbage L. apple M. lettuce N. peas O. tomato

Stem	Leaf	Flower	Fruit	Seed	Root	Bulb
A	B	G	H	C	F	E
	K		L	N	I	J
	M			O		

Directions: Circle the vegetables that are the seeds of the plant.

(pea pod)   cabbage   carrot   (string bean)
cucumber   avocado   broccoli   green pepper
spinach   zucchini   potato   turnip

102

Words About Nutrition

Directions: Read about calcium. Then, try the experiment.

The **skeleton** is a framework of 206 bones that has three main jobs: to hold up your body, to protect your inner organs, and to produce new blood cells inside the bones. It is important to keep our bones healthy. The outer part of a bone contains calcium. Calcium keeps our bones strong. What would happen if our bones lacked calcium?

Materials Needed:
1 chicken bone
1 glass jar with a lid
1 cup vinegar

Directions:
1. Clean the chicken bone.
2. Place the bone in the jar and cover it with vinegar.
3. Cover the jar tightly.
4. Let the jar sit for two weeks.

After two weeks:
How has the chicken bone changed? Answers will vary.

What would happen to your body without calcium? _____

103

Unit 4 Review

Directions: Unscramble the letters of words you have learned in this unit. Use the Word Bank if you need help.

Word Bank			
sports	energy	cereal	genre
nutrition	vegetables	fractions	biography
fantasy	vitamins	expedition	Delaware

1. gereny _energy_
2. sfaynat _fantasy_
3. edexitonpi _expedition_
4. sitavmin _vitamins_
5. grene _genre_
6. laceer _cereal_
7. ewlaread _Delaware_
8. norunitit _nutrition_
9. storps _sports_
10. giopyahrb _biography_
11. sonticarf _fractions_
12. beglestave _vegetables_

104

Words That Are Sounds

Onomatopoeia is the use of words that sound like the noises they represent. These words can make writing more interesting to read.

Example: The bees **buzzed** around my head in an angry swarm. The door made a loud **bang** when it closed.

Directions: Write a sentence for each word. Then, draw a picture to illustrate one of your sentences.

1. chugged Sentences will vary.
2. snap _____
3. hiss _____
4. splash _____
5. boom _____
6. splat _____
7. thump _____
8. pop _____

Pictures will vary.

106

Words That Are Sounds

Animal noises are another example of onomatopoeia.

Directions: Write the noise that each animal makes.

Woof   Meow   Quack   Moo   Baa   Oink

107

Figures of Speech

An **idiom** is a figure of speech. An idiom means something different than what the words actually say.

Directions: Read each story. Then, put an **X** in front of the best example of the idiom in bold type.

1. I was really frustrated on Monday. First, my alarm clock broke, and I overslept. Next, my mom drove over a nail. We got a flat tire, and I was late for school. The **last straw** was when I forgot to bring my lunch to school. It was a horrible day!

_____ The last straw is when there are no more straws for your soda pop.

__X__ The last straw is when a person is pushed to his or her limit and feels angry or frustrated.

_____ The last straw is when the farmer runs out of straw for the barn.

2. Matt decided to change his bad habits and **turn over a new leaf**. From now on, he was going to stop watching T.V. and study more.

_____ Matt will go leaf collecting tomorrow.

_____ Matt will rake leaves instead of watch T.V.

__X__ Matt will change what he is doing and start fresh to make things different and better.

108

Words About U.S. Presidents

Directions: Use the Word Bank to find and circle the names of U. S. presidents in the puzzle. Look across, down, diagonally, and backward.

| N R K L E A L R H R I W |
| S O F E N O X I G J O N D |
| K C T A G N W V M O M C |
| E H I G L O C O S S C R |
| K R L N N I N R H E S R E |
| N O F I O T E C I V E R V O |
| E O E X N F H F O E Y U A |
| D S V D F C T S F L U A H |
| Y L N E Y S O P A T N H |
| T E J H R H N L I W E O |
| K N G R E A G A N X C O |

Word Bank
JEFFERSON
KENNEDY
LINCOLN
REAGAN
ROOSEVELT
WASHINGTON

Directions: Write the correct name from the Word Bank under each description.

1. He was America's first elected president.
   W A S H I N G T O N

2. The teddy bear was named for this president.
   R O O S E V E L T

3. This president wrote the Declaration of Independence.
   J E F F E R S O N

4. He was the youngest man to be elected President.
   K E N N E D Y

5. This president led the Union through the Civil War.
   L I N C O L N

6. This president was a former movie star.
   R E A G A N

109

Words About Plants

Directions: Use the words in the Word Bank to complete the puzzle about plants.

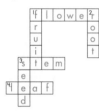

Word Bank
stem
root
leaf
flower
fruit
seed

Crossword:
1. f l o w e r (across)
  r / o
  u / o
  i / t
3. s t e m
  e
4. l e a f
  d

Across
1. I often have bright colors, but my real job is to make seeds.
3. I carry water from the roots to the leaves and food back to the roots.
4. I collect energy from the sun to make food for the plant.

Down
1. I often taste delicious, but my job is to hold and protect the seeds.
2. I hold the plant tight like an anchor but also collect water and minerals from the soil.
3. Someday a new plant will grow from me.

110

Words About Plants

Directions: Plants give us all the fruits, vegetables, grains, spices, and herbs we eat. Use the picture of the garden to write the fruits and vegetables under the correct plant part that can be eaten.

Stem	**Leaf**	**Flower**	**Root**
celery	spinach	broccoli	carrot
asparagus	lettuce	cauliflower	radish
Fruit	**Seed**	**Bulb**	
tomato	lima beans	onion	
watermelon	peanut	garlic	

Directions: On a separate sheet of paper, make a chart like the one below. Complete the chart with as many kinds of fruits and vegetables you can name. Answers will vary.

Vegetable or Fruit	Root	Stem	Leaf	Flower	Bulb	Fruit	Seed
kiwi						✓	

111

Words About Plants

Directions: Read about leaves. Then, use the bold words to complete the sentences. Use the numbered letters to answer the mystery question.

Leaves work like little factories making food for the plant, using a **green** material called **chlorophyll**. In each leaf, chlorophyll is like a little "green machine," changing **water** and air into food. Like most machines, chlorophyll needs energy to work. The green machine gets its energy from **sunlight**. This process is called **photosynthesis**. Without sunlight, the **leaves** could not make food.

1. Food-making material in leaves is called c h l o r o p h y l l
   3 1 2 7

2. Plants make food from air and w a t e r
   4

3. The green machine gets its energy from s u n l i g h t
   8 9

4. Food is made in the plant's l e a v e s
   6

5. The color of chlorophyll is g r e e n
   5

Mystery Question
What is the scientific name for the process of making food with the help of light?
p h o t o s y n t h e s i s
1 2 3 4 5 6 7 8 4 2 5 6 9 6

112

Measurement Words

Look at the units used to measure length, width, and distance.

12 inches = 1 foot
3 feet = 1 yard
5,280 feet = 1 mile

Different units are used to measure weight.

16 ounces = 1 pound
2,000 pounds = 1 ton

Directions: Reach each question. Circle the best estimate.

1. How long is a football field? a. 100 feet (b. 100 yards)
2. How long is a pencil? (a. 6 inches) b. 10 inches
3. How far is it between two cities? a. 100 yards (b. 100 miles)
4. How wide is your bedroom door? (a. 3 feet) b. 3 yards
5. How long is a book? (a. 12 inches) b. 2 feet
6. How long is your bed? a. 15 feet (b. 5 feet)
7. How heavy is your backpack? a. 50 pounds (b. 5 pounds)
8. How long is a crayon? (a. 4 inches) b. 10 inches
9. How heavy is the average dog? (a. 25 pounds) b. 25 tons
10. How long is your arm? (a. 1 1/2 feet) b. 1 1/2 yards
11. How heavy is a can of soda? (a. 12 ounces) b. 2 pounds

Directions: Look around your house and estimate the length, width, and weight of various items. Use a ruler and scale to measure each item to see how close your estimate was.

113

Figures of Speech

An **idiom** is a colorful way of saying something ordinary. The words in an idiom do not mean exactly what they say. The words are read in a figurative way, not a literal one.

Directions: Read each idiom. Draw a picture of its literal meaning. Then, draw a line to match the idiom to its meaning.

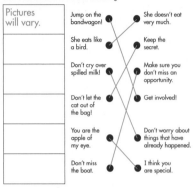

Pictures will vary.

Jump on the bandwagon! — Get involved!

She eats like a bird. — She doesn't eat very much.

Don't cry over spilled milk! — Don't worry about things that have already happened.

Don't let the cat out of the bag! — Keep the secret.

You are the apple of my eye. — I think you are special.

Don't miss the boat. — Make sure you don't miss an opportunity.

114

Figures of Speech

Directions: Read each sentence. Then, write the letter of the phrase that tells what the speaker really means.

He says:		What he means is:
e	1. It's "raining cats and dogs."	a. don't eat very much
d	2. I remember when you were "knee-high to a grasshopper."	b. make me very happy
a	3. You "eat like a bird."	c. robbed the bank
c	4. He "held up the bank."	d. very small
b	5. You "light up my life!"	e. pouring hard
g	6. Which way should I turn "at the fork in the road?"	f. was hoarse
f	7. The speaker "had a frog in her throat."	g. where the road splits

115

Figures of Speech

You can make sentences more interesting by using figures of speech. The following are four popular kinds of figures of speech.

Personification—gives human characteristics to things
Example: The sun smiled down on me.

Hyperbole—great exaggeration
Example: She was so frightened that she said she would never sleep again.

Simile—compares two unlike things using **like** or **as**
Example: He runs as fast as the wind.

Metaphor—suggests a comparison of two unlike things
Example: The empty field was a desert.

Directions: Read each sentence. Identify the figure of speech used. Write **personification, hyperbole, simile,** or **metaphor** on the line.

1. The leaves danced in the wind. _personification_
2. He was an angel during class. _metaphor_
3. I have heard that story at least one hundred times. _hyperbole_
4. After playing in the snow, her hands were as cold as ice. _simile_
5. The old car groaned as it went up the steep hill. _personification_
6. I was not at work yesterday, because I was as sick as a dog. _simile_
7. She is a graceful swan. _metaphor_
8. He was so hungry he could eat a horse. _hyperbole_
9. The storm slept for two days. _personification_
10. He said she was as pretty as a picture. _simile_

116

Words About Leaders

Directions: Circle the correct answer to finish each sentence.

1. The leader of a school is a
   a. principal
   b. student
   c. police officer
   d. firefighter

2. The leader of the United States is a
   a. mayor
   b. governor
   c. president
   d. senator

3. The leader of England is a
   a. president
   b. prime minister
   c. princess
   d. prince

4. The leader of a family is often a
   a. parent
   b. sister
   c. brother
   d. cousin

5. Leaders are usually
   a. responsible
   b. hard working
   c. good with people
   d. all of the above

117

Words About Flowers

Flowers are beautiful to look at and pleasant to smell, but they also have a very important job. Most plants make seeds inside the flower.

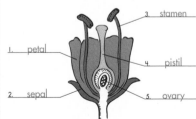

3. stamen
1. petal
4. pistil
2. sepal
5. ovary

Directions: Use the chart to color and label each flower part.

Flower part	Description	Color
pistil	A large center stalk, often shaped like a vase.	yellow
stamen	A tall, thin stalk with a knobbed tip. It holds grains of pollen.	brown
petal	Brightly colored and sweet-smelling leaves.	red
sepal	Small leaf-like part at the base of the flower.	green
ovary	Ball-shaped part at the base of the pistil. This is where the seeds develop.	blue

118

Words About Plants

Directions: Read about dangerous plants. Then, write the correct words on the lines to complete the sentences.

You may have been warned about some plants. Poison ivy and poison oak are two examples of plants to be careful around. The itching and burning some people get from touching or even being around these plants is enough to make them extra careful. Have you ever walked through a field and felt like you had been stung? You probably touched the stinging nettle. This plant with jagged edges should be avoided.

Other plants can be more dangerous. You should not pick and eat any berries, seeds, or nuts without first checking to make sure they are safe. You could get very sick or even die if you ate from one of these poisonous plants. Rhubarb and cherries are two common pie-making ingredients, but never eat the leaves of the rhubarb plant. Also, cherry leaves and branches have poison in them.

1. You should not pick and eat any _berries_ , _seeds_ or _nuts_ without first making sure they are safe.
2. _Poison ivy_ and _poison oak_ might make your skin itch and burn.
3. If you touched a stinging nettle plant, you would _feel like you had been stung._

119

Words About Trees

Directions: Read about trees. Then, answer the questions.

Have you ever seen a tree that has been cut down? If so, you may have seen many circles in the trunk. These are called the **annual rings**. You can tell how old a tree is by counting these rings.

Trees have rings because they grow a new layer of wood every year. The new layer grows right below the bark. In a year when there is a lot of rain and sunlight, the tree grows faster; the annual ring that year will be thick. When there is not much rain or sunlight, the tree grows slower and the ring is thin.

1. The annual ring of a tree tells how big the tree is.
    True   (False)

2. Each year, a new layer of wood grows on top of the bark.
    True   (False)

3. In a year with lots of rain and sunlight, the annual ring that year will be thick.
    (True)   False

4. Trees grow faster when there is more rain and sunlight.
    (True)   False

5. How old was the tree on this page?   _____17_____

120

Measurement Words

Directions: Read about two different kinds of measurement. Then, answer the questions.

Perimeter is the distance around a shape. To find the perimeter, measure the length of all of the sides of the shape and add them together. Each shape, even the funny looking ones, has a perimeter. If the sides of a shape are all the same length, you can multiply one length by the number of sides. You can measure perimeter in inches, feet, yards, and miles. You can also measure it in centimeters, meters, and kilometers.

The number of square units covering a space is called **area**. A square unit is a way to measure. It is a perfect square with all of the sides the same length. For instance, a square inch is like a piece of space that is 1 inch on each side. You can sometimes find area by counting the square units. If you want to find the area of a rectangle, multiply the length times the width. Area is calculated in square units. That means that if you are measuring area in inches, the result is inches squared, or in^2.

1. What is the definition of perimeter?
   Perimeter is the distance around a shape.

2. You have a unit that is 2 inches by 4 inches. Is this a square unit? Why or why not?
   No, it is not a square unit, because the sides are not equal.

3. What is a perfect square?
   A perfect square is shape with all of the sides the same length.

4. Find the perimeter and area of the figure.
   perimeter = perimeter = 16m
   area = area = 15 m²

5 meters
3 meters

121

Foreign Words

Directions: Many foreign words have worked their way into the English language. Read each foreign word. Then, write the letter of the word or phrase that defines it. Use a dictionary if you need help.

1. _m_ au revoir (French)   a. a lobby or entryway
2. _q_ Gesundheit (German)   b. a flat bread made from corn or flour
3. _o_ crepe (French)   c. thin sticks used for eating
4. _b_ tortilla (Spanish)   d. a married woman
5. _p_ pita (Greek)   e. a dip made with avocado
6. _c_ chopsticks (Asian)   f. a scarf worn on the head
7. _i_ oui (French)   g. fabric wrapped to wear as a skirt
8. _g_ sarong (Malaysian)   h. a friend
9. _h_ amigo (Spanish)   i. yes
10. _k_ rendezvous (French)   j. a rich layer cake
11. _f_ babushka (Russian)   k. a meeting place
12. _n_ lasagna (Italian)   l. a flat hat
13. _d_ madam (French)   m. good-bye
14. _e_ guacamole (Spanish)   n. a dish made with long, flat noodles
15. _j_ Torte (German)   o. a thin cloth or pancake
16. _a_ foyer (French)   p. round bread with a pocket
17. _l_ beret (French)   q. "Good health!" to someone who sneezes

122

Foreign Words

Directions: The words in the Word Bank mean **hello** or **good-bye** in different languages. Write each word in the correct column.

Word Bank
Hola (Spanish)
Au revoir (French)
Arriverderci (Italian)
Adiós (Spanish)
Sayonara (Japanese)
Bonjour (French)
Guten tag (German)
Buon giorno (Italian)

Hello	Good-bye
1. Hola	1. Au revoir
2. Bonjour	2. Arrivederci
3. Guten tag	3. Adiós
4. Buon giorno	4. Sayonara

123

Foreign Words

Directions: Match the words with their meanings.

_g_ 1. éclair (France)   a. sauce made of basil, parmesan cheese, and pine nuts
_d_ 2. piñata (Mexico)   b. horn-shaped bread
_i_ 3. quiche (France)   c. type of dance
_h_ 4. chow mein (China)   d. decorated container filled with candy
_e_ 5. limone (Italy)   e. lemon
_a_ 6. pesto (Italy)   f. cold, cooked rice wrapped in seaweed
_j_ 7. cannoli (Italy)   g. pastry filled with custard
_f_ 8. sushi (Japan)   h. fried noodle dish
_c_ 9. flamenco (Spain)   i. an unsweetened custard pie
_b_ 10. croissant (France)   j. a deep fried tube of pastry filled with cheese
_k_ 11. burrito (Spanish)   k. a flour tortilla rolled or folded around a filling

124

Words About U.S. Presidents

Directions: Read about Thomas Jefferson. Then, answer the questions.

Thomas Jefferson was the third president of the United States. He was also an inventor. That means he created things that had never been made before. Thomas Jefferson had many inventions. He built a chair that rotated in circles. He created a rotating music stand. He also made a walking stick that unfolded into a chair. Thomas Jefferson even invented a new kind of plow for farming.

1. The main idea is: (Circle one)
   Thomas Jefferson was very busy when he was president.
   (Thomas Jefferson was a president and an inventor.)

2. What do we call a person who has new ideas and makes things that no one else has made before? an inventor

3. What are three of Thomas Jefferson's inventions?
   Three of the following answers should be written:
   a) a chair that rotated in circles
   b) a rotating music stand
   c) a walking stick that unfolded into a chair
   a new kind of plow for farming

125

Words About Trees

What is the largest plant growing near your home? It is probably a tree. It may be a maple, oak, pine, or palm. All trees have many of the same parts as the plants that grow in your garden—only much larger.

Directions: The riddles below tell about the jobs of the tree parts. Use the tree parts listed in the Word Bank to solve each riddle. Then, label the parts of the tree.

Word Bank
seed
trunk
leaves
roots
bark

1. Green and flat
   Or needle-like,
   We make food by day
   And rest at night.
   leaves

2. From roots to branches,
   Short or long,
   My tough wood
   Keeps me tall and strong.
   trunk

3. Scattered by wind
   When breezes blow,
   I'll make a new tree
   When I sprout and grow.
   seed

4. Thin-like hair,
   Or thick and round,
   We hold the tree
   Firmly in the ground.
   roots

5. Rough or smooth,
   A very tough cover,
   I keep out insects,
   Fire, and weather.
   bark

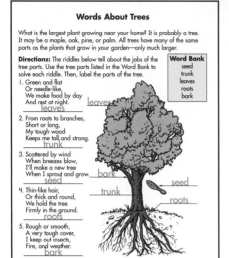

Labels: leaves, bark, seed, trunk, roots

126

Words About Trees

Directions: Read about trees. Then, answer the questions.

Each year, as the hours of daylight grow shorter and colder weather comes, many types of trees lose their leaves. The falling of the leaves is so regular and amazing that the entire autumn season is called "fall."

The trees that lose their leaves are known as **deciduous** (dee-SID-you-us) trees. The word means "falling down." The leaves on these trees are wide, not like the needle-shaped leaves on pine and other **evergreen** trees. Trees lose water through their leaves, and wide leaves lose more water than the ones that look like needles. Water is very important to a tree. Because there is less water in the winter, the tree must drop its leaves to stay alive.

1. In what season do deciduous trees lose their leaves? **autumn**

2. What are the trees that do not lose their leaves called?
   evergreen trees

Directions: Circle the correct answer.

3. Deciduous trees have needle-shaped leaves.   True   **(False)**

4. Trees drop their leaves to save water.   **(True)**   False

127

Words About Plants

Directions: Use the words in the Word Bank to complete the puzzle about plants.

Across
4. Deep-growing type of root
6. Beautiful, seed-making part of plant
7. Brightly colored "leafy" parts of the flower
9. Large part of seed that supplies food
10. Sweet food made by the leaves

Down
1. Making food with the help of light
2. Green food-making material in a leaf
3. Plant's "food factory"
5. Plant's anchor
8. What plants get their energy from

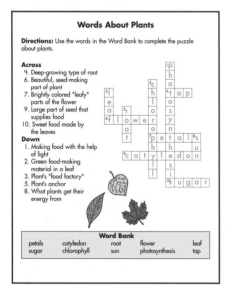

Crossword answers: tap, flower, petals, cotyledon, sugar

Word Bank
petals   cotyledon   root   flower   leaf
sugar   chlorophyll   sun   photosynthesis   tap

128

Unit 5 Review

Directions: Finish the story. Use words from the Word Bank.

Word Bank			
seeds	inches	roots	flower
fruit	light	water	area

Today, I am going to turn over a new leaf. My mom says that I am lazy and need a hobby to keep me busy. I am going to try gardening. I love to be outside, and I'm excited to learn about plants and how to take care of them.

First, I have to plan out how big I want my garden to be.

Stories will vary.

129

Words That Are Antonyms

Antonyms are words that have opposite meanings.

Example: neat — sloppy

Directions: Cut out each frog. Then, glue each frog to the lily pad with its antonym.

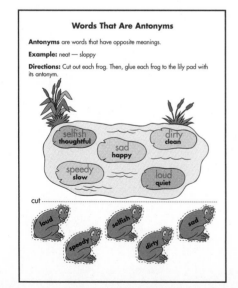

selfish / thoughtful
dirty / clean
sad / happy
speedy / slow
loud / quiet

cut ----

Frogs: loud, selfish, sad, speedy, dirty

131

Words That Are Synonyms

Synonyms are words that mean almost the same thing.

Example: sick — ill

Directions: Use the words from the Word Bank to complete the sentences.

Word Bank				
glad	fast	noisy	filthy	angry

1. When I am mad, I could also say I am **angry** .

2. To be **glad** is the same as being happy.

3. After playing outside, I thought I was dirty, but Mom said I was **filthy** !

4. I tried not to be too loud, but I couldn't help being a little **noisy** .

5. If you're too **fast** , or speedy, you may not do a careful job.

Think of another pair of synonyms. Write the words on the lines

Synonyms will vary.

133

Words About the Statue of Liberty

Directions: Read about the Statue of Liberty. Then, use the bold words to complete the puzzle. Color the picture.

The **Statue of Liberty** is the statue of a woman holding a burning **torch**. There are 25 windows in her **crown** that serve as an observation deck for visitors. Visitors ride ferries to visit the statue, because it is surrounded by **water** in the **New York** Harbor. F.A. Bartholdi designed the statue. **France** presented it as a gift to the United States in 1886. To people all around the world, the statue is a symbol of **freedom**.

Color the picture.

Crossword:
1. freedom
2. torch
3. new york
4. crown
5. water

Across
1. The Statue of Liberty is a symbol of _____ .
3. The statue is located in the state of _____ .
4. There are 25 windows in Lady Liberty's _____ .
Down
1. _____ gave the statue to the United States as a gift.
2. She carries a _____ in her right hand.
5. Liberty Island is surrounded by _____ .

134

Space Words

Directions: Read about the sun's core. Then, use the bold words to complete the sentences.

If we could travel from the sun's **core**, or center, to the surface, we would be at the **photosphere**, which is the surface part of the sun seen from Earth. The flashes of light that scientists have seen on the surface of the sun are called **flares**. The dark patches are called **sunspots**. Sometimes, eruptions of gas, called **prominences**, can also be seen during a solar eclipse. Just above the sun's surface is a layer of bright gases called the **chromosphere**. The **corona**, the region beyond the chromosphere, consists of white concentric circles of light that radiate from the sun.

1. The _photosphere_ is the surface part of the sun that we can see.

2. The _chromosphere_ is the layer of bright gases above the sun's surface.

3. The _corona_ consists of white concentric circles of light.

4. _Prominences_ can be seen during a solar eclipse.

5. The flashes of light on the sun's surface are _flares_ .

6. The sun's center is also known as its _core_ .

7. The dark patches that sometimes appear on the sun are _sunspots_ .

135

Space Words

Directions: Unscramble each space word. Use the numbers below the letters to tell you what order the letters belong in.

1. o r b i t
   i r t b o
   4 2 5 3 1

2. c o u n t d o w n
   u t o n c w d n o
   3 5 7 9 1 8 6 4 2

3. a s t r o n a u t
   a t s r a t n o u
   7 9 2 4 1 3 6 5 8

4. f u e l
   u l e f
   2 4 3 1

5. s h u t t l e
   t e h t s u l
   5 7 2 4 1 3 6

Directions: Write a space word beside each definition. Use the words that you unscrambled above.

1. A member of the team that flies a spaceship.
   astronaut

2. A rocket-powered spaceship that travels between Earth and space.
   shuttle

3. The material, such as gas, used for power.
   fuel

4. The seconds just before take-off.
   countdown

5. The path of a spaceship as it goes around Earth.
   orbit

136

Space Words

On a clear night, you can see about two thousand stars in the sky. Scientists use giant telescopes to see billions of stars.

Stars in groups form pictures called **constellations**. People have been able to recognize these constellations for hundreds of years. Ancient people named many constellations for animals, heroes, and mythical creatures. We still use many of these names.

We can see some constellations every night of the year. Others change with the seasons.

Since all stars are constantly moving, these same constellations that we now see will be changed thousands of years from now.

Connect the stars to form the constellation called the Little Dipper.

Directions: Read about constellations. Then, complete the activities. There may be more than one correct answer

Write:
Stars in groups form pictures called _constellations_ .
   telescopes   constellations
Check:
Ancient people named many constellations for:
☑ animals   ☑ heroes   ☐ oceans   ☑ mythical creatures

Circle Yes or No:
Some constellations can be seen every night.   (Yes)   No
Some constellations change with the seasons.   (Yes)   No
In thousands of years, all constellations will be the same.   Yes   (No)

137

Geometric Shape Words

Directions: Read about geometric shapes. Then, follow the instructions.

Your kitchen is full of shapes.

You drink from **cylinders**. Color the glass. Then, draw two foods that come in cylinders.

Color
Pictures will vary.

You put your food in a **hemisphere**. Color the bowl.

Color

You eat **spheres, cubes, triangular prisms,** and **rectangular prisms.** Color the grapes, cheese, cake, and candy bar. Then, draw one other food that shares each shape.

Color
Pictures will vary.

138

Words That Are Antonyms

Directions: Write each word from the Word Bank on the correct "antonym ant."

Word Bank					
careful	save	sour	fat	dirty	pretty
cry	far	poor	under	winter	low

spend — save
ugly — pretty
thin — fat
summer — winter
rich — poor
sweet — sour
clean — dirty
careless — careful
high — low
over — under
near — far
laugh — cry

139

Words That Are Synonyms

Directions: Circle a synonym for the underlined word in each row below. Then, write another synonym from the Word Bank on the line.

Wow, you're speedy!

You're rather swift yourself!

Word Bank		
assist	rich	daring
processed	same	easy

1. prosperous   mansion   (wealthy)   _rich_
2. simple   (plain)   plan   _easy_
3. artificial   flavor   (fake)   _processed_
4. bold   (brave)   warrior   _daring_
5. uniform   soldier   (attire)   _same_
6. support   (help)   bridge   _assist_

140

Words That Are Synonyms

Directions: Read the words on the kite tails. Choose a synonym for each word from the Word Bank. Then, write it on the correct tailpiece.

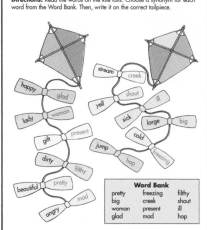

stream — creek
happy — glad
lady — woman
gift — present
dirty — filthy
beautiful — pretty
angry — mad
yell — shout
ill — sick
large — big
cold — freezing
jump — hop

Word Bank		
pretty	freezing	filthy
big	creek	shout
woman	present	ill
glad	mad	hop

141

Words About the White House

The **White House** has been the home of every president in United States history except George Washington. However, George Washington chose the site and approved the construction of the home in 1792.

Directions: Use the Word Bank to find and circle the words about the White House. Look across and down.

Word Bank
president
Washington
oval
white
house
government
office

```
v s e v o a v b o p
l o h i f b m t u i
t v i s f t s x h c
w a s h i n g t o n
n l t m c e s c u l
g h r o e s e z s m
k e y r w h i t e s
d p r e s i d e n t
g o v e r n m e n t
```

142

Space Words

Planets vary greatly in size. Look at the list of planets and their diameters.

Planet	Diameter (in miles)
Mercury	3,000
Venus	7,500
Earth	7,900
Mars	4,200
Jupiter	88,700
Saturn	74,600
Uranus	31,600
Neptune	30,200

Color the picture.

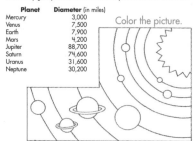

Directions: Write the names of the planets in size order starting with the planet that has the largest diameter. Then, color the picture.

1. Jupiter   6. Venus
2. Saturn   7. Mars
3. Uranus   8. Mercury
4. Neptune
5. Earth

143

Space Words

Directions: Read about our solar system. Then, complete the activities. There may be more than one correct answer.

Our **solar system** is made up of the sun and all the objects that go around, or **orbit**, the sun.

The sun is the only star in our solar system. It gives heat and light to the eight planets in the solar system. The planets and their moons all orbit the sun.

Draw the eight planets around the sun.

The time it takes for each planet to orbit the sun is called a **year**. A year on Earth is 365 days. Planets closer to the sun have shorter years. Their orbit is shorter. Planets farther from the sun take longer to orbit, so their years are longer.

Underline:
The solar system is: the sun without the planets.
                         the sun and all the objects that orbit it.

Check:
☑ is the center of our solar system
☑ is the only star in our solar system.
☐ is a planet in our solar system.
☑ gives heat and light to our solar system.

Write:
A _year_ is the time it takes for a planet to orbit the sun.
  month   year

Match:
Planets closer to the sun . . .   have a longer year.
Planets farther from the sun . . .   have a shorter year.

144

Space Words

Directions: Read about the Milky Way. Then, complete the activities. There may be more than one correct answer.

The **Milky Way** galaxy is made up of our solar system as well as many other stars and solar systems. There are over 100 billion stars in the Milky Way!

The Milky Way is shaped much like a record. The outer part spins around the center.

The Milky Way is always spinning slowly through space. It is so large that it would take 200 million years for the galaxy to turn one complete time.

Many stars in the Milky Way are in clusters. Some star clusters contain up to one million stars!

Milky Way

Our solar system

Put a red circle around our solar system.

Check:
The Milky Way galaxy is made up of
☑ Earth.
☐ no Sun.
☑ our solar system.
☑ 100 billion stars.

Circle Yes or No:
The Milky Way is shaped like a pencil.   Yes   (No)
The Milky Way is always slowly moving in space.   (Yes)   No
Many stars in the Milky Way are in clusters.   (Yes)   No
Some star clusters have one million stars.   (Yes)   No

Circle:
It would take (200)   90   million years for the galaxy to spin once.
              600

Underline:
Which object is the Milky Way shaped much like?
 record   ruler

145

Geometric Shape Words

Objects are **congruent** if they are the same size and shape.

These cones are congruent:

Objects are **similar** if they have the same shape, but are not the same size.

A grapefruit and a grape are similar because they are both spheres. They are not congruent because they are not the same size.

Directions: Circle **similar** or **congruent** to describe each set of items.

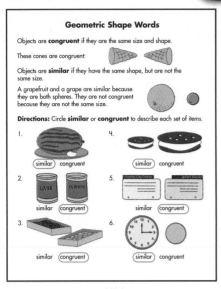

1. (similar) congruent
2. similar (congruent)
3. similar (congruent)
4. (similar) congruent
5. similar (congruent)
6. (similar) congruent

146

Words That Are Antonyms

Word Bank			
allow	blossom	bud	capture
forbid	release	tender	tough

Directions: Use the words in the Word Bank to write each antonym pair.

1. tender ___tough___   3. bud ___blossom___
2. capture ___release___   4. allow ___forbid___

Directions: Use the word pairs from items 1–4. Complete the sentences by writing an antonym pair.

5. To _capture_ an animal means to catch it. To _release_ an animal means to let it go.

6. School rules _allow_ us to yell on the playground. But the rules _forbid_ us to yell in class.

7. A flower _bud_ 's petals are tightly closed. A _blossom_'s petals are open.

8. It is easy to chew _tender_ meat. But _tough_ meat is hard to chew.

147

Words That Are Antonyms

Directions: Write a word from the Word Bank to complete each sentence.

Word Bank					
open	right	light	full	late	below
hard	clean	slow	quiet	old	nice

1. My car was dirty, but now it is ___clean___ .
2. Sometimes my cat is naughty, and sometimes she's ___nice___ .
3. The sign said, "Closed," but the door was ___open___ .
4. Is the glass half empty or half ___full___ ?
5. I bought new shoes, but I like my ___old___ ones better.
6. Skating is easy for me, but ___hard___ for my brother.
7. The sky is dark at night and ___light___ during the day.
8. I like a noisy house, but my mother likes a ___quiet___ one.
9. My friend says I'm wrong, but I say I'm ___right___ .
10. Jason is a fast runner, but Adam is a ___slow___ runner.
11. We were supposed to be early, but we were ___late___ .
12. A roof is above a house, and a basement is ___below___ it.

148

Words That Are Synonyms

Directions: Read each sentence. Write a synonym from the Word Bank that can take the place of the underlined word.

Word Bank		
runs	throw	dress
quilt	ribbon	

1. My friend and I like to toss the ball. ___throw___
2. The mouse scurries across the kitchen floor. ___runs___
3. I decorated each package with a pretty bow. ___ribbon___
4. He likes to sleep with the blanket his mother made for him. ___quilt___
5. Her gown is beautiful. ___dress___

149

Words About the American Flag

Directions: How much do you know about the American flag? Write a sentence using each of the words or phrases from the Word Bank.

Word Bank			
stars	stripes	pledge	red, white, and blue
American	parade	fifty	thirteen

1. _Sentences will vary._
2. _____
3. _____
4. _____
5. _____
6. _____
7. _____
8. _____

150

Space Words

Directions: Read about Venus. Then, complete the activities. There may be more than one correct answer.

Venus is the nearest planet to Earth. Because it is the easiest planet to see in the sky, it has been called the **Morning Star** and **Evening Star**. The Romans named Venus after their goddess of love and beauty.

Venus is covered with thick clouds. The sun's heat is trapped by the clouds. The temperature on Venus is nearly 900 degrees! Space probes can report information about the planet to scientists. But they can last only a few hours on Venus because of the high temperature.

West   East
Draw the sun rising on Venus.

Venus turns in the opposite direction from Earth. So, on Venus, the sun rises in the west and sets in the east!

Circle:
Venus is the (nearest) ~~farthest~~ planet to Earth.

Check:
It is called the
☐ Evening Sun
☑ Morning Star because it is so easy to see.
☑ Evening Star

Circle:
The Romans named Venus for their: (goddess of love and beauty) god of light goddess of truth

Circle Yes or No:
Half of Venus is frozen with ice and snow. Yes (No)
On Venus, the sun rises in the east and sets in the west. Yes (No)

151

ANSWER key

Space Words

Directions: Read about Saturn. Then, complete the activities. There may be more than one correct answer.

Saturn is a planet famous for its rings. The rings are made of billions of tiny pieces of ice and dust. They are very wide and very thin. If you look at the rings from the side, they are almost too thin to be seen.

Saturn is the second largest planet in our solar system. It is so big that 758 Earths could fit inside it!

Saturn is covered by clouds. Strong, fast winds move the clouds quickly across the planet.

Draw 22 moons around Saturn!

Saturn has 22 moons! Its largest moon is called **Titan**.

Circle:
Saturn is most famous for its — spots. (rings).

Write:
Saturn's rings are made of ___ice___ and ___dust___.
mud   ice   dust   moons

Check:
Saturn's rings are ☐ red, yellow, and purple.
☑ wide, but thin.

Underline:
Saturn... is the second largest planet in our solar system.
is big enough to hold 758 Earths inside it.
is farther from the sun than any other planet.
is covered by fast, strong winds.
has a moon called Titan.

152

Space Words

Directions: Read about Pluto. Then, complete the activities. There may be more than one correct answer.

Pluto is a dwarf planet. It is farther from the sun than the eight planets of our solar system.

If you could stand on Pluto, the sun would look just like a bright, distant star in the sky. Pluto is so far away that it gets little of the sun's heat. That is why it is freezing cold on Pluto.

Some scientists think that Pluto was once one of Neptune's moons that escaped from orbit and drifted into space. Others believe it has always been a planet in our solar system.

Pluto is so far away from the sun that it takes 247 Earth years just to orbit the sun once!

Draw how the sun would look from Pluto.

Circle:
Pluto is a (dwarf planet).
planet.

Write:
Pluto is (closer to) ___ the sun than any of the planets of our solar system.
(farther from)

Check:

Pluto Facts
☑ On Pluto, the sun looks like a bright star.
☑ Pluto gets very little of the sun's heat.
☐ Pluto has very hot weather.
☑ Pluto takes 247 Earth years to orbit the sun.

Circle:
Some scientists believe that Pluto was once Neptune's (moon).

153

Unit 6 Review

Directions: Read each sentence. Look at the bold word. Write its antonym on the line to correct the sentence.

1. If you run **slow**, you will win the race. — fast
2. The **sweet** candy made my lips pucker. — sour
3. She was too **healthy** to go to work. — sick
4. Some constellations can be seen every **day**. — night
5. If I **spend** my money, I know I will have enough for a new bike. — save
6. The Milky Way is always spinning **quickly** though space. — slowly
7. We were told to be **loud** in the library. — quiet
8. It was **hot** enough for me to wear a coat. — cold
9. The girls are so **different** that you would think they were sisters. — similar
10. He is so **poor** that he owns three restaurants. — rich
11. Her **cowardly** deeds brought her great fame. — brave
12. Pluto, the dwarf planet, is the **closest** planet from the sun. — farthest
13. The Statue of Liberty carries a torch in her **left** hand. — right
14. The flower was so **ugly** that it won first prize in the gardening show. — pretty

154

Words That Are Abbreviations

An **abbreviation** is the general term for the shortened form of a word of phrase used in writing.

An **acronym** is a kind of abbreviation in which a word is formed by putting together the first letters or parts of a series of words in a longer phrase.

Example: SCUBA
Self **C**ontained **U**nderwater **B**reathing **A**pparatus

Directions: Write acronyms that you know. Then, write what they stand for. The first one is done for you.

1. DARE — Drug Abuse Resistance Education
2. _____ — Answers will vary.
3. _____ — _____
4. _____ — _____
5. _____ — _____
6. _____ — _____
7. _____ — _____
8. _____ — _____
9. _____ — _____

156

Words That Are Abbreviations

Initialism is a kind of abbreviation formed from the first (initial) letter or series of letters of several words. Each letter is pronounced individually. **TV**, **AM**, and **PM** are examples of initialism.

Directions: Initialism is used often when referring to computers and technology words. Use the Word Bank to complete each sentence with the correct initialism.

Word Bank
TV	PC	CD	URL	DVD	www

1. Let's listen to my classic rock ___CD___.
2. We can watch movies on my ___DVD___ player.
3. I watch cartoons on ___TV___ every Saturday morning.
4. My new ___PC___ has computer games and Internet access.
5. The "World Wide Web" is commonly referred to as ___www___.
6. My teacher wants me to list the ___URL___ of each website I used.

157

Words That Are Abbreviations

Some abbreviations are formed by using the first and second or first and last letters of a word.

Examples: **Dr.** - doctor
St. - street

Some abbreviations are formed with the first and last letters of a word as well as letters in between.

Example: **Blvd.** - boulevard

Directions: Rewrite each sentence by spelling out each bold abbreviation.

1. **Mr.** Stevens is out today.
Mister Stevens is out today.

2. The car turned onto Front **St.**
The car turned onto Front Street.

3. We need to find **Dr.** Hamilton.
We need to find Doctor Hamilton.

4. Franklin **Ave.** crosses Stuart **Blvd.**
Franklin Avenue crosses at Stuart Boulevard.

158

Holiday Words

Thanksgiving is a holiday in the United States held on the fourth Thursday in November. On Thanksgiving, Americans remember the good harvest of the Pilgrims in 1621 and show thanks for what they have now.

Directions: Use the Word Bank to find and circle the hidden Thanksgiving words in the puzzle. Look across and down. Then, color the picture.

Color the picture.

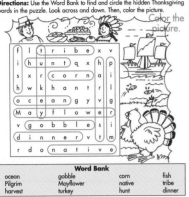

f	l	t	r	i	b	e	x	v
i	h	u	n	t	q	x	h	p
s	x	r	c	o	r	n	a	i
h	w	k	h	a	n	t	r	l
o	c	e	a	n	g	y	v	g
M	a	y	f	l	o	w	e	r
v	g	o	b	b	l	e	s	i
d	i	n	n	e	r	v	t	m
r	d	o	n	a	t	i	v	e

Word Bank

ocean	gobble	corn	fish
Pilgrim	Mayflower	native	tribe
harvest	turkey	hunt	dinner

159

Conservation Words

To **conserve** is to keep safe from loss, destruction, or waste. In order to take care of our planet, we must conserve the materials and resources that we take from the planet. April 22 is designated as Earth Day, a day to remember how important it is to be good to our planet.

Directions: Make a poster to celebrate Earth Day or to inspire others to conserve resources. Use words from the Word Bank on your poster. Use the space below to plan out your poster.

Word Bank				
polluting	Earth	solar	creatures	conserve
energy	clean	reduce	reuse	recycle

Posters will vary.

STOP POLLUTING MOTHER EARTH!

Let's use more windmills, electric cars, and solar power!

All living creatures need clean air.

160

Conservation Words

To **recycle** is to put through a process that allows used things to be reused.

What do you throw away every day? What could you do with these things? You could change an old greeting card into a new card. You could make a puppet with an old paper bag. Old buttons make great refrigerator magnets. You can plant seeds in plastic cups. Cardboard tubes make perfect rockets. So, use your imagination!

Directions: Write a sentence to tell what you could do to reuse each item.

1. A cardboard tube Answers will vary.

2. Buttons _____

3. An old greeting card _____

4. Paper bag _____

5. Plastic cups _____

161

Conservation Words

Directions: Circle the letter of the word or phrase that means the same as the underlined word.

1. Riding a bike saves energy and <u>reduces</u> pollution.
   a. decreases   c. increases
   b. cleans   d. eliminates

2. This house runs on <u>solar</u> power instead of gas or electricity.
   a. from the phone company   c. from the sun
   b. from Mars   d. from water

3. We try to <u>reuse</u> paper at school.
   a. write on   c. put away
   b. use again   d. throw away

4. In the morning, we <u>carpool</u> to school.
   a. share the ride   c. walk
   b. ride a bike   d. go for a swim

5. We need more laws against <u>polluting</u> our air and water.
   a. dirtying   c. protecting
   b. cleaning   d. studying

162

Geometry Words

Geometry is the branch of mathematics that has to do with **points**, **lines**, and **shapes**.

A **line** goes on and on in both directions. It has no end points.

Line CD

A **segment** is part of a line. It has two endpoints.

Segment AB

A **ray** has a line segment with only one endpoint. It goes on and on in the other direction.

Ray EF

An **angle** has two rays with the same end point.

Angle BAC

Directions: Write the name for each figure. The first one is done for you.

1. Line MN

2. 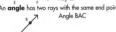 Line EF

3. Ray YX

4. Angle BAC

5. Segment AB

6. Line OP

163

Words That Are Abbreviated

An **abbreviation** is the shortened form of a word. Most abbreviations begin with a capital letter and end with a period. Look at the abbreviations in the box.

Mr.	Mister	St.	Street
Mrs.	Missus	Ave.	Avenue
Dr.	Doctor	Blvd.	Boulevard
A.M.	before noon	Rd.	Road
P.M.	after noon		

Days of the week: Sun. Mon. Tues. Wed. Thurs. Fri. Sat.
Months of the year: Jan. Feb. Mar. Apr. Aug. Sept. Oct. Nov. Dec.

Directions: Write the abbreviation for each word.

1. street   St.   5. doctor Dr.   9. Tuesday Tues.
2. road   Rd.   6. mister Mr.   10. avenue Ave.
3. missus Mrs.   7. October Oct.   11. Friday Fri.
4. before noon A.M. 8. March Mar.   12. August Aug.

Directions: Rewrite each sentence using abbreviations.

1. On Monday at 9:00 before noon, Mister Jones had a meeting.
   On Mon. at 9:00 A.M. Mr. Jones had a meeting.

2. In December, Doctor Carlson saw Missus Zuckerman.
   In Dec., Dr. Carlson saw Mrs. Zuckerman.

3. One Tuesday in August, Mister Wood went to the park.
   One Tues. in Aug., Mr. Wood went to the park.

164

Words That Are Abbreviated

A person's title is often abbreviated. Look at the abbreviations and their meanings.

Full Title	Abbreviation	Definition
Mister	Mr.	title for a man
Missus	Mrs.	title for a married woman
Doctor	Dr.	title for someone with a doctoral degree
Junior	Jr.	a son with the same first, middle, and last name as his father

Directions: Draw a line through each word that could be abbreviated. Then, write the abbreviation above the word. The first one is done for you.

1. Liz, should I call your mother ~~Missus~~ Marks or ~~Doctor~~ Marks?
   Mrs. _Dr._

2. ~~Doctor~~ Martin Luther King, ~~Junior~~, was a great man.
   _Dr._ _Jr._

3. Our neighbor's name is ~~Mister~~ Samuels.
   _Mr._

4. I have an appointment with ~~Doctor~~ Garza.
   _Dr._

5. My mom likes to be called ~~Missus~~ Reed.
   Mrs.

165

Words That Are Abbreviated

Sometimes, measurement words are abbreviated. Read the abbreviations in the box.

oz.	ounce(s)
lb./lbs.	pound/pounds
in.	inch(es)
ft.	foot or feet

Directions: Rewrite each sentence without abbreviations. Some sentences have more than one abbreviation.

1. I weigh 73 lbs.
   I weigh 73 pounds.

2. My height is 4 ft., 5 in.
   My height is 4 feet, 5 inches.

3. My baby sister is 21 in. long.
   My baby sister is 21 inches long.

4. She weighs only 7 lbs., 6 oz.
   She weighs only 7 pounds, 6 ounces.

5. Our dad is 77 in. tall. That is over 6 ft.
   Our dad is 77 inches tall. That is over 6 feet!

166

Holiday Words

Directions: Use the words in the Word Bank to complete the puzzle about holidays.

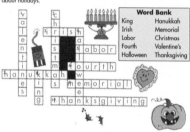

Word Bank

King	Hanukkah
Irish	Memorial
Labor	Christmas
Fourth	Valentine's
Halloween	Thanksgiving

Across
3. St. Patrick's Day is an _____ holiday.
5. _____ Day is the first Monday in September.
6. The _____ of July is Independence Day.
7. _____ is a Jewish holiday.
9. _____ Day is a day of remembrance.
10. _____ Day began with Pilgrims and Indians.

Down
1. Hearts are all around on _____ Day.
2. _____ is celebrated in December.
4. _____ is a time to trick-or-treat.
8. Martin Luther _____, Jr., is honored in January.

167

Conservation Words

The things we throw away affect the environment. Things that are biodegradable will eventually break down and become part of the earth. Things that are not biodegradable stay with us forever as litter. Check out what is, or is not, biodegradable with this long-term activity. Find an adult to help you.

You will need: a trowel, apple cores, large lettuce leaves, a plastic wrapper, Styrofoam cups, craft sticks, markers

Directions:

1. Find a spot where it is all right to dig four holes. Dig all about the same size—2 inches deep by 3 inches square.

2. Put the apple cores, lettuce leaves, plastic wrapper, and Styrofoam cups in their respective holes and cover them with dirt.

3. Write the name of each item on a craft stick. Put each craft stick in the ground to mark the spots.

4. In a month, go back and dig up the items. Discuss with an adult what you discover.

168

Conservation Words

Directions: Many people devote their lives to helping the earth. Here are some job titles those people have. Can you think of others?

solid waste technician	geologist
air pollution inspector	ecologist
sewage plant worker	forester
pollution scientist	oceanographer
city planner	marine biologist
park ranger	forest naturalist
forest ranger	conservationist

Answers will vary.

Select from the list above a career about which you would like to learn. Write a report about it. If someone in the community holds one of those jobs, you should write the person to ask for an interview and/or on-site visit, or ask if they might send information about their job. You may also learn about environmental careers from reference books or by obtaining material from one of the organizations below.

Air and Waste Management Association
One Gateway Center, 3rd Floor
Pittsburgh, PA 15222

American Institute of Architects
1735 New York Avenue NW
Washington, D.C. 20006

American Forests
1516 P Street NW, P.O. Box 2000
Washington, D.C. 20005

American Water Works Association
6666 W. Qunicy Avenue
Denver, CO 80235

American Geological Institute
4220 King Street
Alexandria, VA 22302

Conservation Fund
1800 N. Kent Street, Suite 1120
Arlington, VA 22209

169

Conservation Words

Many places in your community do things to help the environment.

aquarium	national park	library
science museum	landfill	recycling center

Directions: Visit one of the places listed above. After your trip, write a list of what this place is doing to protect the environment. Also, write ways that you can help.

Answers will vary.

170

Geometry Words

A **triangle** is a figure with three sides and three angles. The angles of a triangle always add up to 180 degrees.

Triangles are organized sometimes by the characteristics of their sides.

> An **isosceles triangle** has two equal sides.
> A **scalene triangle** has no equal sides.
> An **equilateral triangle** has three equal sides.

Directions: Write the name of each triangle.

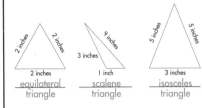

equilateral triangle

scalene triangle

isosceles triangle

171

Words That Are Abbreviated

Recipes sometimes contain abbreviations. Look at the common abbreviations in the box.

c.	cup
tsp.	teaspoon
tbsp.	tablespoon
min.	minute
hr.	hour

Directions: Read the recipe. Circle the abbreviations. With the help of an adult, try the recipe!

Peanut Butter Balls

Ingredients:
1 (c.) creamy peanut butter
1 (c.) honey
2 (c.) powdered milk
2 (tbsp.) chocolate chips

Get a large bowl and a big, strong spoon. Put all of the ingredients in the bowl. Mix them together for 5 (min.) Roll the mixture into balls. Arrange the balls on a plate. Chill them in the refrigerator for 1 (hr.) Enjoy!

172

Names for the Parts of a Letter

Directions: Read about the parts of a letter.

123 Main Street
Plainsville, NY 41698
January 30, 2007

Dear Frank,
Our class just went on a field trip to the aviation museum. I know how much you like airplanes, so it reminded me of you. I saw an open cockpit biplane like the ones used in World War I. Wouldn't it be cool to ride in one of those?
I hope you are having fun in school. Does your class take any field trips?

Your friend,
Jack

Heading:
This can be your address and the date, or just the date. It starts halfway across the page.

Greeting:
It is the opening of the letter. It usually starts with **Dear**. Then, add the person's name and a comma. It starts on the left side of the page.

Body:
This is the main part of the letter. Each paragraph has its own main idea. Each new paragraph is indented.

Closing:
It is the ending of the letter. It usually says good-bye with phrases like **Your friend, Your grandson,** or **Love**. The first letter in the first word is capitalized, and a comma follows the phrase.

Signature:
Write your name. It goes below the closing.

173

Names for the Parts of a Letter

Directions: Label the parts of a letter. Then, write a letter to a friend or relative about your favorite holiday.

Heading

Letters will vary.   Greeting

Body

Closing
Signature

174

Holiday Words

Directions: Use the Word Bank to write the correct holiday to complete each sentence.

Word Bank		
Valentine's Day	Halloween	
The Fourth of July	Thanksgiving	St. Patrick's Day

1. Halloween takes place on October 31. Children celebrate this holiday by dressing up in costumes and going from house to house begging for treats.

2. St. Patrick's Day takes place on March 17. It is a day to celebrate the patron saint of Ireland.

3. Valentine's Day takes place on February 14. It is a day to celebrate love and friendship.

4. The Fourth of July is also called Independence Day. It is a day that Americans celebrate the signing of the Declaration of Independence from England in 1776.

5. Thanksgiving is held on the fourth Thursday of November. On this day, Americans remember the good harvest of the Pilgrims in 1621 and show thanks for what they have now.

175

Conservation Words

When you **recycle**, you find a way to use something again. With an adult, follow the directions to make recycled paper.

You will need: newspaper, a blender or beater, a bowl, a dishpan (or large, deep pan), a piece of window screen, paper towels, sections of the newspaper, pens, a measuring cup, a large board, water, tape.

Put tape around the edges of the screen. Then, follow the directions. An adult should work with you on the activity after the first soaking (step #1).

Directions:

1. Tear enough old paper into tiny pieces to fill six cups. Put the pieces in a pan. Cover the paper with water. Soak this overnight.

2. Blend or beat a small handful of the soaked paper with two or three cups of water. Add water if blending or beating is too difficult. Empty the pulp into a large bowl. Continue making small batches of pulp.

3. Add enough water to the pan so that when you stir the mixture with your fingers, you cannot feel the pulp.

4. Tilt the screen and slide it to the bottom of the pan. Using your fingers, spread the pulp evenly over the screen. Let it settle a minute.

5. Open a section of newspaper to its center. Cover one side of it with paper towels.

paper towels   newspaper

6. Lift the screen straight up over the pan. Let it drain.

screen
pan

176

Conservation Words

7. Place the screen with the pulp onto the side of newspaper without towels. Close the paper making sure the towels are over the screen.

8. Carefully flip the entire newspaper section so that the screen is on top of the pulp.

9. Put the board on top of the newspaper. Press on the board to squeeze out the excess water.

10. Open the newspaper. Remove the screen. Carefully remove the paper towel with the pulp on it to a dry piece of newspaper. Let the pulp dry.

11. When dry, carefully peel the pulp away from the paper towel.

12. Write a message about recycling on the paper you made.

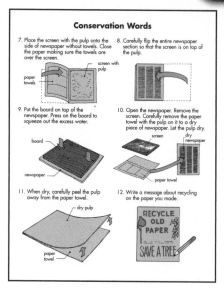

177

Conservation Words

Directions: Draw a line to match each conservation word with its definition.

1. landfill — to put through a process that allows used things to be reused
2. biodegradable — able to be broken down by the action of living organisms such as bacteria
3. pollute — an artificial substance that can be formed into many materials and products
4. litter — full of or covered with living plants, trees, and grass
5. plastic — to make messy by scattering rubbish or other objects
6. recycle — a place to dispose of garbage and rubbish
7. green — everything that surrounds a living thing and affects its growth and health
8. environment — to make something dirty or harmful by mixing in or adding waste material

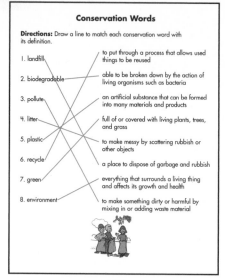

178

Unit 7 Review

Directions: Write a letter to your local state representative. Write five things that you would like your representative to do to preserve the environment in your community.

Remember the parts of a letter, abbreviations, and conservation words that you have learned in this unit.

_____
_____
_____

Letters will vary.

_____
_____
_____
_____
_____
_____
_____
_____

_____
_____

179

Classifying Words

Classifying means putting similar things into groups.

Directions: Write each word from the Word Bank on the correct line.

Word Bank

baby	donkey	whale	family	fox
uncle	goose	grandfather	kangaroo	policeman

people

baby

family

grandfather

policeman

uncle

animals

goose

whale

fox

kangaroo

donkey

181

Classifying Words

Directions: Read the three words in each box. Then, add one more word that is like the others.

Words will vary.

1. cars trucks airplanes ____	6. cows pigs chickens ____
2. bread bagels muffins ____	7. pens pencils paints ____
3. square triangle rectangle ____	8. violets tulips iris ____
4. milk yogurt cheese ____	9. mom dad sister ____
5. merry-go-round swings sandbox ____	10. snowpants boots jacket ____

Suggested answers:

Challenge: Can you write the theme of each group?

1. transportation
2. bakery items
3. shapes
4. dairy products
5. playground equipment
6. farm animals
7. drawing utensils
8. flowers
9. family
10. cold weather clothes

182

Classifying Words

Directions: The words in each box form a group. Choose the word from the Word Bank that describes each group. Then, write it on the line.

Word Bank

clothes	family	noises	colors	flowers
fruits	animals	coins	toys	

rose buttercup tulip daisy	crash bang ring pop	mother father sister brother
flowers	noises	family
puzzle wagon blocks doll	green purple blue red	grapes orange apple plum
toys	colors	fruits
shirt socks dress coat	dime penny nickel quarter	dog horse elephant moose
clothes	coins	animals

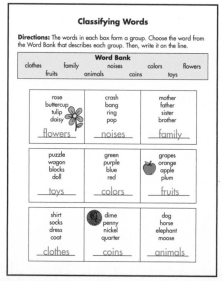

183

332

Words About Canada

Directions: Unlike the United States, Canada is not divided into states. Follow the directions to label the ten provinces and two territories that make up Canada.

1. The Yukon Territory is connected to Alaska. The Northwest Territory is the large area to its east. Label them.
2. British Columbia is south of Yukon. Label the province and color it yellow.
3. East of British Columbia is Alberta. Label it and color it red.
4. The province between Alberta and Manitoba is called Saskatchewan. This is where Big Foot supposedly lives. Draw him there and label the provinces.
5. Winnipeg is a city in Manitoba. Label the city and color the province brown.
6. The province north of the Great Lakes is Ontario. Color it orange.
7. The largest province is Quebec. Label the province and color it green.
8. New Brunswick borders Quebec on the southeast, and Nova Scotia is attached to it. Label them and color them purple.
9. Nestled above the two provinces is Prince Edward Island. Color this province black.
10. The last province is Newfoundland. This province borders Quebec and includes the large island near it. Label both parts.

184

Weather Words

Directions: Read about lightning. Then, complete the activities. There may be more than one correct answer.

Clouds are made of many water droplets. All of these droplets together contain a large electrical charge. Sometimes these clouds set off a large spark of electricity called **lightning**. Lightning travels very fast. When it cuts through the air, it causes the air to move violently. The sound the air makes is called **thunder**.

Lightning takes various forms. Some lightning looks like a zigzag in the sky. **Sheet lightning** spreads and lights the sky. **Ball lightning** looks like a ball of fire.

Underline:
Lightning is a flash of light
1. caused by sunshine.
2. <u>caused by electricity in the sky.</u>

Circle Yes or No:
Sometimes clouds set off a huge spark of electricity. (Yes) No
Lightning is caused by dry weather. Yes (No)
Lightning travels very fast. (Yes) No
Lightning can cause thunder. (Yes) No

Unscramble and write in the puzzle above:

1. <u>ball</u>   2. <u>sheet</u>   3. <u>zigzag</u>
   l a b l   t e h s e   g a i z g z
   3 2 1 4   5 3 2 1 4   3 5 2 1 6 4

185

Weather Words

Directions: Read about hurricanes. Then, complete the activities. There may be more than one correct answer.

A **hurricane** is a powerful storm that forms over some parts of an ocean. A hurricane can be several hundred miles wide.

A hurricane has two main parts: the **eye** and the **wall cloud**. The eye is the center of the storm. In the eye, the weather is calm. The storm around the eye is called the wall cloud. It has strong winds and heavy rain. In some hurricanes, the wind can blow 150 miles an hour!

As the storm moves across the water, it causes giant waves in the ocean. As the storm moves over land, it can cause floods, destroy buildings, and kill people who have not taken shelter.

Circle:
A hurricane has two main parts: tornado (wall cloud) (eye)

Match:
The calm center of the hurricane. —— wall cloud
The wind and rainstorm around the eye. —— eye

Check:
A hurricane ☑ can be several hundred miles wide.
☑ can have winds that move 150 miles an hour.
☐ is a small storm.
☑ can cause giant waves in the ocean.
☑ can cause floods and hurt people.

186

Weather Words

Directions: Read about tornados. Then, complete the activities. There may be more than one correct answer.

Did you know that a tornado is the most violent windstorm on Earth? A **tornado** is a whirling, twisting storm that is shaped like a funnel.

A tornado usually occurs in the spring on a hot day. It begins with thunderclouds and thunder. A cloud becomes very dark. The bottom of the cloud begins to twist and form a funnel. Rain and lightning begin. The funnel cloud drops from the dark storm clouds. It moves down toward the ground.

A tornado is very dangerous. It can destroy almost everything in its path.

Circle:
A thunder (tornado) is the most violent windstorm on Earth.

Check:
Which words describe a tornado?
☑ whirling   ☑ twisting   ☐ icy   ☑ funnel-shaped   ☑ dangerous

Underline:
A funnel shape is: ○ ▢ ⬭ ▽ ✕

Write and Circle:
A tornado usually occurs in the <u>spring</u> on a (cool/(hot)) day.
                              autumn/spring

Write 1 - 2 - 3 below and in the picture above.
③ The funnel cloud drops down to the ground.
① A tornado begins with dark thunder clouds.
② The dark clouds begin to twist and form a funnel.

187

Number Words in Spanish

Directions: Draw a line to match the number words one through twenty from Spanish to English. The first one is done for you.

uno — one
siete — seven
catorce — fourteen
cuatro — four
doce — twelve
dieciséis — sixteen
dos — two
ocho — eight
dieciocho — eighteen
seis — six
diez — ten
diecisiete — seventeen
tres — three
quince — fifteen
once — eleven
cinco — five
trece — thirteen
diecinueve — nineteen
nueve — nine
veinte — twenty

188

Classifying Words

Directions: After each sentence, write three words from the Word Bank that belong to the group described.

Word Bank			
eagle	whistle	horn	frog
dime	wheel	throat	ball
sun	airplane	penny	marble
banana	balloon	dollar	heart
camel	grasshopper	horse	kangaroo
chipmunk	lemon	butterfly	mouth

1. These are things that can hop.
   grasshopper   frog   kangaroo
2. These things all have wings.
   eagle   airplane   butterfly
3. These are types of money.
   dime   penny   dollar
4. These are four-legged animals.
   camel   chipmunk   horse
5. These are parts of your body.
   throat   heart   mouth
6. These things are yellow.
   sun   banana   lemon
7. These things can roll.
   wheel   ball   marble
8. These are things you can blow.
   whistle   balloon   horn

189

Classifying Words

Directions: Write the word from the Word Bank that tells what kinds of things are in each sentence.

Word Bank				
birds	toys	states	insects	women
men	numbers	animals	flowers	letters

1. A father, uncle, and king are all __men__
2. Fred has a wagon, puzzles, and blocks. These are all __toys__
3. Iowa, Ohio, and Maine are all __states__
4. A robin, woodpecker, and canary all have wings. They are kinds of __birds__.
5. Squirrels, rabbits, and foxes all have tails and are kinds of __animals__.
6. Roses, daisies, and violets smell sweet. These are kinds of __flowers__.
7. A, B, C, and D are all __letters__. You use them to spell words.
8. Bees, ladybugs, and beetles are kinds of __insects__.
9. A mother, aunt, and queen are all __women__.
10. Seven, thirty, and nineteen are all __numbers__.

190

Classifying Words

Directions: Write a word from the Word Bank to complete each sentence. If the word names an article of clothing, write **1** on the line in front of the sentence. If it names food, write **2** on the line. If it names an animal, write **3** on the line. If the word names furniture, write **4** on the line.

Word Bank				
jacket	chair	shirt	owl	mice
bed	cheese	dress	bread	chocolate

__1__ 1. Danny tucked his ____shirt____ into his pants.
__2__ 2. __Chocolate__ is my favorite kind of candy.
__3__ 3. The wise old ____owl____ sat in the tree and said, "Who-o-o."
__4__ 4. I can't sit on the ____chair____ because it has a broken leg.
__1__ 5. Don't forget to wear your ____jacket____ because it is chilly today.
__2__ 6. Will you please buy a loaf of ____bread____ at the store?
__1__ 7. She wore a very pretty ____dress____ to the dance.
__3__ 8. The cat chased the ____mice____ in the barn.
__4__ 9. I was so sleepy that I went to ____bed____ early.
__2__ 10. We put ____cheese____ in the mouse trap to help catch the mice.

191

Words About Canada

Canada is located north of the United States on the continent of North America. Canada's largest province, **Quebec**, is unique because most of its inhabitants speak French. The people there have long been referred to as French-Canadians.

Montreal is Quebec's most famous city and is often called the "Heart of French Canada." By day or night, it is an exciting city with fine universities, the National Hockey League (Montreal Canadiens), incredible museums, and the one-of-a-kind Cirque du Soleil.

Cirque du Soleil means "Circus of the Sun." This circus is unique because it has only human performers and no animals. Quebec funds a school called the Ecole Nationale de Cirque. With an enrollment of 20 youngsters, the school provides an academic education while the students learn the arts of the big top on the trapeze, stilts, trampoline, and tightrope.

Directions: Imagine that you are a student at the school. On a separate sheet of paper, write about what a typical day is like for you. Then, draw a picture of yourself performing.

192

Weather Words

Wind is the air as it moves naturally over the surface of the earth. You probably already know of the dangerous aspects of wind. Hurricanes and tornadoes cause property damage, topple down trees, and knock down electric wires and telephone wires.

Think of some of the helpful aspects of wind. Wind can create energy with windmills, cool you off on a hot day, move sailboats, dry wet areas, transport seeds, etc.

Directions: Divide a large sheet of paper in half. Label one side **Destructive Wind Forces** and the other side **Helpful Wind Forces**. Cut out newspaper articles and draw pictures to show the effects of wind. Glue each article and picture on the correct side of the paper.

193

Weather Words

The three major types of clouds are **cirrus**, **cumulus**, and **stratus**. You can become more familiar with these types of clouds when you do this project.

You will need: cotton balls, dryer lint or gray flannel, glue, poster board (11 inches x 18 inches), a pencil, crayons, markers, white paint, paintbrushes, and glitter.

Directions: Use a pencil to divide the poster board into six sections. Use the top sections to simulate the three major types of clouds by following the directions below.

 1. **Cirrus Clouds**—high, white clouds with a feathery appearance. To create this type of cloud, paint white streaks at the very top of your poster board and sprinkle glitter sparingly while the paint is still wet to represent the ice that may be present in these high clouds.

 2. **Cumulus Clouds**—puffy, white, low clouds with flat bottoms. In the second top box, glue cotton balls of various sizes approximately 1/3 of the way down the poster board.

3. **Stratus Clouds**—wide, often gray, low clouds that can drip snow flurries and drizzle. Glue dryer lint or gray flannel across the top of the third top box covering the length of the box.

After each of the three major cloud types is completed, draw pictures in the box underneath each cloud. The pictures should show activities you could do if you were to observe that particular type of cloud on any given day.

194

334

Weather Words

An **idiom** means something different than what the words actually say. Many idiomatic expressions contain weather words.

Example:
Ray has his **head in the clouds.**

This expression means that Ray is not paying attention.

Directions: Read each idiom that uses weather words. Write what it means on the line.

Suggested answers:

1. raining cats and dogs — raining very heavily
2. under the weather — sick
3. fair-weather friend — someone who is only your friend when you are happy and successful
4. come rain or shine — nothing, not even the weather, will stop you from being somewhere
5. shoot the breeze — chat
6. wet behind the ears — inexperienced
7. cold feet — loss of courage
8. cloud nine — extremely happy
9. steal someone's thunder — taking credit for someone else's accomplishment

195

Number Words in Spanish

Addition means **putting together** or adding two or more numbers to find the sum. For example, 3 + 5 = 8.

Más means **plus** in Spanish.

Directions: Add to solve the problems. Write the correct answer on the line.

Example: uno más tres = <u>4</u>
     1   +   3

1. siete más catorce = <u>21</u>
2. cuatro más doce = <u>16</u>
3. dieciséis más dos = <u>18</u>
4. cinco más tres = <u>8</u>
5. tres más diez = <u>13</u>
6. nueve más veinte = <u>29</u>
7. once más quince = <u>26</u>
8. ocho más uno = <u>9</u>
9. diez más seis = <u>16</u>

196

Words That Are Homophones

Homophones are words that sound alike but are spelled differently and have different meanings.

Directions: Underline the wrong homophone in each sentence. Then, write the correct homophone on the line.

1. How much do you think I <u>way</u>? — weigh
2. My brother <u>blue</u> the car's horn loudly. — blew
3. She needed to <u>so</u> Mr. Rogers's torn shirt. — sew
4. The <u>son</u> shone through the curtains. — sun
5. Mom baked the cake with <u>flower</u>. — flour
6. My friend went on a <u>plain</u> to visit her aunt. — plane
7. She swept the <u>stares</u>. — stairs
8. Mr. Rogers's shirt was bright <u>read</u>. — red
9. The boy was stung by a <u>be</u>. — bee
10. We rode a Ferris wheel at the <u>fare</u>. — fair

197

Words That Are Homophones

Directions: On the line before each homophone, write the letter of the phrase that best defines its meaning.

F 1. hare — A. any creature hunted for food
N 2. hair — B. a mass of unbaked bread
H 3. peer — C. a body part used to smell
K 4. pier — D. something that is owed
J 5. doe — E. the end of an animal's body
B 6. dough — F. an animal related to the rabbit
M 7. bare — G. a large, furry animal with a short tail
G 8. bear — H. to look closely; to gaze
P 9. dew — I. to beg or ask for by prayer
D 10. due — J. a female deer, hare, or rabbit
C 11. nose — K. a platform built out over water
O 12. knows — L. a story
A 13. prey — M. naked; without any covering
I 14. pray — N. growth that covers the scalp of a person or the body of a mammal
E 15. tail — O. understands; to be certain of something
L 16. tale — P. water droplets

198

Words That Are Homophones

Directions: Circle the words that are not used correctly. Use the Word Bank to write the correct word above the circled word. The first one is done for you.

Word Bank

| road | see | one | be | so | I | brakes | piece | there |
| wait | not | some | hour | would | no | deer | you | heard |

Jake and his family were getting close to Grandpa's. It had taken them nearly an ~~our~~ (hour) to get ~~their~~ (there) but Jake knew it was worth it. In his mind, he could already ~~sea~~ (see) the pond and could almost feel the cool water. It had been ~~sew~~ (so) hot this summer in the apartment.

"~~Wood~~ (Would) ~~ewe~~ (you) like a ~~peace~~ (piece) of my apple, Jake?" asked his big sister Clare. "~~Eye~~ (I) can't eat any more."

"~~Know~~ (No) thank you," Jake replied. "I still have ~~sum~~ (some) of my fruit left."

Suddenly, Dad slammed on the ~~breaks~~ (brakes).

"Did you see that ~~dear~~ (deer) on the ~~rode~~ (road)? I always ~~herd~~ (heard) that if you see ~~won~~ (one) there might ~~bee~~ (be) more."

"Good thinking, Dad. I'm glad you are a safe driver. We're ~~knot~~ (not) very far from Grandpa's now. I can't ~~weight~~ (wait)!"

199

Words About North America

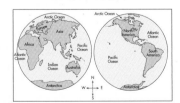

Directions: Fill in the circle beside the answer that best completes each sentence.

1. The United States is a
   A. continent.
   B. country.
   C. hemisphere.
   D. state.

2. Mexico is in the continent of
   A. South America.
   B. North America.
   C. Africa.
   D. Europe.

Directions: Read each statement. Decide whether it is true or false. Then, fill in the correct circle.

3. Canada is in the continent of North America.
   A. True   B. False

4. The United States is in the continent of South America.
   A. True   **B. False**

5. To travel from North America to Antarctica, you need to cross the Indian Ocean.
   A. True   **B. False**

200

Weather Words

Directions: Word webs are a good way to classify weather words. Look at the groups below. Add more words in each group.

Words will vary.

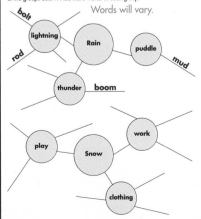

bolt, lightning, rod — Rain — puddle, mud

thunder — boom

play — Snow — work, clothing

201

Weather Words

Directions: Does color have anything to do with temperature? Try this experiment to find out.

You will need:
2 identical glasses
one 9" x 12" sheet of black paper
one 9" x 12" sheet of white paper
masking tape
a pencil
a pen
an outside thermometer
water
scissors

Directions:
Wrap one glass with black paper and one with white paper. Tape the paper closed. Cut off the excess paper. Fill each glass with the same amount of water. Set both glasses in a sunny spot. Leave them there for at least an hour. Then, put the thermometer into each glass and record the temperature of each on the Cool Color chart. Also, write on the chart what you concluded from this experiment. Do this experiment at least two more times to verify your conclusion. Try other colors to see if there is any difference.

Note: The water in the jar wrapped with black paper should be warmer because the black paper absorbs more heat than the white.

Cool Color Chart			
Paper Color	Time	Temperature	Conclusion
Answers will vary			

202

Weather Words

Directions: Use the weather words from the Word Bank to complete the sentences.

Word Bank				
sunny	temperature	foggy	puddles	rainy
windy	rainbow	cloudy	lightning	snowy

1. Sometimes, the school closes on very ___snowy___ days.
2. I will wait for a ___rainy___ day so I can use my new umbrella.
3. Today is a ___sunny___ day, so I'm wearing sunglasses.
4. The day is ___cloudy___ with a chance of showers.
5. The ___lightning___ flashed during the thunderstorm.
6. After it rains, I like to jump in ___puddles___ .
7. The ___temperature___ cooled down in the evening.
8. A colorful ___rainbow___ appeared in the sky in the light rain.
9. This morning it was so ___foggy___ that the air was thick.
10. It was so ___windy___ that I almost blew away!

203

Unit 8 Review

Directions: Read each word in the Word Bank. Then, write the word in the correct group.

Word Bank				
storm	nueve	mother	lightning	baby
territory	sister	sunny	clouds	twenty
trece	four	ocean	Canada	uncle
island	diez	temperature	father	continent

Family Words
mother
baby
sister
uncle
father

Number Words
nueve
twenty
trece
four
diez

Weather Words
storm
sunny
temperature
lightning
clouds

Geography Words
territory
ocean
Canada
island
continent

204

Commonly Misused Words

The word **this** is an adjective that refers to things that are near. **This** always describes a singular noun. **Singular** means one.

Example: I will buy **this** coat.
(**Coat** is singular.)

The word **these** is also an adjective that refers to things that are near. **These** always describes a plural noun. **Plural** means more than one thing.

Example: I will buy **these** flowers.
(**Flowers** is a plural noun.)

Directions: Write **this** or **these** on each line to finish the sentence correctly. The first one is done for you.

1. __this__ A cat with orange and black stripes sits on this/these fence.
2. __these__ I will buy this/these gloves for my dad.
3. __this__ She would like to try this/these new recipe.
4. __this__ He said he would take this/these bag with him.
5. __These__ This/These dresses look very expensive.
6. __this__ The hen is sitting on this/these nest to keep its eggs warm.
7. __these__ Would you like to taste this/these cookies?
8. __this__ How long will it take to get this/these situation corrected?
9. __these__ I would like to borrow this/these books from the library.
10. __these__ Did you write this/these letters to me?
11. __this__ He took this/these bus to school.
12. __this__ Are you on this/these soccer team, too?

206

Commonly Misused Words

The word **can** means **am able to** or **to be able to**.

Example: I **can** do that for you.
Can you do that for me?

The word **may** means **be allowed to** or **permitted to**. **May** is used to ask or give permission. **May** can also mean **might** or **perhaps**.

Example: **May** I be excused?
You **may** sit here.

Directions: Write **can** or **may** on each line to finish the sentence correctly. The first one is done for you.

1. __Can__ Can/May you take this suit to the dry cleaner?
2. __Can__ Can/May you tell me how to get to the post office?
3. __may__ I can/may be able to help you if I can get my own work finished.
4. __may__ You can/may borrow this video.
5. __Can__ Can/May you help your little brother tie his shoes?
6. __May__ Can/May I have a piece of cake?
7. __may__ The baby can/may see his sister from his highchair.
8. __may__ I can/may play outside after I do my chores.
9. __may__ She can/may have a cold.
10. __can__ The boy can/may swim.
11. __can__ The casserole can/may be taken out of the oven in an hour.
12. __can__ He is smart enough that he can/may solve the problem himself.
13. __may__ I can/may have to go out of town tomorrow.
14. __May__ Can/May I sit beside you?

207

Words That Are Contractions

The word **your** shows possession.

Examples: Is that **your** book? I visited **your** class.

The word **you're** is a contraction for **you are**. A **contraction** is two words joined together as one. An **apostrophe** shows where letters have been left out.

Examples: **You're** doing well on that painting.
If **you're** going to pass the test, you should study.

Directions: Write **your** or **you're** on each line to finish the sentence correctly. The first one is done for you.

1. __Your__ Your/You're mom is very nice.
2. __You're__ Your/You're going to get in trouble when your parents see the broken lamp.
3. __your__ Did your/you're friend buy that gift for you?
4. __your__ How do your/you're brother and sister get along?
5. __you're__ Do you think your/you're going to finish this work on time?
6. __your__ Why are your/you're cheeks so red?
7. __your__ What is your/you're grandfather like?
8. __you're__ If your/you're going on the class trip, let me know.
9. __your__ I thought your/you're art project was the best one.
10. __your__ What is your/you're opinion?
11. __your__ What is your/you're favorite color?
12. __your__ Did your/you're team score the winning goal?
13. __You're__ Your/You're going to enjoy this performance.
14. __your__ What are your/you're parents doing tonight?

208

ANSWER key

Words About Africa

Directions: Read about Africa. Then, answer the questions.

Africa is the second largest continent. South of Europe, Africa is between the Atlantic and Indian Oceans. It is in the Eastern Hemisphere.

Northern Africa is almost entirely covered by the **Sahara**, the largest desert in the world. Ancient Egypt, one of the first great civilizations, is located in northern Africa along the **Nile River**. The Nile is the longest river in the world.

Central Africa stretches from Senegal in the west to Tanzania in the east. The Rift Valley, in Kenya, Uganda, and Tanzania, is called the birthplace of humanity. It is here that the very earliest traces of our ancestors have been found, dating back to over four million years ago.

Southern Africa holds the country South Africa, which has three capitals, one for each main branch of its government. The capitals are Cape Town, Pretoria, and Bloemfontein.

1. How big is Africa compared to the other six continents of the world?
   Africa is the second largest continent.

2. If you were a scientist, which part of Africa would you most like to visit? Why?
   Answers will vary.

3. Compare what you know of Africa to North America, where we live.
   Answers will vary.

209

Words About Magnets

A **magnet** is an object that produces an invisible force that attracts, or draws near, iron or steel. Magnets are often made of iron or steel.

Directions: Gather some of the objects listed in the chart. Hold a small magnet next to these objects. Which objects will the magnet pull? Add some of your own objects to the list.

Object	Magnet Attracts	Magnet Does Not Attract
scissors	✓	
wood ruler		✓
eraser		✓
paper clip	✓	
thumbtack	✓	
paper		✓
aluminum foil		✓

Directions: Magnets do not attract all metals. Find and circle the six metals in the word search. The metals listed up and down are attracted to magnets. The metals written across are not attracted. Write each metal in the correct group.

```
B N B R A S S X
Z I K L N T I A
A C O P P E R D
N K T R O E O S
T E K G N U N P
A L U M I N U M
```

Attracted to Magnets
nickel
steel
iron

Not Attracted to Magnets
brass
copper
aluminum

210

Words About Magnets

All magnets are strongest at their **poles**. The poles are at opposite points of the magnet. They are referred to as the **north pole** and the **south pole**. Opposite poles attract each other. The north pole of one magnet attracts the south pole of another magnet. Matching poles repel, or push away from, each other. The north pole of one magnet repels the north pole of another magnet. The invisible force that attracts materials to magnets is called **magnetism**.

Directions: After each magnet word, write its meaning.
Suggested answers:
attract _to draw near_

repel _to push away from_

north pole _one end of a magnet; the opposite end from the south pole_

south pole _one end of a magnet; the opposite end from the north pole_

magnetism _the invisible force that attracts materials to magnets_

Directions: Draw a picture below to show how the north and south poles of magnets attract each other.

Pictures will vary.

211

Words About Magnets

Some materials, such as wood and water, do not seem to respond to magnets. But actually, all materials respond to a magnetic force. Some just respond so weakly to the force that it is not observable in everyday life.

There are even certain materials that are not attracted to magnets. These metals include gold, silver, lead, zinc, copper, aluminum, and brass.

Directions: Use the Word Bank to unscramble the words about magnets.

Word Bank				
scissors	force	attract	repel	iron
steel	metals	poles	opposites	field

1. slope _poles_
2. noir _iron_
3. estel _steel_
4. stalem _metals_
5. cerof _force_
6. difel _field_
7. perel _repel_
8. sopitopes _opposites_
9. scosrsis _scissors_
10. arttact _attract_

212

Metric Words

Directions: Read about metric measurement. Then, answer the questions.

The **metric system** is one way we use to measure. The basic units of the metric system are **meters**, **liters**, and **grams**. Meters measure length. Liters measure volume. Grams measure weight. There are also smaller and larger measurements in the metric system. It is very easy to convert between larger and smaller units because the metric system is based on units of 10. Look at the graphic below. You can convert either higher or lower in the metric system by moving the decimal point. Each new unit has a different prefix. To move to a smaller unit, you go left on the graphic and move the decimal point to the right. To move to a larger unit, you go right on the graphic and move the decimal point to the left.

For example, you have 1 liter of paint and want to know how many milliliters you have. Simply move left. Milli- is three to the left of liters, so you move the decimal point right 3 spaces. One liter is equal to 1,000 milliliters.

milli-　centi-　deci-　meters liters grams　deca-　hecto-　kilo-

1. What is the unit of volume in the metric system?
   liters

2. On what number is the metric system based?
   _10_

3. When converting to a larger unit, in which direction do you move the decimal point?
   left

4. 45 milliliters = _0.045_ liters
5. 6.7 grams = _6700_ milligrams
6. 23 hectoliters = _723,000_ milliliters
7. 528 meters = _0.528_ kilometers

213

Commonly Misused Words

Use the word **good** to describe a noun. **Good** is an adjective.

Example: She is a **good** teacher.

Use the word **well** to tell or ask how something is done or to describe someone's health. **Well** is an adverb. It describes a verb.

Example: She is not feeling **well**.

Directions: Write **good** or **well** on each line to finish the sentence correctly. The first one is done for you.

1. _good_ I could use a good/well book on how to fix bikes.
2. _well_ She did good/well on her oral presentation.
3. _well_ Do you feel good/well enough to go with us to the park?
4. _good_ That television program about penguins was good/well.
5. _well_ You should treat your family and friends good/well.
6. _well_ The baby can walk good/well.
7. _well_ Did you see how good/well he kicked the ball?
8. _good_ You did a good/well job writing that report.
9. _good_ Keep up the good/well work!
10. _good_ Complaining too much is not a good/well thing to do.
11. _well_ We went out to dinner, because I did good/well on my report card.
12. _well_ The dog does those tricks good/well.

214

Words That Are Contractions

The word **they're** is a contraction for **they are**.

Examples: **They're** our very best friends!
Ask them if **they're** coming over tomorrow.

The word **their** shows ownership.

Examples: **Their** dog is friendly.
It is **their** bicycle.

The word **there** shows place or direction.

Examples: Look over **there**. **There** it is.

Directions: Write **they're**, **their**, or **there** on each line to finish the sentence correctly. The first one is done for you.

1. **There** They're/Their/There is the boy that has been teasing me.
2. **their** Who are they're/their/there parents?
3. **Their** They're/Their/There cat keeps coming into our backyard.
4. **there** We're going over they're/their/there to play ball.
5. **they're** Do you know what they're/their/there serving for dinner?
6. **their** I would like to know they're/their/there address so I can send a postcard.
7. **there** He has to be they're/their/there by seven o'clock.
8. **there** The clouds over they're/their/there look very dark.
9. **They're** They're/their/there going to be here soon.
10. **there** The animals they're/their/there are fun to watch.
11. **their** She wants they're/their/there stay to be pleasant.
12. **They're** They're/their/there meeting us here for lunch.

215

Commonly Misused Words

The word **sit** means to rest.

Examples: Please **sit** here!
Will you **sit** by me?

The word **set** means to put or place something.

Examples: **Set** your purse there.
Set the dishes on the table.

Directions: Write **sit** or **set** on each line to finish the sentence correctly. The first one is done for you.

1. **sit** I would like you to sit/set beside me.
2. **set** You can sit/set your bag on the counter.
3. **set** He sit/set the dirty dishes in the sink.
4. **sit** Please sit/set here and wait for the nurse.
5. **set** She sit/set her watch back an hour.
6. **set** Can you sit/set these papers on the desk?
7. **sit** I would like to sit/set here with you, but I have to go.
8. **set** The farmer sit/set the food in the trough.
9. **Set** Sit/Set the table, please.
10. **sit** Instead of cleaning up the mess, he decided to sit/set down to rest.
11. **Set** Sit/Set the blocks on top of each other.
12. **Sit** Sit/Set still!

216

Words About Japan

Directions: Follow the directions from 1 to 9 to complete the map of Japan.

1. Label the islands in capital letters:
   KYUSHU-southernmost
   HOKKAIDO-northernmost
   HONSHU-south of Hokkaido
   SHIKOKU-north of Kyushu
2. Add a red (set a star) and label the capital city, Tokyo.
3. Draw a mountain at Mount Fuji's location.
4. Label **Nagasaki** (by the dot on Kyushu Island.)
5. Label the **Sea of Japan** and the **Pacific Ocean**. Add blue waves.
6. Label **Osaka** by the dot on Honshu Island.
7. Outline the islands in these colors:
   Hokkaido-orange
   Honshu-green
   Shikoku-red
   Kyushu-yellow
8. Along the northern edge of the box, label the map **JAPAN**, using a different color for each letter.
9. Draw the flag of Japan under the map.

217

Words About Magnets

The ends of a magnet are called its **poles**. One pole is called the north-seeking pole or north pole; the other is the south-seeking pole, or south pole.

When the poles of two bar magnets are put near each other, they have a force that will either pull them together or push them apart. If the poles are **different**, then they will pull together, or **attract** each other. (One pole is a south pole and one pole is a north pole.) If the poles are the **same**, then they will push apart, or **repel** each other. (They are either both south poles or both north poles.) The push and pull force of a magnet is called **magnetism**.

Directions: Write attract or repel on each line to tell what happens when the magnets are brought toward each other.

1. repel
2. repel
3. attract
4. repel

218

Words About Magnets

Directions: Read about Earth and magnets. Then, follow the directions below to complete the map.

Earth is like a big magnet and has magnetic poles just like a magnet.

A **compass** is a free-turning magnet. Compasses that you buy are made with a thin magnet, called a **needle**, that turns freely inside a case. The case is made of a non-magnetic material. The north-seeking pole of the magnet is attracted toward Earth's magnetic north pole. The other end points to the magnetic south pole. A compass helps you find the directions north and south.

There is a **compass rose** in the bottom right corner of the map. The compass rose gives the eight compass directions: North (N), South (S), East (E), West (W), Northeast (NE), Southeast (SE), Southwest (SW), and Northwest (NW).

Directions:
1. Start at the star.
2. Go North 5 steps.
3. Go East 9 steps.
4. Go Southwest 4 steps.
5. Go East 2 steps.
6. Go South 2 steps.
7. Go Northeast 4 steps.
8. Draw an X to show your final location!

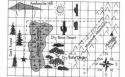

219

Words About Magnets

Electromagnets are made of wire that is tightly wound around an iron core and connected to a source of electricity. When electricity flows through the wire, the iron core behaves like a permanent magnet. When the flow of electricity stops, the iron core is no longer magnetic. Electromagnets are some of the strongest magnets in the world.

Directions: You can find electromagnets all around your home. The words in the Word Bank name machines or devices that contain electromagnets. Use the Word Bank find and circle the hidden words. Look across and down.

Word Bank

doorbell	motor	radio	refrigerator
stereo	tape recorder	telephone	television

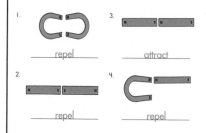

220

Metric Words

Directions: Solve each metric problem. Write your answer on the line.

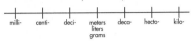

milli- centi- deci- meters deca- hecto- kilo-
                        liters
                        grams

1. Rafael wants to measure the hallway to find out how much room on the wall he has for his mural. What metric unit of measure should he use and why?
   He should use meters, because he wants to measure length.

2. Elma has a 4-liter bottle of glue for refilling smaller bottles. The small bottles hold 200 milliliters. How many small bottles can she fill from the big one?
   20

3. Meg has a plastic art case that is 4 centimeters by 4 centimeters. She found a shell for a project she's making that is 34 millimeters long. Will it fit in her case?
   yes

4. Rena made a woven mat that is 1.27 meters long. How long is it?
   a. in centimeters 127
   b. in decimeters 12.7
   c. in millimeters 1,270

5. Shane knows that he needs 3,500 milliliters of paint to finish his project. Paint is sold in 1-liter bottles. How many bottles does he need to buy in order to have enough paint?
   4

6. Natasha is using glitter to decorate stars for the school play. Is the glitter measured in grams or meters?
   grams

221

Words That Are Contractions

The word **its** shows ownership.

Examples: **Its** leaves have all turned green.
Its paw was injured.

The word **it's** is a contraction for **it is**.

Examples: **It's** better to be early than late.
It's not fair!

Directions: Write **its** or **it's** on each line to finish the sentence correctly. The first one is done for you.

1. It's Its/It's never too late for ice cream!
2. Its Its/It's eyes are already open.
3. It's Its/It's your turn to wash the dishes!
4. Its Its/It's cage was left open.
5. Its Its/It's engine was beyond repair.
6. Its Its/It's teeth were long and pointed.
7. its Did you see its/it's hind legs?
8. it's Why do you think its/it's mine?
9. it's Do you think its/it's the right color?
10. its Don't pet its/it's fur too hard!
11. It's Its/It's from my Uncle Harry.
12. it's Can you tell its/it's a surprise?
13. its Is its/it's stall always this clean?
14. It's Its/It's not time to eat yet.

222

Commonly Misused Words

The word **than** is used to show a difference.

Example: Your feet are bigger **than** mine.

The word **then** means next.

Example: Let's go to the end of the block. **Then**, I'll race you.

Directions: Write **than** or **then** on each line to finish the sentence correctly. The first one is done for you.

1. than You are much taller then/than I.
2. then If you invited me, than/then I would go.
3. then I was planning on going, and then/than I had a change of plans.
4. than This movie is funnier than/then the last one we saw.
5. Then Read the story. Then/Than, answer the questions.
6. than I would rather play soccer then/than watch cartoons.
7. then I settled into the car, and then/than I put on my seatbelt.
8. than Today is a colder day than/then yesterday.
9. Then First the leaves turned yellow. Then/Than, they fell off the tree.
10. than No season is more colorful then/than the fall.

223

Words That Are Contractions

The word **who's** is a contraction meaning **who is**.

Example: **Who's** your teacher this year?

The word **whose** indicates possession.

Example: **Whose** book is this?

Directions: Write **who's** or **whose** on each line to finish the sentence correctly. The first one is done for you.

1. Whose Whose/Who's responsibility is it to erase the board?
2. Who's Who's/Whose on your baseball team, Jake?
3. who's This is the girl who's/whose a great dancer.
4. Who's Whose/Who's ready to answer the question?
5. whose Anthony, whose/who's desk is across from mine, is very smart.
6. Who's Who's/Whose your best friend in school?
7. Who's Who's/Whose sitting at Sara's desk?
8. whose Terrance, whose/who's mom owns a bakery, brought muffins today.
9. who's I need to know whose/who's not going on the trip.
10. who's Raoul, whose/who's absent today, is not going.

224

Words About Africa

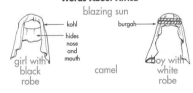

blazing sun

kohl

burgah

hides nose and mouth

girl with black robe

camel

boy with white robe

desert sand

Drawings will vary.

Tunisia is located in northeastern Africa. Much of the land is desert, so the people must protect themselves from sun and blowing sand. For this reason, many children wear special head coverings like the ones pictured.

Directions: Finish the picture above by following the instructions.

1. Use pencil to draw a boy wearing the burgah.
2. Draw a girl wearing the kohl.
3. Draw a white robe on the boy.
4. Draw a black robe on the girl.
5. Draw desert sand under their feet.
6. Draw the blazing sun.
7. Draw a camel nearby.
8. Color the boy and the girl.

225

Words About Magnets

Permanent magnets are the most familiar to us. The magnets on a refrigerator, for example, are permanent magnets. Once this type of material is magnetized, it never loses its level of magnetism.

Permanent magnets may be stronger or weaker depending upon the materials from which they are made. Certain materials are easily magnetized, including iron, steel, nickel, cobalt, and ceramics.

You Will Need: 1 magnet, 2 needles or straight pins, and paper clips

Directions:
Hold a needle close to a pile of paper clips. The needle and the paper clips are not attracted to each other.
Now, stroke the magnet 50 times in one direction (not back and forth) across the needle.
Hold the needle close to the pile of paper clips again. Count the number of paper clips that are attracted to the needle.
Stroke the magnet 75 times in one direction across the second needle.
Hold this needle close to the pile of paper clips. Count the number of paper clips that are attracted to the needle.

1. Did you pick up more paper clips with the first or second needle?
   Answers will vary.

2. What do you think this means?

226

Words About Magnets

Directions: Read about electromagnets. Then, answer the questions.

Some of the most powerful magnets are made with electricity. These magnets are called **electromagnets**. A strong magnet can be made by winding wire around an iron bar. As soon as the current from a battery is switched on, the bar becomes a strong electromagnet. The magnet can be switched off by stopping the flow of current.

Larry and Eddie each made an electromagnet. Only one of them worked.

 Larry   **Eddie**

1. Whose electromagnet worked? __Larry's__
2. Why wouldn't the other electromagnet work? __Eddie's wouldn't work, because the flow of current was switched off.__
3. Electromagnets have many uses and can be found in many places. Write a sentence to tell how and where you use each electromagnet.
   a. doorbell __Sentences will vary.__
   b. radio _____
   c. motor _____
   d. television _____
   e. telephone _____
   f. refrigerator _____

227

Words About Magnets

Directions: Write a word from the Word Bank to fit each clue. When you are finished, the letters in the squares will form a word that means "attracted to a magnet."

Word Bank			
paper clip	attract	locker	chain
refrigerator	nail	can	metal

1. It is shiny and can be melted. m e t a l
2. Soup is sold in it. c a n
3. Cold food is inside. r e f r i g e r a t o r
4. A carpenter uses this. n a i l
5. Where to store your coat in school l o c k e r
6. To pull close a t t r a c t
7. Many metal links c h a i n
8. This holds papers together. p a p e r c l i p

228

Unit 9 Review

Directions: Write the letter of the definition in the right column that matches the word on the left.

1. __n__ Sahara
2. __l__ well
3. __k__ may
4. __a__ their
5. __l__ attract
6. __b__ Tokyo
7. __m__ meters
8. __e__ these
9. __h__ compass
10. __f__ electromagnets
11. __d__ kohl
12. __i__ you're
13. __g__ Africa
14. __c__ poles

a. a word that shows ownership
b. the capital of Japan
c. opposite points of a magnet
d. a head covering that hides the nose and mouth
e. an adjective that refers to things that are near
f. some of the strongest magnets in the world
g. the second largest continent
h. a free-turning magnet
i. a contraction of "you are"
j. an adverb used to describe a verb
k. a word that means be allowed to or permitted to
l. draw near
m. metric unit used to measure length
n. the largest desert in the world

229

Words to Use Instead

It's easy to use certain words again and again. Try giving these "tired" words a break! Instead of a "wonderful" time, try using a different word.

Example: I had an **extraordinary** time at the party!
I had a **marvelous** time at the party!

Directions: Write three words that can replace the first.

1. nice __Words will vary.__ _____
2. beautiful _____ _____ _____
3. good _____ _____ _____
4. many _____ _____ _____

Directions: Write a paragraph about a class field trip. Use the words that you wrote above to make your paragraph interesting.

__Paragraphs will vary.__ _____

_____

_____

_____

_____

_____

231

Words to Use Instead

Specific words tell the reader more information than vague or unclear words. Read the examples in the box.

vivid verb:	The bubble broke. The bubble **burst**.
added names:	The teacher cried when she read the book. **Mrs. Brenner** cried when she read **The Invisible Man**.
specific word:	He saw something in the water. He saw a **jellyfish** in the water.

Directions: Read each sentence. Then, circle the revised sentence that makes it clearer. A hint after each sentence tells what kind of specific word is needed.

1. He stood by the fire and looked out at the snow. (name)
   a. The old man stood by the fire and looked out at the snow.
   b. (Old Mr. Janski stood by the fire and looked out at the snow.)

2. My friend broke the mirror in the bathroom. (vivid verb)
   a. Someone broke the bathroom mirror.
   b. (My friend shattered the mirror in the bathroom.)

3. The thief left some stuff in the safe. (specific word)
   a. The thief left some valuables in the safe.
   b. (The thief left some diamonds in the safe.)

4. A scientist looked through the microscope. (name and specific words)
   a. (Dr. Singh, the famous chemist, looked through the microscope.)
   b. The scientist looked through the old microscope.

232

Words to Use Instead

Good writing helps the reader to see something in his or her mind. When writing, **don't tell** the reader about what is happening. **Show** the reader. Use words to paint a picture for the reader to see.

Examples: tell: The meadow was pretty.

show: The alpine meadow glittered with the early morning dew. Tiny, white wildflowers bloomed among the meadow grass. The air was cool.

Directions: Read the sentences. Then, circle the letter of the sentence that shows the reader what is happening.

1. a. Trey ran all the way back to the school.
   b. He went back to school.
   c. (Trey bolted three blocks back to school.)

2. a. The bees flew around Beth's head.
   b. (Thirty bees buzzed around Beth's head.)
   c. There were lots of bees near Beth.

3. a. (She stomped her feet and screamed at me.)
   b. She was mad at me.
   c. She got mad and yelled at me.

4. a. The player was dirty.
   b. The player had mud on his clothes.
   c. (The player's clothes were crusted with black dirt.)

5. a. Rebbie was happy for her father.
   b. (Rebbie smiled proudly at her father.)
   c. Rebbie felt very happy for her dad.

233

Transportation Words

Directions: Read about "horseless carriages." Then, answer the questions.

Do you know how people traveled before cars? They rode horses! Often the horses were hooked up to wagons. Some horses were hooked up to carriages. Wagons were used to carry supplies. Carriages had covered tops. They were used to carry people. Both wagons and carriages were pulled by horses.

The first cars in the United States were invented shortly before the year 1900. These cars looked a lot like carriages. The seats were high off the ground. They had very thin wheels. The difference was that they were powered by engines. Carriages were pulled by horses. Still, they looked alike. People called the first cars "horseless carriages."

1. Write one way wagons and carriages were the same.
   Suggested answer:
   Wagons and carriages were pulled by horses.

2. When were the first cars invented?
   The first cars were invented shortly before the year 1900.

3. Why were the first cars called "horseless carriages"?
   Suggested answer:
   The first cars looked like carriages but were not pulled by horses.

4. What was the difference between a carriage and a "horseless carriage"?
   A carriage was pulled by a horse. A "horseless carriage" was powered by an engine.

234

Words About Simple Machines

Look at the children in the picture. How are they moving their friends? A push or a pull on something is called a **force**. Forces can cause an object to move, slow down, speed up, change direction, or stop.

Directions: You use pushing and pulling forces to move objects. Write five ways that you use each of these forces.

Pushing Forces *Suggested answers:*
1. pushing a vacuum cleaner
2. shoveling the driveway
3. mowing the lawn
4.
5.

Pulling Forces *Suggested answers:*
1. pulling window blinds shut
2. starting a lawnmower
3. shutting a door
4.
5.

Directions: It takes more force to move some objects than it does to move others. Circle the object in each picture that would take more force to move.

235

Words About Simple Machines

Simple machines have been used for hundreds of years. The castle builders in Europe did not have modern machines. But they did have some simple machines to help them make their castles.

Directions: Look carefully at the men building the castle. They are working hard, but their simple machines are missing. Use the Picture Bank to draw the missing machines.

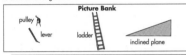

Picture Bank

pulley   lever   ladder   inclined plane

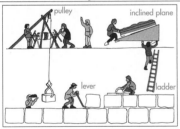

pulley   inclined plane
lever   ladder

236

Words About Simple Machines

Machines help to make work like pushing, pulling, and lifting easier. A machine is often made up of different parts that move, is sometimes big and complicated, and is other times small and simple.

Read the examples and definitions of some simple machines.

Lever—A hammer can be used as a kind of lever. This type of machine helps to move things with less force.

Wheel and axle—(such as those on a wagon or car) Wheels can be used to move things more easily from one place to another.

Pulley—A pulley can be used to hoist a flag or sail. Pulleys can be used to lift loads more easily.

Screw—Screws are typically used to hold things together. Sometimes screws are used to lift hinges such as the seat of a chair.

Wedge—An ax is an example of a kind of wedge. Wedges help cut or split things.

Inclined plane—A ramp up to a building is an example of an inclined plane. This type of simple machine can be used to move things from a lower place to a higher place and vice versa.

Directions: On another sheet of paper, make a collage of machines you use or see every day. Use books about machines, drawing paper, crayons, markers, magazines, and newspapers.

237

Early Algebra Words

In math, there are some basic rules that always apply.

The **commutative property** says that you can add or multiply numbers in any order without changing the outcome.

Examples: $1 + 2 = 2 + 1$ $2 \times 3 = 3 \times 2$

The **associative property** says that you can group numbers when adding or multiplying in any way without changing the outcome.

Examples: $(5 + 6) + 1 = 5 + (6 + 1)$ $(4 \times 2) \times 3 = 4 \times (2 \times 3)$

Directions: Look at the addition and multiplication problems. Decide which property each problem demonstrates. Then, write **commutative property** or **associative property** on the line.

1. $1 + 2 + 3 + 4 + 5 = 2 + 1 + 3 + 5 + 4$ commutative property

2. $1 \times 1 \times 8 = 1 \times 8 \times 1$ commutative property

3. $8 + 9 + (10 + 11) = 8 + (9 + 10) + 11$ associative property

4. $25,262 \times (4,000,000 \times 3) =$
   $(25,262 \times 4,000,000) \times 3$ associative property

238

Words to Use Instead

Some verbs, such as **went** or **said**, are used too often. Changing an overused verb to an exciting or **vivid verb** can add more meaning to a sentence. It can also make your sentence more fun to read.

overused:	vivid:
went	skipped
went	zoomed
said	yelled
said	whispered

Directions: Circle a vivid verb to complete each sentence. Then, write it on the line.

1. A train _zoomed_ into the tunnel. (went, (zoomed))
2. A person was _strapped_ to the tracks. ((strapped), tied)
3. She _cried_, "Help!" (said, (cried))
4. I _streaked_ across the sky. ((streaked), flew)
5. The train _roared_ louder. (seemed, (roared))
6. Its headlight _burned_ brightly. ((burned), shone)
7. I _rescued_ the girl just in time. (found, (rescued))
8. I _pulled_ her from the tracks. (got, (pulled))
9. The train _thundered_ past us. (went, (thundered))
10. The girl _shouted_, "You saved my life!" ((shouted), said)

239

ANSWER key

Library Words

Reference books are books that tell basic facts. Usually, you cannot check them out from the library. **Dictionaries** and **encyclopedias** are reference books. A dictionary tells you about words. Encyclopedias give you other information, such as when the president was born, when the Civil War took place, and where Eskimos live. Encyclopedias usually come in sets of more than 20 books. Information is listed in alphabetical order, just like the words in a dictionary. There are other kinds of reference books, too, like books of maps called **atlases**. You likely will not need to read a reference book from cover to coverr.

Directions: Draw a line from each sentence to the correct type of book. The first one is done for you.

1. I can tell you the definition of **divide**.

2. I can tell you when George Washington was born.

3. I can give you the correct spelling for many words.

4. I can tell you where Native Americans live.

5. I can tell you the names of many butterflies.

6. I can tell you what **modern** means.

7. I can give you the history of dinosaurs.

8. If you have to write a paper about Eskimos, I can help you.

240

Library Words

Directions: Read about periodicals. Then, complete the activities.

Libraries have **periodicals**, such as **magazines** and **newspapers**. They are called periodicals because they are printed regularly within a set period of time. There are many kinds of magazines. Some discuss the news. Others cover fitness, cats, or other topics of special interest. Almost every city or town has a newspaper. Newspapers are usually printed daily, weekly, or even monthly. Newspapers cover what is happening in your town and in the world. They usually include sections on sports and entertainment. They present a lot of information.

1. Choose an interesting magazine.
   What is the name of the magazine? <u>Answers will vary.</u>
   Write the titles of three articles in the magazine.
   _____
   _____
   _____

2. Now, look at a newspaper.
   What is the name of the newspaper? _____
   The title of a newspaper story is called a **headline**.
   Write two headlines from your local newspaper.
   _____
   _____
   _____

241

Transportation Words

Directions: Read about the first trains. Then, answer the questions.

A train is a connected series of cars that moves along tracks. Trains have been around much longer than cars or trucks. The first train that Americans used came from England. The United States brought it back in 1829. Because it was light green, people nicknamed it "Grasshopper." Unlike a real grasshopper, this train was not fast. It traveled only 10 miles an hour.

In the same year, an American built another train. Compared to the Grasshopper, the American train was fast. It traveled 30 miles an hour. People were amazed. They called this train the "Rocket."

1. Where was the first train made that was used by the United States?
   <u>The first train used in the United States was made in England.</u>
2. What did people call this train?
   <u>People called this train "Grasshopper."</u>
3. How fast did it travel?
   <u>The Grasshopper traveled 10 miles an hour.</u>
4. What year did the Grasshopper arrive in the United States?
   <u>The Grasshopper arrived in the United States in 1829.</u>
5. What American train was built that same year?
   <u>The Rocket was the American train built that same year.</u>

242

Words About Simple Machines

A doorknob is a simple machine you use every day. It is a **wheel-and-axle** machine. The wheel is connected to the axle. The axle is a center post. When the wheel moves, the axle does, too.

Opening a door by turning the axle with your fingers is very hard. But by turning the doorknob, which is the "wheel," you use much less force. The doorknob turns the axle for you. The doorknob makes it easy because it is much bigger than the axle. You turn the doorknob a greater distance, but with much less force.

Sometimes the "wheel" of a wheel-and-axle machine doesn't look like a wheel. But look at the path the doorknob makes when it is turned. The path makes a circle, just like a wheel.

Directions: Color only the wheels of the wheel-and-axle machines. Then, answer the questions.

1. A screwdriver is a wheel and axle. What part of a screwdriver is the wheel? <u>the handle</u>
2. What part of a screwdriver is the axle? <u>the blade</u>
3. Which screwdriver has the largest wheel? <u>the one on the right</u>
4. Which screwdriver would take the least amount of force to turn? <u>the larger one</u>

243

Words About Simple Machines

An eggbeater has a special kind of wheel. It is called a **gear**. A gear is a wheel with teeth. The teeth allow one gear to turn another gear.

Gears are often used to increase or decrease speed. If the large gear turns one time, the small gear will turn two times.

Directions: You can find gears in many machines. Find and circle all of the machine words in the puzzle. Look across, down, and diagonally. Then, write only the machines that use gears.

```
S T K N Z O R K G
H A M M E R U T K
O P S O R P R C N
V G Z V F A O T S
E L B O I C L G X
U Z N E C B J Y Z
D C K T P W I T G
C R T R U C K G K
R K T M O X Y T U
A T N J S C L V H
K N N E G R L V M
E P S C Q E W T Z
P L K C G Z T E S
Z U T R A M P N P
```

Machines with Gears
<u>clock</u>
<u>truck</u>
<u>eggbeater</u>
<u>movie projector</u>
<u>bicycle</u>

244

Words About Simple Machines

Directions: Use the words in the Word Bank to complete the sentences.

Word Bank		
machine	easier	force
inclined	shorter	longer

Simple machines help people do work. In the picture above, the ramp makes the man's work a lot <u>easier</u>. The ramp is a simple <u>machine</u> called an inclined plane.

An <u>inclined</u> plane makes work easier. It lessens the amount of force needed to move a load. By using the ramp, the man moves the barrel with much less force than if he tried to lift the barrel himself. With the ramp, the man moves the barrel a <u>longer</u> distance, but with much less force. By just lifting the barrel onto the truck, he would move it a <u>shorter</u> distance, but he would need to use much more <u>force</u>.

Directions: People use ramps in many different places. They are especially useful for people in wheelchairs. Write the names of places where you have seen ramps in your community.

1. <u>Answers will vary.</u>
2. _____
3. _____

245

Early Algebra Words

The **distributive property** is important when an addition problem is multiplied by something. According to this property, you can add first and then multiply the sum, or you can multiply first and then add together the products. You "distribute" the multiplication across the problem.

Examples: $3 \times (4 + 5) = (3 \times 4) + (3 \times 5)$

Directions: On the lines below, write an explanation for the distributive property in your own words. Then, write your own example.

Answers will vary.

246

Library Words

Directions: Use the words in the Word Bank to complete the crossword puzzle about the library.

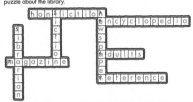

Word Bank
reference	nonfiction	newspaper	magazine
librarian	encyclopedia	fiction	adult's

Across:
1. A book based on facts is _____.
4. You can research Abraham Lincoln's life in this book.
6. If you are not in the children's section, then you may be in the _____ section.
7. This is a kind of periodical.
8. Dictionaries and encyclopedias are included in this section.

Down:
2. A story that someone has made up is _____.
3. This can be delivered to your home every day.
5. If you cannot find what you are looking for, ask this person for help.

247

Library Words

A **library** is a place filled with books. People can borrow the books and take them home. When they are finished reading them, people return the books to the library. Most libraries have two sections: One is for adult books and one is for children's books. A **librarian** is there to help people find books.

Directions: Read the title of each library book. On each line, write **A** if the book is written for an adult or **C** if it is written for a child.

1. Sam Squirrel Goes to the City — C
2. Barney Beagle Plays Baseball — C
3. Sammy's Silly Poems — C
4. Understanding Your Child — A
5. Learn to Play Guitar — A
6. Bake Bread in Five Easy Steps — A
7. The Selling of the President — A
8. Jenny's First Party — C

248

Library Words

Directions: Paul and Maria want to learn about the moon. Answer the questions to help them find the information they are looking for.

1. Should they look in the children's section or in the adult's section? — children's
2. Should they look for a fiction book or a nonfiction book? — nonfiction
3. Who at the library can help them? — librarian
4. What reference books should they look at? — encyclopedias
5. Where can they find information that might have been in the news? — newspapers
6. What word would they look up in the encyclopedia to get the information they need? — moon

249

Transportation Words

Directions: Read about the first cars. Then, use the bold words to complete the puzzle.

Can you guess how many cars there were in the United States about 100 years ago? Only four! Today, nearly every family has a car. Most families have two cars. **Henry** Ford started the Ford **Motor** Company in 1903. His first car was called the **Model T**. People thought cars would never be used in place of **horses**. Ford had to sell his cars through department **stores**! Soon, cars became popular. By 1920, there were 200 different U.S. companies making **cars**!

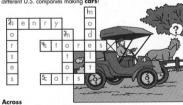

Across
2. _____ Ford began making cars in 1903.
4. At first, cars were sold in department _____.
5. By 1920, there were 200 different companies making these.

Down
1. Henry Ford's first car was called a _____.
2. At first, people thought cars would never replace _____.
3. Ford's company was called the Ford _____ Company.

250

Words About Simple Machines

Directions: Use the words in the Word Bank to complete the sentences. Then, label the picture with these words: **load**, **force**, and **fulcrum**.

Word Bank
simple	force
easier	load
fulcrum	distance

Mandy wants to try to lift her dad off the ground. Where should Mandy stand on the board? By standing on point B, Mandy can lift her dad.

The board resting on the log is an example of a _simple_ machine called a lever. A **lever** has three parts—the **force**, the **fulcrum**, and the **load**. Mandy is the force. The point on which the lever turns is called the _fulcrum_. And Mandy's dad, the object to be lifted, is called the _load_. The greater the _distance_ between the _force_ and the fulcrum, the _easier_ it is to lift the load. The closer the distance between the **force** and the **fulcrum**, the harder it is to lift the load.

Directions: Label the force, fulcrum, and load on the levers.

251

Words About Simple Machines

Directions: Read the story. Then, answer the questions.

"Poof!" Leroy just shrank himself again in his "Super Electro Shrinking Machine." He is trying to decide which would be easier—climbing around and around the threads of a screw to get to the top or just climbing straight up the side of the screw. He found that the distance up the winding ramp is a lot farther, but the traveling is much easier than going straight up the side. The winding ramp of the screw is like a spiral stairway.

1. Would you travel a farther distance climbing a spiral stairway up three floors or climbing a ladder straight up three floors?
   climbing a spiral stairway

2. Which would take more force to climb—the stairway or the ladder? the ladder

3. When you climb a spiral stairway, you travel a greater _____distance_____ , but you use less _____force_____ .

Directions: Read about special inclined planes. Then, label each picture with the word **wedge** or **screw**.

A **screw** is a special kind of inclined plane. A spiral stairway is also an inclined plane. Two or more inclined planes that are joined together to make a sharp edge or point form a wedge. A **wedge** is a special kind of inclined plane. It is used to pierce or split things. A knife is an example of a wedge.

screw   wedge   wedge   wedge

252

Words About Simple Machines

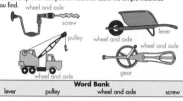

levers

gears

wheel and axle

Many of the machines that you use each day are made up of two or more simple machines. Look at the simple machines labeled on the bicycle. Machines that are made out of two or more simple machines are called **compound machines**.

Directions: Look at the compound machines. Find the simple machines that make up each compound machine. Label the simple machines you find.

wheel and axle

screw

pulley

wheel and axle

wheel and axle

lever

wheel and axle

gear

Word Bank			
lever	pulley	wheel and axle	screw

253

Unit 10 Review

Directions: Pretend that you are an inventor. Think of a machine that you could invent that would make your life or someone else's life easier. Do research at the library to get ideas. Write about your invention and what it can do. Use vivid and specific words to describe your machine. Then, draw a picture of your invention. Label the simple machines that you used.

Answers will vary.

Pictures will vary.

254

Poetry Words

Poetry tells about feelings, ideas, or events, often with fewer words than regular writing. Some poems rhyme and some poems do not. A poem can be whatever the writer wants it to be. Poems do not need to have complete sentences.

A **couplet** is a pair of rhyming lines. Poems can be made by combining couplets. Line **a** rhymes with another line **a**, and line **b** rhymes with another line **b**.

Sometimes the rhymes are together, like this:

a Carrots, beans, or peas?
a Who wants to eat these?
b I won't tell a lie.
b We'd like cake and pie.

Sometimes the rhymes are apart, like this:

a A timeless tree stood
b on the edge of a dream,
a and thought that he could
b run like the stream.

Directions: Choose the correct word to complete each couplet. Then, write it on the line.

1. a City noises, dirty air, crowded street.
   a Country sun, soaring birds, rows of _wheat_ .
      i. corn   ii. wheat   iii. streets

2. a In an alley paved with trash, a flower grows.
   b It stands alone, an upturned bell.
   a How did it get there? The cruel wind knows,
   b A secret the wind will never _tell_ .
      i. knows   ii. stirs   iii. tell

3. a A shower of tears rains down on the stone.
   a This mountain and I are both soaked to the _bone_ .
      i. clothes   ii. bone   iii. skin.

256

Poetry Words

A **cinquain** is a special five-line poem. It does not have to rhyme, but the lines follow a specific format.

Line 1: Noun (topic of poem)
Line 2: Two adjectives (describe the topic)
Line 3: Three verbs (actions that relate to the topic)
Line 4: Two more adjectives
Line 5: Noun (another word for the topic)

Directions: Read the cinquain. Then, write your own. Draw a picture to go along with your poem.

Example:

Spring
Bright, cheerful
Raining, blooming, dancing
Fresh, new
Beginning

Poems and pictures will vary.

noun

_____ adjective _____ adjective

_____ verb _____ verb _____ verb

_____ adjective _____ adjective

_____ noun

257

Poetry Words

Directions: A **cinquain** follows the format described below. Write your own cinquain about the sun, moon, or stars.

Star Maiden
Beautiful, bright
Shining, glittering, sparkling
Came to live on earth
Water Lily

Line 1: a noun (topic of poem)
Line 2: two adjectives that describe the noun
Line 3: three verbs with ing endings that tell what the noun does
Line 4: a phrase or sentence that tells something special about the noun
Line 5: a synonym for the noun. Repeat the noun if there is no synonym.

Poems will vary.

258

Job Words

Directions: Follow the instructions below.

1. In each sentence, circle the word that means the same as **teacher**.

   My (educator) is a tall man.
   I will ask the (professor) for help.
   We played basketball outside with the (instructor).

2. Look at the word **teacher**. Within this word, underline the smaller word that tells what a teacher does. Then, study the list of verbs in the box. Circle the verbs that mean almost the same as the word you underlined.

(educate)	sing	(inform)	dance
(instruct)	(train)	stand	read

3. Write one or two complete sentences that tell about your favorite **teacher**. Why do you like him or her? What does he or she teach? Draw a picture of your special **teacher**.

   <u>Answers will vary.</u>

   Pictures will vary.

259

Electricity Words

Have you ever scuffed your feet as you walked across the carpet and then brought your finger close to someone's nose? Zap! Did the person jump? The spark you made was **static electricity**.

Static electricity is made when objects gain or lose tiny bits of electricity called **electrical charges**. The charges are either positive or negative.

Objects that have electrical charges act like magnets, attracting or repelling each other. If two objects have **like charges** (the same kind of charges), they will repel each other. If the two objects have **unlike charges** (different charges), the objects will attract each other.

Directions: Find out more about static electricity. Unscramble the word(s) in each sentence. Then, write the words on the lines.

1. Flashes of (ghtlining) <u>lightning</u> in the sky are caused by static electricity in the clouds.

2. Electrical charges are either (ospivite) <u>positive</u> or (givnatee) <u>negative</u>.

3. Small units of electricity are called (srgache) <u>charges</u>.

4. Two objects with unlike charges will (arcttat) <u>attract</u> each other.

5. Sometimes electric charges jump between objects with (unkile) <u>unlike</u> charges. This is what happens when lightning flashes across the sky.

260

Electricity Words

A **circuit** is a path along which electricity travels. It travels in a loop around the circuit. In the circuit pictured below, the electricity travels through the wire, battery, switch, and bulb. The electricity must have a source. What is the source in this circuit? You're right if you said the battery.

If the wire in the circuit was cut, there would be a **gap**. The electricity wouldn't be able to flow across the gap. Then, the bulb would not light. This is an example of an **open circuit**. If there were no gaps, the bulb would light. This is an example of a **closed circuit**.

Directions: Follow the instructions below.
1. Draw in the wire to the battery, switch, and bulb to make a closed circuit.

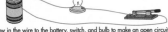

2. Draw in the wire to the battery, switch, and bulb to make an open circuit.

Directions: Unscramble the word at the end of each sentence. Then, write the word on the line.

1. Even the tiniest <u>gap</u> can stop the electricity from flowing. (apg)
2. A <u>circuit</u> is a path along which electricity flows. (rictuc)
3. If there are no gaps, or openings, a <u>closed</u> circuit is formed. (sodelc)

261

Electricity Words

The bulb won't light in the circuit above. What's wrong with the circuit? It has a gap. How could you fill the gap to make a closed circuit? The easiest way would be to connect the two wires, but with what?

What would happen if you placed a paper clip across the gap? How about a nail? The bulb would light up. The nail or paper clip will form a bridge across the gap. The nail and paper clip carry, or **conduct**, electricity. They are both **conductors**.

Some materials will not carry the electricity well enough to make the bulb light. Try a rubber band. The bulb won't light. Rubber is a poor conductor of electricity. It is called an **insulator**.

C O T T O N P
O K G T S O R
P A P E R X K
P L A S T I C
E U D T O R D
R M K E L O S
T I X E R N N
N N G U A S S
R U B B E R Z
K M G R X Z P

Directions: Find the different materials hidden in the word search. The materials listed up and down are conductors. Those written across are insulators. Write these materials in the correct group.

Conductor	Insulator
copper	cotton
aluminum	paper
steel	plastic
iron	glass
	rubber

Directions: Now that you know which materials make good conductors and which make good insulators, write **C** under each object that is a conductor and **I** under each object that is an insulator.

 C   I   C   I

262

Calendar Words

Directions: Use the calendar to answer the questions. Circle the correct answer.

April

S	M	T	W	T	F	S
				1	2	3
4	5	6	7	8	9	10
11	12	13	14	15	16	17
18	19	20	21	22	23	24
25	26	27	28	29	30	

1. If today is Friday, what day will tomorrow be?
   (A) Tuesday
   (B) Monday
   (C) Sunday
   (D) Saturday

2. If today is Friday, what day will the day after tomorrow be?
   (A) Tuesday
   (B) Monday
   (C) Sunday
   (D) Saturday

3. A carpenter who is building a deck will not work on May 2. What day is that?
   (A) Sunday
   (B) Monday
   (C) Tuesday
   (D) Saturday

4. Imagine that today is Thursday, April 8. What will the date be 3 weeks from now?
   (A) April 22
   (B) April 15
   (C) May 6
   (D) April 29

263

Poetry Words

A **diamante** is a special poem that is shaped like a diamond. You can write a diamante poem about any subject.

The diamante has a special format:

Line 1: Noun or pronoun — Monkey
Line 2: Two adjectives — Furry, small
Line 3: Three verbs — Swinging, walking, gathering
Line 4: Four-word phrase — Chewing leaves and twigs
Line 5: Three more verbs — Communicating, caring, moving
Line 6: Two more adjectives — Wild, climber
Line 7: Noun or pronoun — Primate

Directions: Write a diamante about yourself, a feeling, or even a science project!

<u>Poems will vary.</u>

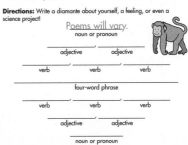

noun or pronoun

adjective   adjective

verb   verb   verb

four-word phrase

verb   verb   verb

adjective   adjective

noun or pronoun

264

Poetry Words

An **acrostic poem** has a special format. First, write a word vertically down the page. Then, choose describing words or phrases that begin with each letter of the word.

Example:

Light and breezy
Ever flowing in the wind
Autumn dawns
Fall to the ground

Directions: Write your own acrostic poem. Draw a border around your poem to show what it is about.

Poems and pictures
will vary.

265

Poetry Words

A **free-verse poem** does not have a special format. It can be in whatever form you like.

Directions: Complete the phrases below to help you write a free-verse poem about you! Then write your final poem in the box. Your poem doesn't have to rhyme!

I am _Answers will vary._
I hear _____.
I see _____.
I wish _____.
I feel happy when _____.
I feel frustrated when _____.
I get angry when _____.
I am puzzled by _____.
I dream about _____.
I wonder _____.
I plan to _____.
I hope _____.
I know _____.
I understand _____.
I learn _____.
I value _____.
I love _____.
I am afraid of _____.

Poems
will vary.

266

Job Words

Directions: It takes many people to build a shopping center. Write a sentence that explains how each person helps to build the shopping center.

1. architect

Sentences will vary.

2. carpenter

3. painter

4. plumber

5. gardener

6. roofer

7. electrician

267

Electricity Words

A **light bulb** changes electricity into light. Electricity passes through the very thin wire, called a **filament**, inside the bulb. As electricity flows through the filament, the wire gets hot and gives off light.

Look very closely at the filament in a light bulb. It is made of tiny coils of wire. By using coils, more wire can fit inside the bulb, and the bulb can produce more light.

Directions: Use the words in the Word Bank to label the parts of the light bulb.

Word Bank
coil filament
glass bulb
wire support
glass support
base

base
glass bulb
glass support
coil filament
wire support

For further investigation:
The first light bulb ever made had a filament made out of cotton! It burned brightly but didn't last long. Find out who invented the first light bulb and when it was invented.

268

Electricity Words

Directions: Read about electricity. Then, answer the questions.

"Jane, did you remember to turn off the TV?" Jane's parents want Jane to remember to conserve electricity. It takes a lot of fuel to make electricity. We have to be careful not to waste electricity.

Your house has an **electric meter** that measures the amount of electricity your family uses. The meter measures the electricity in **kilowatt hours**. It would take one kilowatt hour to light ten light bulbs (100 watts each) for one hour.

1. Would a 75-watt light bulb use more or less power than the 100-watt light bulb? _less_

2. Look at Jane's home. How could Jane conserve electricity?
Answers can include:
1. _turn off the fan_
2. _turn off the television_
3. _turn off the stereo_
4. _close the refrigerator door_
5. _close the door when the air conditioning is on_
6. _turn off the light when no one is in the room_

3. The electric meter on Jane's house is shown in Picture **A**. It reads 2,563 kilowatts. Picture **B** shows Jane's electric meter after one month. Write the number of kilowatts shown on the meter. Then, figure out the number of kilowatt hours Jane's family used in one month.

A. 2 5 6 3 kilowatts

B. _2 9 7 5_ 2 9 7 5 kilowatts
_- 2 5 6 3_
_4 1 2_ kilowatt hours

269

Electricity Words

Directions: Read about the telegraph. Then, complete the activities.

In 1877, Samuel Morse used electricity to make the first telegraph. This invention allowed people to communicate directly with one another over long distances.

1. Study the picture of the simple telegraph. Notice how the switch, light bulb, battery, and wire form a circuit. Use the symbols in the key to draw a diagram of the telegraph.

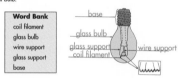

Simple Telegraph Diagram	Key
wire battery switch light bulb	⊣⊢ wire ⚬ battery ⊖ switch ◯ light bulb

Directions: Study the Morse Code. Then, decode the message below it.

Morse Code

A ·—	F ··—·	K —·—	P ·——·	U ··—
B —···	G ——·	L ·—··	Q ——·—	V ···—
C —·—·	H ····	M ——	R ·—·	W ·——
D —··	I ··	N —·	S ···	X —··—
E ·	J ·———	O ———	T —	Z ——··

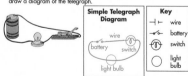

_W R I T E   A   S E C R E T_
_M E S S A G E   T O   A_
_F R I E N D_

270

Calendar Words

Directions: Use the calendar section to answer the questions.

Sun.	Mon.	Tues.	Wed.	Thurs.	Fri.	Sat.
		1	2	3	4	5
6	7	8				

1. Will there be a Friday the thirteenth this month?
   __no__

2. What date is the third Monday of the month?
   __21__

3. If today is Wednesday, how many days are there until Monday?
   __5__

4. What day of the week is the sixteenth?
   __Wednesday__

5. Will the fourteenth fall on a Sunday or a Monday?
   __Monday__

6. If today is Thursday, the day before yesterday was
   __Tuesday__.

7. If today is Tuesday, the day after tomorrow will be
   __Thursday__.

8. If yesterday was Monday, tomorrow will be
   __Wednesday__

9. If tomorrow will be Thursday, yesterday was
   __Tuesday__.

10. If the day after tomorrow will be Saturday, what was the day before yesterday?
    __Tuesday__

271

Poetry Words

Shape poems are words that form the shape of the thing being written about.

Example:

Directions: Create your own shape poem.

Poems will vary.

272

Poetry Words

Haiku is a form of Japanese poetry that is often about nature. There are 3 lines. The first line has 5 syllables. The second line has 7 syllables. The third line has 5 syllables.

Example:

The rain falls softly,	5
Touching the leaves on the trees,	7
Bathing tenderly.	5

Directions: Choose a topic in nature that would make a good haiku. Think of words to describe your topic. Then, write and illustrate your haiku.

Poems will vary.

Pictures will vary.

273

Poetry Words

A **limerick** is a fun type of rhyming poem. It has five lines in a special format. Limericks are usually funny or silly! Look at the format below.

	Number of Syllables	Rhyme Scheme
Line 1:	9	a
Line 2:	9	a
Line 3:	5	b
Line 4:	5	b
Line 5:	9	a

Example:
There once was a girl who was silly.
She lived in a place that was hilly.
She sneaked out at night
To fly her new kite.
It tossed her about willy-nilly.

Directions: Write your own limerick.

Poems will vary.

274

Job Words

Directions: This is a **Venn diagram**. It shows how things are the same or different. Write the ideas from the Word Bank where they belong in the Venn diagram. Three are done for you.

Word Bank			
help people	fight fires	ride cars	ride fire engines
fight crime	are brave	use sirens	give traffic tickets

police officers
give traffic tickets
fight crime

police officers and firefighters
help people
use sirens

firefighters
fight fires

ride cars   are brave   ride fire engines

Directions: Use the information in the Venn diagram to complete this compare-and-contrast paragraph.

Police officers and firefighters are brave. They both __use sirens__ to alert people on the road, but police officers __ride cars__, while firefighters __ride fire engines__. They both help people, but in different ways. Police officers __fight crime__ and firefighters __fight fires__. My dad only wishes that police officers didn't also __give traffic tickets__

275

Electricity Words

Steve and Lenny really enjoyed listening to the radio while they fished. Radios need electricity to work. Where did Steve's radio get its power? From a **dry cell battery**, of course. Dry cells are sources of portable power.

Most portable radios use dry cells. A dry cell makes electricity by changing chemical energy into electrical energy. Chemicals in the dry cell act on each other and make **electrons** flow. The flow of electrons is called **electricity**.

Directions: Use the words in the Word Bank to label the parts of the dry cell. You can use a science book for help, but first try to figure out each part by yourself.

Word Bank
chemical paste
carbon rod
zinc case
terminal

zinc case
terminal
chemical paste
carbon rod

Directions: Write the names of the appliances, tools, or toys in your house that are powered with dry cells.

Answers will vary.

276

Electricity Words

Directions: Someone is responsible for inventing each of these appliances. Try to think of your own invention. Describe it below.

Answers will vary.

277

Electricity Words

Directions: Make your own battery with the help of an adult.

You will need:
a lemon
two different pieces of metal (for example, a brass thumbtack and a steel paperclip)
copper wire
a flashlight bulb

Directions:
Push the two pieces of metal into the lemon. Make sure that the two metals do not touch one another!
Wrap copper wire around the ends of the metals and connect the other ends of the wire to a flashlight bulb.
The light bulb should light up.

The acid in the lemon acts as the electrolyte that allows particles to move to the electrodes (the thumbtack and the paperclip). The electricity then flows through the light bulb until the electrolyte (acid) around the metal pieces is no longer able to react.

278

Unit 11 Review

Directions: Draw a line to match each word to its description.

1. teacher — someone who educates
2. month — 12 of these make up a year
3. circuit — the path along which electricity travels
4. terminal — part of a battery
5. Haiku — a form of Japanese poetry
6. couplet — a rhyming pair of lines
7. cotton — a type of insulator
8. filament — the thin wire inside a light bulb
9. positive and negative — types of electrical charges
10. free verse — a poem that has no special format
11. conductor — a material that carries electricity
12. seven — the number of days in a week
13. cinquain — a special five-line poem
14. police officer — a protector

279

Words in an Expository Paragraph

An **expository paragraph** gives detailed information about a topic. It tells facts, opinions, or both.

Example: My favorite sport is swimming. It is not only fun and refreshing on a hot day, but it is also a great way to exercise. I go swimming almost every day in the summer.

Directions: Write an expository paragraph to tell about each subject.

1. My favorite pastime is
   Paragraphs will vary.

2. Summer is important to me because

3. My ambition in life is to be a

4. If I could be anywhere in the world,

281

Words in a Compare-and-Contrast Paragraph

To **compare** is to notice the similarities and differences between two things. Another way to say this is **compare and contrast**.

Directions: Compare books and movies. Write a list of the ways they are the same and a list of the ways they are different.

Ways they are the same:
Answers will vary.

Ways they are different:

Directions: Use your ideas to write a paragraph about the similarities between books and movies and a paragraph about their differences. Begin both paragraphs with topic sentences.
Paragraphs will vary.

282

Words in a Persuasive Paragraph

A **persuasive paragraph** is a way to express strong opinions and to try to make others feel the same way.

To write a persuasive paragraph:
- Choose a topic.
- Write a topic sentence that states your strong opinion and why you feel this way.
- Write several supporting sentences that give your reasons. Try to include several facts as well as feelings.
- End with a concluding sentence that summarizes your strong opinion.

Directions: Follow the steps to plan a persuasive paragraph.

1. Topic (state your opinion)
   Answers will vary.

2. Topic Sentence

3. Supporting Sentences

4. Concluding Sentence

283

Words About Famous People

Directions: Read the paragraph about Neil Armstrong. Then, answer the questions.

Neil Armstrong was born on August 5, 1930. From an early age, Armstrong took a great interest in planes and began flying lessons as soon as he was old enough. In college, he studied aerospace engineering. After college, Armstrong worked in a number of different fields of flight, finally joining the National Aeronautics and Space Administration (NASA) in 1962. It wasn't until 1969 that Armstrong participated in the legendary flight of Apollo 11 to the moon, serving as the first human being to ever set foot on its surface. When Armstrong took his first step, he made the famous statement, "That's one small step for [a] man, one giant leap for mankind."

1. What does "aerospace" mean?
   Aerospace refers to the Earth's atmosphere and the space outside it.

2. Summarize Armstrong's life leading up to his flight on Apollo 11.
   Armstrong was interested in planes, took flying lessons as a young man, studied aerospace engineering in college, worked in different fields of flight, and finally joined NASA.

3. Imagine you were Armstrong, taking your first step on the moon. Describe your experience.
   Answers will vary.

284

Words About Earth

Thousands of years ago, people made up stories to explain things that happened in their world. Those stories are called **myths**.

Directions: Read the myths about Earth. Then, complete the activity at the bottom of the page.

1. Some ancient cultures believed that Earth was held by huge figures. For example, the Greeks believed that Atlas carried the sky on his shoulders. When he shrugged his shoulders, an earthquake took place.

2. Another Greek legend says that when Poseidon, the sea god, was angry, he banged the sea floor with his trident (or spear), causing storms at sea.

3. Aerial views of craters look like giant eyes. Mount Vesuvius's crater may have inspired the Greek myth of the Cyclops, a tribe of one-eyed giants.

4. It is said that the powerful goddess, Pele, lives in the crater Halemaumau at the summit of Kilauea on Hawaii and makes mountains, melts rocks, destroys forests and builds new islands.

Extension activity:
Look up natural disasters in almanacs and/or encyclopedias. On a separate sheet of paper, write a myth to explain its event. Give the main characters (quakes, volcanoes, gods, animals, etc.) human characteristics and motions. The name of your story should be the name of the natural disaster.

285

Words About Earth

Directions: Follow the recipe to learn more about Earth's layers.

You will need:
an adult, 2 large bowls (one that can go in the freezer), a rolling pin, a wooden spoon, a large wooden cutting board, a saucepan, measuring spoons, a long sharp knife, paper plates, plastic forks, the ingredients listed below
Cover the inside of the bowl that will go in the freezer with a nonstick spray.

INGREDIENTS:

Crust   4 tablespoons powdered sugar
               1/2 cup butter
               2 cups graham crackers

Mantle   1/2 cup crushed, unsalted peanuts
               chocolate ice cream

Outer Core   orange, red, and yellow sorbet M&M's™

Inner Core   vanilla ice cream
               red and green food coloring

— crust
— mantle
— outer core
— inner core

CRUST: Crush graham crackers on the cutting board. Mix powdered sugar with melted butter in a bowl. Line all sides of sprayed bowl with the mixture. Pat it inside the bowl to about 1/4 - 1/2 " thickness. Put it in the freezer until frozen.

Make layers in the order shown above, one layer at a time. Freeze each layer in the bowl before you go on to the next step. (Before mixing and adding each layer, let the ice cream soften, without completely melting.)

When Earth's cross section is frozen, take it out of the freezer. Cut it in half and then in fourths. Remove one quarter at a time. Slice it like a cake so that each serving has a little of each of Earth's layers. Put it on plates and serve.

286

Words About Earth

Erosion is the wearing away of Earth's surface by wind or water. Complete the following activity to learn about the effects of erosion on Earth.

You will need:
dirt, five 12" square pieces of thick cardboard, 5 roasting-type pans (you may wish to purchase disposable ones), grass seed, small rocks, leaves, twigs, paper towels, a small watering can, water, a quart-size jar

Directions: Cover the 5 pieces of cardboard with at least an inch or two of moist dirt. Then, do one of the following with each piece of cardboard:

1. Leave one piece of cardboard as is.
2. Set the leaves into the dirt in one.
3. Set the twigs into the dirt in one.
4. Set the rocks into the dirt in one.
5. Plant grass seed in one. Water it and wait for a good crop of grass to grow. When the board is dry and there is a good crop of grass, follow the directions below.

Lean the cardboard against the inside of a pan. Fill a quart jar with water and pour it into a watering can. Holding the spout about 2" above the cardboard, sprinkle water over it and observe the water flowing over the dirt into the pan.

To compare the amount of dirt that has been eroded, fold a paper towel into a cone shape. Place it in the mouth of the jar and pour the muddy water from the pan into it. Compare what each piece of cardboard looks like and the amount of dirt on the paper towels. Why do you think there are differences?

287

Words About Place Value

The **place value** of a digit or numeral is shown by where it is in the number. For example, in the number **23**, **2** has the place value of **tens** and **3** is **ones**.

Directions: Add the tens and ones. Then, write your answers on the lines.

Example:

          3 tens   +   3 ones =   33

1. 7 tens + 5 ones =   75   4. 4 tens + 0 ones =   40
2. 2 tens + 3 ones =   23   5. 8 tens + 1 one   =   81
3. 5 tens + 2 ones =   52   6. 1 ten + 1 one   =   11

Directions: Draw lines to match the numbers. The first one is done for you.

2 tens + 5 ones   38
3 tens + 8 ones   25
1 ten + 0 ones   6
0 tens + 6 ones   10

288

349

Words in a How-To Paragraph

A **how-to** paragraph gives instructions to the reader about how to do something. The paragraph should give step-by-step instructions.

Directions: Number the sentences in order from 1 to 7 as they should appear in a how-to-paragraph.

How to Use a Hula Hoop

   7 Let go of the hoop.
   3 Bring the hoop up around your waist.
   4 Twist the hoop.
   6 Keep swiveling your hips.
   1 Hold the hoop in both hands.
   5 Swivel your hips.
   2 Step into the hula hoop.

Directions: Write a paragraph that explains how to use a hula hoop using the steps above. Add your own topic sentence and concluding sentence. Add details to make your instructions more interesting.

Paragraphs will vary.

289

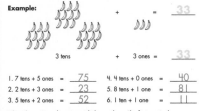

Words in an Informative Paragraph

An expository paragraph gives information or explains something. One type of expository writing is an **informative paragraph**. It gives information.

Directions: Only five of these sentences belong in a paragraph together. Draw a line through the sentences that do not belong. Then, rewrite the paragraph.

There are many kinds of snakes. ~~Kenny has two snakes.~~ Some pythons are as long as a bus. Water snakes live in rivers or lakes. ~~The snake at the zoo is named Monty.~~ Garter snakes are very small. ~~I like snakes.~~ All snakes are reptiles.

<u>There are many kinds of snakes. Some pythons are as long as a bus. Water snakes live in rivers or lakes. Garter snakes are very small. All snakes are reptiles.</u>

290

Words in a Descriptive Paragraph

A **descriptive paragraph** tells about something that can be observed or experienced. Notice how the paragraph below begins with a topic sentence. It is followed with support sentences that give descriptive details.

Example:

The banana split was an ice-cream lover's dream come true. A large blue oval dish was lined with long slices of bananas. On the bananas were three huge scoops of ice cream: chocolate fudge, vanilla, and strawberry. Drizzled over the vanilla scoop was loads of hot fudge sauce. Butterscotch sauce was dripping down the other two scoops. Lastly, chopped nuts were sprinkled over the sauce with a puff of whipped cream and a cherry to top it off!

Directions: Choose a topic from the list in the box. Then, write a list of details that could describe it.

My Classroom	My Favorite Outfit	Sledding
In-Line Skating	Around the Campfire	My Pet
Thanksgiving Dinner	Riding a Roller Coaster	

Topic: <u>Answers will vary.</u>
Details:

291

Words About Famous People

Directions: Read about Christopher Columbus. Then, answer the questions.

What do you know about Christopher Columbus? He was a famous sailor and explorer. Columbus was 41 years old when he sailed from southern Spain on August 3, 1492 with three ships and 90 men. Thirty-three days later, they landed on Watling Island in the Bahamas. The Bahamas are islands located in the West Indies. The West Indies are a large group of islands between North America and South America.

1. How old was Columbus when he set sail from southern Spain?
   <u>Columbus was 41 years old.</u>

2. How many ships did he take?
   <u>He took three ships.</u>

3. How many men were with him?
   <u>Ninety men went with Columbus.</u>

4. How long did it take him to reach land?
   <u>It took 33 days to reach land.</u>

5. Where did Columbus land?
   <u>Columbus landed on Watling Island in the Bahamas.</u>

6. What are the West Indies?
   <u>The West Indies are a large group of islands between North and South America.</u>

292

Words About Earth

Directions: Earth is made of **rocks** and **minerals**. A rock is a solid mass made up of minerals. Minerals are substances that are not made of animals or plants. Gold, silver, iron, and salt are minerals. Here is how you can make your own crystal rock candy.

You will need:
an adult, 4 cups of sugar, water, string, pencils, glasses that will not break when hot water is added, saucepans, spoons, measuring cups, a magnifying glass, food coloring, a stove, a pen, scissors, a stainless steel spoon, 9" x 12" sheets of drawing paper cut into four equal pieces

Directions:

Pour one cup of water into a saucepan. Add two cups of sugar. Stir over heat until sugar is dissolved. Add two more cups of sugar and continue heating and stirring until clear. Pour sugar water into glasses. (As a precaution against breakage, put a stainless spoon in each glass while pouring.)

Tie a piece of string to the center of each pencil—one per glass. The string should be long enough so that the string will hang in the solution, just above the bottom of the glass. Measure off and tie two more pieces of string to the same pencil. Cut them off and let them hang in the solution, too. Add food coloring if you want the crystals to have color.

In a few hours, examine the string in the glass. Some crystals should have formed. Look at them with a magnifying glass and draw a picture of them. Taste one. If you like it, you can eat it.

293

Words About Earth

Directions: The Seven Summits are the highest mountains of each of the seven continents. Use the Word Bank to write the name of each mountain on the correct continent. Then, color the continents.

Word Bank		
Everest	Aconcagua	Mount McKinley
Kilimanjaro	Elbrus	Vinson Massif	Kosciuszkor

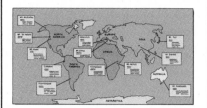

294

Words About Earth

Color the continents.

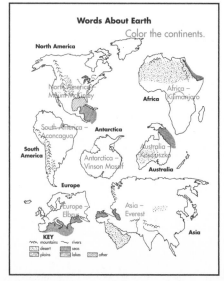

North America – Mount McKinley

Africa – Kilimanjaro

South America – Aconcagua

Antarctica – Vinson Massif

Australia – Kosciuszko

Europe – Elbrus

Asia – Everest

KEY
mountains   rivers
desert   seas
plains   lakes   other

295

Words About Place Value

The **place value** of a digit, or numeral, is shown by where it is in the number. For example, in the number 1,234, 1 has the place value of **thousands**, 2 is **hundreds**, 3 is **tens**, and 4 is **ones**.

Hundred Thousands	Ten Thousands	Thousands	Hundreds	Tens	Ones
9	4	3	8	5	2

943852

Directions: Draw lines to match the numbers in Column A with the place values listed in Column B. The first one is done for you.

A	B
62,453	two hundred thousand
7,641	three thousand
486,113	four hundred thousand
11,277	eight hundreds
813,463	seven tens
594,483	five ones
254,089	six hundreds
79,841	nine ten thousands
27,115	five tens

296

Words in a Cause-and-Effect Paragraph

Expository writing gives information or explains something. A **cause-and-effect paragraph** is expository writing that explains why something happened.

Directions: Draw a line to match each cause to its effect. Notice that the cause happens before the effect.

Cause	Effect
Don't pet the snake from tail to head.	The wrong food will make a snake sick.
Snakes should not be kept in a cold place.	Doing this could hurt its scales.
Never feed a snake something it should not eat.	A snake cannot make itself warm, and it could get sick.

Directions: Read the cause-and-effect paragraph. Underline the causes. Circle the effects. (Hint: There are three of each.)

I have to watch my snake, Jake, more closely. Yesterday, I took him out of his cage to clean it. He got away when I was not looking. He slithered as fast as lightning into the kitchen. My mom screamed loudly and jumped on a chair. Jake hid under the stove. I looked for a long time before I found him. Now, he is back in his cage. Next time, I plan to put him in a box while I clean his cage.

297

Words in an Expository Paragraph

Compare-and-Contrast Paragraph	Persuasive Paragraph	How-To Paragraph
topic sentence	state opinion	topic sentence
first comparison or contrast	first reason for	materials
second comparison or contrast	second reason for	first step
third comparison or contrast	third reason for	second step
concluding sentence	concluding sentence	third step
		concluding sentence

Directions: Read each paragraph. Decide what type of paragraph it is. Write its name on the line.

1. persuasive
   Mom and Dad, I think I should be able to have a birthday party for three reasons. First, I think it would be fun to spend time with my friends. We also have not had cake and ice cream lately. My sister and brothers would enjoy the party, too. Surely, it is a good idea to have a party.

2. how-to
   This is how I can invite all my friends to my birthday party. My dad and I will buy invitations at the store. The first thing I will do is write the day and time inside each invitation. Next, I will write each friend's name on the outside of each envelope. Last, I will give them to my friends. I cannot wait for the party!

3. compare-and-contrast
   I wonder if I should ask for a puppy or a video game. Both would be fun to have, but a dog would take a lot of care. A video game cannot snuggle at night, but it takes very little care. A dog has many other costs, such as food, vets, and grooming. I think the video game would be best for me.

298

Words in an Expository Paragraph

Informative Paragraph	Descriptive Paragraph	Cause-and-Effect Paragraph
topic sentence	topic sentence	topic sentence
first fact	descriptive sentence	cause or effect
second fact	descriptive sentence	cause or effect
third fact	descriptive sentence	cause or effect
concluding sentence	concluding sentence	concluding sentence

Directions: Read each paragraph. Decide what type of paragraph it is. Write its name on the line.

1. descriptive
   What a beautiful birthday cake I have! Mom made it look just like a puppy. It has floppy ears with a shiny, black gumdrop nose. The dog cake even has a blue frosting collar that says, "Snoopy." When I saw the cake, I was sure I was getting a video game. I think Mom and Dad are hinting that my cake is the only dog I'm going to get.

2. cause-and-effect
   My birthday cake was nearly ruined. First, Felix tried to pin the tail on the cat. The poor cat ran through the kitchen and jumped up on the table. Mom grabbed the cake just before the cat ran into it. We almost had a cat in our dog cake!

3. informative
   I had my birthday party on Saturday. Four boys and three girls came to the party. Everyone had a piece of my dog birthday cake with a scoop of vanilla ice cream. My parents gave me a white beagle puppy named "Snoopy." Everyone who came to the party said that it was really fun, and they all loved my new dog!

299

Words About Famous People

Directions: Read about Babe Ruth. Then, answer the questions.

The great baseball champion **Babe Ruth** was born in Baltimore, Maryland on February 6, 1895. He could hit a ball farther than most major-league players when he was only 13 years old. He did not have a very good home life, so he spent most of his early years living in a school for boys. He played baseball whenever he could, so he became very good.

His real name was George Ruth. People gave him the nickname "Babe" when he was 19 years old and the minor-league team manager Jack Dunn became his legal guardian. The other players on the team called him "Jack's Babe." Later, they shortened it to "Babe."

1. When was Babe Ruth born?
   Babe Ruth was born on February 6, 1895.

2. Where was he born?
   He was born in Baltimore, Maryland.

3. What did the players originally call Babe Ruth?
   The players originally called him "Jack's Babe."

4. How old was Babe when he got his nickname?
   Babe was 19 years old when he got his nickname.

300

Words About Earth

Directions: Write a descriptive shape poem about a type of natural disaster. List different kinds of natural disasters, such as tornadoes, floods, monsoons, volcanic eruptions, earthquakes, typhoons, and hurricanes. Under each one, list words associated with that disaster.

Choose one of the natural disasters to be the theme of your **shape poem**. A shape poem takes the shape of the subject it describes. Use the words you have listed to create the picture of the disaster.

Poems will vary.

301

Words About Earth

Earth is made of several layers. This is what they are called and their composition (what they are made of), from the inside out:

Inner core: solid iron and nickel
Outer core: melted iron and nickel
Mantle: thick layer of solid rock
Crust: upper layer that is brittle and can break

Directions: Complete the activity to understand Earth's composition.

You will need:
green, blue, red, gray, white, and yellow plasticine clay; knives; a lemon, a small apple, an orange, a small grapefruit (or their equivalent sizes); paper; pen or chalk

Directions: Put the fruit on display. Make Earth's inner core using gray plasticine. Roll it into a ball about the size of a lemon. Then, add red plasticine around it to make the outer core. The total size should now be equal to that of an apple. Next, add yellow clay to make the mantle. When this is added, the clay should be about the size of an orange. The last layer of Earth is the crust. Put a 1/4" white layer of clay around the mantle. Next, put on what is visible—a thin layer of blue (water) and green (continents). Cut out a wedge to show the cross section of Earth's different layers.

blue
white
yellow
red
gray
green

302

Words About Earth

A **volcano** is an opening in Earth's crust through which melted rock, ash, and gases are forced out.

Directions: Complete the activity to make a volcano erupt!

You will need:
vinegar, red food coloring, a large cardboard box, baking soda, a narrow plastic beaker, sand, a paper towel tube, scissors, clay, a flat box (3-4" high), a knife, masking tape

Cut and tape a flat box together so that it is about 10" square. Color the vinegar with red food coloring. Wear old clothes for the eruption.

Directions:

1. Fill half of a beaker with baking soda.

2. Cut two or three holes in the paper towel tube. Put it over the beaker.

3. Mold clay around the tube. Leave the top and the holes you poked open.

4. Make tunnels out of clay that lead down to the holes.

5. Put the beaker with the tube molded with clay in the large box. Pile damp sand around the clay volcano. Pat it to make it into a volcano shape. Leave the top and tunnels exposed.

6. When it is time to make it erupt, take it outside. Pour red vinegar into the beaker. Stand back. **VOOM!**

303

Unit 12 Review

Directions: Use a word in the Word Bank to complete each sentence.

Word Bank				
concluding	baseball	Atlas	ones	wind
minerals	similarities	natural	Spain	how
crust	inner	opinion	aerospace	

1. Christopher Columbus set sail from ___Spain___ to discover the new world.
2. ___Atlas___ is the mythical man who carried the sky on his shoulders.
3. In a compare-and-contrast paragraph, you write about the ___similarities___ and differences between two things.
4. Hundreds, tens, and ___ones___ are words used to describe place value.
5. The wearing away of the earth's surface is caused by ___wind___ and water.
6. ___Minerals___ are substances formed in the earth that are not made of animals or plants.
7. Neil Armstrong studied ___aerospace___ engineering to prepare himself to become an astronaut.
8. Floods, earthquakes, and hurricanes are kinds of ___natural___ disasters.
9. Each paragraph should end with a ___concluding___ sentence.
10. The ___crust___ is the layer of the earth's surface that is brittle and can break.
11. A ___how___-to paragraph gives step-by-step instructions.
12. If you wanted to express your ___opinion___ on a topic, you would write a persuasive paragraph.
13. Babe Ruth was a famous ___baseball___ player.
14. The layer closest to the center of the earth is called the ___inner___ core.

304